Software Process Automation

Alan M. Christie

Software
Process Automation

The Technology and Its Adoption

With 48 Figures and 19 Tables

 Springer

Alan M. Christie
Software Engineering Institute
Carnegie Mellon University
Pittsburgh, Pennsylvania 15213-3890
USA

ISBN-13:978-3-642-79254-0   e-ISBN-13:978-3-642-79252-6
DOI:10.1007/978-3-642-79252-6

CIP data applied for

© Springer-Verlag Berlin Heidelberg 1995
Softcover reprint of the hardcover 1st edition 1995

Cover Design: Künkel+Lopka, Ilvesheim
Typesetting: Camera ready by author
SPIN 10478695   45/3142 – 5 4 3 2 1 0 – Printed on acid-free paper

To Evelyn

Preface

Software production has historically been a very labor-intensive, highly skilled, and costly business. In addition, the more technically advanced Western nations have led the way in the rapidly changing field of software engineering. However, other nations, whose labor costs are far below those of the West, are catching up. These facts, coupled with the efficiency of global communications, suggest that the competitive position of the Western nations in software development may soon erode. Software is a strategic technology, from both defense and commercial points of view, and loss of this competitive edge could have profound consequences.

So what are the implications for software development? Several elements are necessary to compete successfully. First, one needs a vibrant infrastructure (such as Silicon Valley) where intense competition drives technology ahead of outside competition. Second, one needs an educated workforce that is capable of using new technologies and rapidly adapting to new circumstances. Third, there must be an emphasis on continuously improving software quality and hence on organizational performance. Since the process with which a product is built has a direct bearing on quality, understanding one's process is required. Finally, with a well-defined process, automating that process may be undertaken as a means to assure process consistency and to reduce cost. Automation of the process includes, but is not limited to, providing software organizations with appropriate tools to perform specific tasks, relieving developers and managers of as much tedium as possible, eliminating error-prone activities, and guiding process-critical tasks. Such support should allow developers and managers to concentrate on the creative non-automatable part of their jobs. If such cost-reducing, quality-enhancing measures are not taken, the competitive advantage currently held by countries that have relatively high labor rates will likely disappear.

A note of caution should, however, be stated with respect to automating software production. With mechanical or electrical products, the number of component variants is usually smaller relative to the number of software variants, logical complexity is less, and initial requirements are usually better understood than with software products. These factors often result in mechanical and electrical products having logically simpler manufacturing processes. In addition while much of hardware manufacturing can be performed repetitively by machines, software production, having a higher intellectual (and non-standardized) content, tends to be manually produced. Thus any approach to software automation cannot simply rely on principles developed for hardware. In particular, software automation forces a very tight and complex relationship between the computer environment and the software developer. Thus an understanding of human-computer interaction is particularly important for process-centered environments (PCEs) to be effective. Simply automating the software production process without giving due importance to end-user, process, and even social issues could result in the erroneous conclusion that automation does not work.

In essence, this book addresses four basic questions:

1. What is the technical basis for process definition and automation?
2. What are the characteristics of currently available commercial products that support the implementation of software process automation?
3. What are the important process, organizational, and social issues that one will have to addressed to effectively adopt a process-centered environment?
4. How does software process automation fit within the wider context of traditional manufacturing automation, and what can we learn from this wider view?

Thus there are several related groups of people who will find this book of interest:

1. Implementers of software process environments within projects. These people may wish to become more aware of the technical and non-technical issues that they will need to address in designing, implementing, and deploying such environments.
2. People involved in software process improvement or active in software engineering process groups (SEPGs). These people may wish to increase their understanding of PCE technology and how it can support process improvement.
3. Developers of commercial PCE products. These people may wish to broaden their understanding of less technical issues as such issues may affect the features implemented within their products.
4. Technologists interested in process definition, enactment, and verification and the relationship among these topics.

The book should also be of use to those who are involved with business process re-engineering as the technical and organizational issues being addressed by both communities are very similar. To date, there is little experience with day-to-day commercial application of software process automation, and this book was motivated to a considerable extent by the desire to promote the technology.

Software Engineering Institute   Alan M. Christie
December 1994

Acknowledgments

I'd like to thank Mike Baumann of Hewlett Packard, and Jean-Luc Meunier and Larry Proctor of Cap Gemini for all their support and patience while I developed the process models. Without their help, I could not have performed the in-depth analysis that I did. In particular I would like to thank Mike for helping develop parts of the process script and the supporting function *getTerm* and Jean-Luc for helping to develop parts of the ProcessWeaver model and supporting functions. I'd also like to thank Granville Gosa and Paul Zarella whose local technical support was invaluable. I'd like to thank Christer Fernstrom, Jean-Luc Meunier, and Gerald Perdreau of Cap Gemini for their technical review of the ProcessWeaver section of the book and Dave Pugmire of Hewlett Packard for his review of the Synervision section. I'd also like to thank Edward Averill, Alan Brown, Michael Caldwell, Susan Dart, David Carney, Marc Kellner, Priscilla Fowler, Leonard Green, Patricia Oberndorf, Dennis Smith, and Kurt Wallnau for the wealth of excellent suggestions they gave me from their reviews. A special thanks goes to Peter Feiler who reviewed the complete draft. These reviews have significantly improved the quality of the document. I also appreciate the support of those who participated in the end-user evaluations and who provided me the excellent insights that resulted from that experience (Jim Armitage, Edward Averill, Cliff Huff, Ed Morris, Neal Reizer, and Paul Zarella). I'd like to thank my publisher Springer-Verlag and in particular Hans Wössner for their support and encouragement during the writing process. Finally, I much appreciate the copy-editing support provided by Sandra Bond, Julia Deems, and Barbara White of the Software Engineering Institute and J. Andrew Ross and H. Matthies of Springer-Verlag. Of course, I take full responsibility for any remaining errors.

Some of the material for Chapter 2 has been taken from two papers published in *Information and Software Technology*: A graphical process definition language and its application to a maintenance project (Vol. 35, No. 6/7, 1993) and Enactable process specification in support of process-centered environments (Vol. 36, No. 10, 1994). This material is reproduced here with the permission of Butterworth-Heinemann Ltd., Oxford, UK. In addition, some material in Chapter 4 was previously published in *CrossTalk: The Journal of Defense Software Engineering*: Software process automation: a technology whose time has come? (Vol. 7, No. 7, 1994).

This work was sponsored by the U.S. Department of Defense.

Contents

1 Software Process Automation in Perspective

Consider two scenarios:

Jim is the manager responsible for developing the software performance requirements on a flight control computer. Since he is, as usual, overloaded, he asks Bob, one of his engineers, to determine the timing constraints on the system. Bob, who is new to the job, performs the task but significantly overestimates the values. He e-mails these to Jim who inserts them into the requirements document. At the requirements review, Mary who is familiar with timing constraints realizes that something is wrong and requests a recalculation. Jim readily agrees, but because he is preoccupied, forgets to inform Bob about the problem, and corrective action is never taken. When the system is built, a major crisis develops when it is found that the control computer cannot perform the job...

The Nala Corporation has decided that, in order to compete for government contracts, it must improve its software development process. It has taken to heart the belief that you cannot understand what you do not measure, and it therefore initiates a major metrics program. The program's primary focus is to measure programmer productivity and task schedules. To perform this collection task, upper management requests that developers and project managers fill out an electronic form each week identifying task status and lines of code written. Unfortunately, the perception within the ranks is that this is an intrusive bureaucratic hassle that does not help in supporting the on-going projects, many of which are behind schedule and in need of every staff-hour they can get. Thus the forms are resented, only sometimes filled in, and when they are, many errors are made. The result is that no meaningful improvements are made on the basis of the results...

These scenarios represent two fictitious, but realistic, examples of how ineffective processes can put an organization in jeopardy. A well-defined and implemented process will go a long way to resolving these problems, but manual implementation of this process can, in the short run, be time consuming even if, in the long run, it is beneficial. In a competitive commercial environment there is therefore an enormous temptation to skip anything that gets in the way of developing the final product. In the manufacture of mechanical and electrical products, process automation has

made dramatic impacts in improving productivity; there is no reason why similar approaches cannot work with software. Process automation represents a technology that can help manage this problem by:
- guiding sequences of activities that compose the project,
- managing the products that are being developed,
- invoking tools that developers require to do their tasks,
- performing automatic actions that do not need human intervention,
- allowing communication between the persons who are building the product,
- gathering metric data automatically,
- supporting personal task management
- reducing human errors, and
- providing project management with current, accurate status information.

However, there are also pitfalls and these, along with the advantages, will be discussed in Chapter 4.

1.1 The Origins of Software Process Automation

In the manufacture of mechanical and electrical products, process automation has had a long time to mature. With the introduction of interchangeable parts and the assembly line in the early 1900s, automation in the form of mass production made a dramatic impact on productivity. It replaced highly skilled craftsmen with semi-skilled laborers who often had to perform repetitive and tedious tasks that were dehumanizing. However, once it was established, mass production reduced the cost of goods so dramatically that few companies, not using this technique, could compete [Hounshell 84]. In the mass production environment, workers had little or no control of what they did – they simply acted as extensions of the machines they operated. Thus, mass production made little use of the employees intelligence, a valuable resource that was wasted.

At the end of the Second World War, Japanese companies, particularly Toyota, could not afford the massive investments required to produce automobiles on the US scale, and were forced to think anew about manufacturing process. They developed a variety of approaches to reducing cost and improving quality. Examples of these changes include the introduction of quick-change die techniques, just-in-time inventory control, statistical quality control, and new styles of leadership and teamwork. In particular, management actively encouraged workers to show initiative, to identify and resolve engineering problems, to change roles so as to broaden their experience, and in general encouraged workers at all levels to think about improving productivity and quality. This was mass production with a human face [Womack 1990, Humphrey 91a]. Thus it can be argued that automation as such was not dehumanizing. Rather, it was the assignment of roles in which workers were treated as unthinking cogs in a large machine that make it so.

Let us now turn to the question of software production. While specific solutions may be different in the software arena, many of the underlying human and organizational issues referred to above are the same. There has been a wide variety of efforts, both by major US and Japan companies, to adapt the concept of the factory to software production [Cusumano 91]. The Japanese activities were pioneered by companies such as NEC and Hitachi, while in the US companies such as GTE and IBM led the way. (There was, however, a reluctance on the part of many US companies to call their organizations "factories.") These initiatives were motivated by a need to reduce cost and improve quality through standardizing the way in which software was produced. The factory concept was primarily geared to producing large, well understood systems by adapting existing software. Computer operating systems and telecommunications systems are examples of this type of product. Software that was conceptually new did not fit well into the factory paradigm and was generally developed outside this framework.

Software factories attempted to rationalize the means of software production through a variety of techniques. They attempted to standardize on their processes through manual implementation or partial automation. Metrics data was collected in order to analyze and improve the processes and standards. Technical support to the projects was often provided by a group local to the site, rather than remotely from a corporate location. Reuse of software designs, code and documentation was encouraged, and CASE tools were adopted. Throughout, training in the use of tools, development standards and processes was provided. These efforts were started back in the late 1960s and continue today. In the US, the Capability Maturity Model (CMM) [Paulk 93a], developed by the Software Engineering Institute (SEI), evolved out of the experiences within IBM. The CMM has made significant impact in improving the performance of software organizations. In Japan, companies like Hitachi continue to pursue the factory concept for software development. However, the effectiveness of the majority of Japanese software organizations still lags behind those of major corporations like Hitachi [Humphrey 91b].

Software process automation, as described in this book, goes beyond what the software factories have attempted. Process automation, as defined here, has only recently become practical as a result of the widespread use of personal computers and workstations, and the growth in networking capability These two technologies now allow for powerful distributed computing and human communications that was not available before. Such process automation can be viewed as the next logical step in the software factory concept.

1.2 Automation in a Process Improvement Context

In performing goal-oriented tasks, people have an impressive ability to muddle through without having a clear understanding of the process they are following. Of course the more complex the task, or the greater the number of people involved in the task, the more this approach will run into difficulty. Traditional craft industries have relied on individuals or small groups of highly skilled artisans to produce high quality goods. The need for a formal understanding of organizational process has not usually been critical to success. In its early days, software engineering showed characteristics similar to those of craft industries. Small programs (by today's standards) were developed by groups containing small numbers of people. Great importance was placed on, and respect given to technical skills.

Craft industries either remained small or, like the automobile industry, evolved into entities that were significantly different is size, structure, and outlook. However, despite growth in the software industry, and despite the efforts discussed in [Cusomano 91], the software industry has, in many ways, yet to outgrow its craft origins. This is beginning to change with the application of the CMM to process improvement and the development of the ISO 9000-3 standard [ISO 91]. These initiatives are providing both a carrot and a stick for organizations to improve their software processes.

Process automation cannot be viewed as an end in itself, but part of an on-going effort in continuous process improvement. Such an effort requires many elements [Humphrey 89a], but one particularly important element is having an understanding of ones processes. Only through such an understanding can one improve these processes. A first step is thus to find out how the current process is actually performed (as opposed to how it is specified in some company document). Processes can be described through one of several textual or graphical techniques, some of which will be reviewed later. Having such a description of the process allows interested parties to agree that this does indeed reflect the true process, to reason about the process and to identify potential improvements. In particular, such a model allows management and staff to agree on what actually happens as the perception of these two groups may be different. Additional power can be given to this model if process metrics are captured during actual day-to-day operations. These metrics can provide quantitative insights into the dynamics of the process, for example, indicating where bottlenecks occur.

In designing new or improved processes, an ability to simulate these processes is very valuable. Such simulations are based on the process models discussed above, and allow one to sequence through the process tasks in an interactive manner. Thus one can evaluate the effectiveness of candidate processes, assess their behavior, and ask "what-if" questions associated with proposed modifications. Such simulations have another application. With the help of quantitative data, these simulations can also be run in a statistical (Monte Carlo) sense where parameters such as task durations can be varied about some mean value. This technique provides additional insights in to the behavior of the planned process [Kellner 91].

The process models described above can potentially be used as the basis for process automation as they contain much of the information necessary to build a process-centered environment. However, in the current commercial state-of-the-practice, tools whose origins lie in process definition may allow simulation, but are not generally designed to support real-time execution. On the other hand, commercial products for building PCEs are beginning to provide graphical front ends for process definition and simulation. Thus in the future we may see modularized products which allow us to purchase a process definition module, a process simulation module or a real-time process enactment module or some compatible combination of these.

Process models may have a further use in supporting the verification of as-performed processes. In certain applications where high integrity software is required, assurance that the defined process has been followed may be essential. If appropriate process data is collected (for example decisions taken, product versions used), then it is possible to trace back through the process model and verify that the process has indeed been accurately followed.

Section 1.3 expands on the discussion of this section, providing a overview of how many of the issues described above are addressed in subsequent chapters of the book.

1.3 A Process Development and Usage Scenario

Figure 1.1 proposes a process development and usage scenario. It provides a roadmap through which a process-centered environment can be implemented, and links the major themes of this book. This process lifecycle model is analogous to the software development lifecycle. Step 1 is associated with requirements definition, steps 2 through 5 are associated with process specification and validation (and has much in common with the software design phase), step 6 is associated with coding and testing, while steps 7 through 9 support deployment of the process.

Prior to developing any process model, it is necessary to identify the needs of those who will work within the automated environment. From these needs a set of associated requirements can be developed (step 1).[1] In step 2, an appropriate graphical representation of the process, that incorporates the requirements, is constructed. It is important that this process model be defined graphically so that communication between the model builders and end-users of the automated process is facilitated. In step 3, the graphical model is compiled into an executable form through appropriate transformations. Technical details on one approach to such a transformation are discussed in Sections 2.3.[2] Through this executable form, the dynamics of the process can be studied at a high level, without being encumbered, at this point, with lower-

---

1. In the following text, the numbers down the left hand side of Figure 1.1 are called steps.

2. Material in Section 2.3 (and 2.4) is somewhat technical and is likely to be of more interest to technology implementers than technology users. However, understanding this section is not necessary in order to read subsequent chapters.

<u>Step</u>

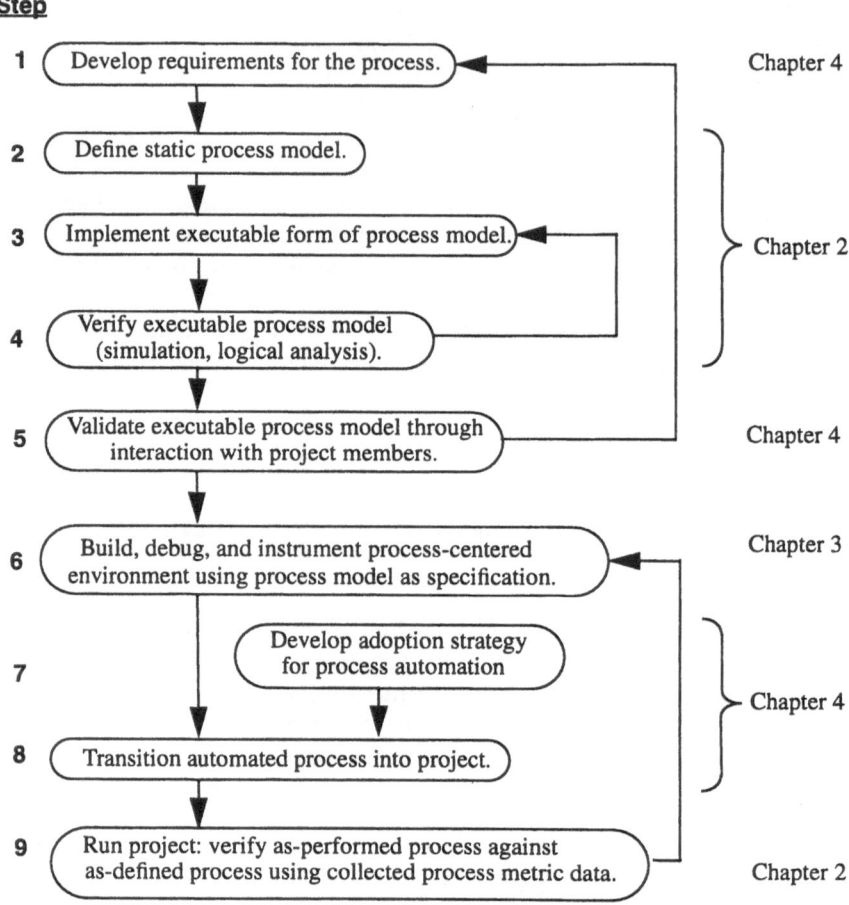

Fig. 1.1. A process development and usage scenario

level implementational detail. At this stage the internal workings of the activities are not defined; only the relationships between the activities, as specified through activity inputs and outputs, are provided. Verifying the correctness of the model (step 4) may involve logical (static) analysis to check for deadlock and reachability and (dynamic) simulation to test the system's behavioral characteristics. After verification, validation of the executable model is performed with the support of the managers and/or developers who will subsequently use the process (step 5). This validation also encourages the buy-in that is essential if the process is to gain acceptance. Thus end-users are involved at steps 1, 2 and 5. It should be noted that, besides generating early buy-in by the end-users, this approach is likely to catch errors in the process at an early stage, before they become increasingly expensive to fix.

As we have seen above, our specification has a dynamic component. This allows us not only to be precise and formally consistent (in a static sense), but also to be more behaviorally correct. By allowing behavior in the specification, we can address, in a preliminary way, some basic end-user issues prior to investing in the full-scale implementation. The enactable specification now defines all significant high-level artifacts in the process, the agents who will perform the activities, the decisions that are made or acted upon throughout the process, and the products that are generated by the activities. Details of how this may be accomplished are described in Chapter 2.

The executable specification developed in step 3 is now used as the basis for developing the process-centered environment. Having gained a solid understanding of the behavioral issues through this specification, development of the PCE can proceed with much greater confidence. The architecture of the PCE (Step 6) may take many forms. At one end of the spectrum, tools can be coupled directly together to allow for simple process enactment. Software environments available today generally have some capability to model and control process although they may not have constructs that are at a sufficiently high-level to make process enactment easy. Recently, a number of commercial process support and enactment tools have become available, in addition to those that have academic origins. These may prove to be a critical ingredient in a total PCE solution. They are the subject of Chapter 3, which provides a detailed review of two major products: SynerVision and ProcessWeaver.

The assessment of these products is conducted using an adaptation to a technique originally designed to consistently evaluate software environments [Weiderman 86]. In this adaptation, a standard process model and a set of product-independent evaluation criteria are first established. The process model is then implemented in each product, and each product is then measured against the evaluation criteria. Being product-independent, the methodology described may be useful to organizations who wish to assess the capabilities of other process-centered environments. However, the investigation conducted here is aimed at assessing the technology by looking at specific examples of commercial products; it is not designed to rank the products. As it turns out both of these products excel in some ways and are weak in others.

The manner in which the PCE is introduced into a project is critical to success. The automation of tasks, impersonal delegation of responsibilities, and a greater degree of interaction with the computer will be issues requiring sensitive solutions. Work habits will necessarily change in significant ways and this requires the development of an effective adoption strategy (step 7). Transitioning the automated process into use is another challenge (step 8). To some extent the degree of challenge will depend on whether the automated process is being "back-fitted" into an existing manual process or being used on an entirely new process. The former case is likely to be more difficult for two reasons. First, there has to be a tailoring with the existing process and the cross-over from the manual to the automated process could result in a mismatch. Second, the people who work within the existing process have expectations of how things should be done and these may be inconsistent with the automated process. With a new project there are likely to be fewer expectations. These issues are discussed in Chapter 4.

Once an automated process is in place, process improvement may be significantly helped by the automated collection of metrics. Having a defined model of ones process helps determine which process metrics to gather. Metrics gathered may include decisions taken, intermediate product versions used, reviews completed, and what agents are involved in what activities. Upon completion of the project, these data can also be used, if required, to verify that the process sequence was correctly followed (step 9). In developing an executable process model, one should be able to select process variables whose values can be automatically collected during the running of the process. As will be shown in Chapter 2, the collected data can allow for a formal procedure through which process verification can be performed.

A final step in the usage scenario (not discussed to any extent in subsequent chapters) is to capture demonstrably effective processes for reuse, and place them in a reuse library. Executable processes leave little room for ambiguity as to what was meant. This precision is a distinct advantage in reuse over processes that have been defined but have not been developed through to executability. In addition, through reuse, one automatically acquires a model that is known to work, and into which process improvement lessons may have been embedded.

Because process automation requires that a project works within a well-defined process, a clear understanding of one's operating procedures is an important prerequisite. Indeed to be most effective, process automation must be viewed within the context of process improvement. This is so since experience gained in working within the process should be incorporated into the process program to make it more effective. Process automation products are qualitatively different from standard CASE tools since the latter do not significantly affect organizational behavior. (CM tools are the exception, but they emphasize data management rather than process management.) Thus Chapter 4 also discusses the relationship of process automation to process improvement and in particular the Capability Maturity Model. This discussion addresses CASE tools and how they fit within this context.

The final chapter (Chapter 5) picks up again on the themes introduced in Sections 1.2 and 1.3. That is, it provides some insights on software process automation as viewed from the perspective of traditional manufacturing automation. While the two fields have obvious differences, many of the organizational and human challenges are quite similar.

The book also contains a number of appendices providing expanded information for those who wish to dig deeper. Appendix A lists a demonstration process execution program, while Appendix B lists a process verification program (both written in Prolog). Appendix C provides information on specific commercial products, and what platforms they operate on, while Appendix D lists the process program for the SynerVision experiment. Appendix E reviews some of the process-related terminology used in this report. A brief note on this terminology is needed here. A process

automation product may fall into the category of either a process-centered environment (PCE) or a process-centered framework (PCF) depending on whether or not
the product includes end-user applications. The relationship between PCEs and
PCFs and other process concepts is discussed and clarified in Appendix E. For simplicity, when we are later discussing the products under review, we will use the term
PCE for either, unless there is a need to differentiate between a PCE and a PCF. Finally, Appendix F lists the scenario script and questionnaire given to the participants
of the SynerVision and ProcessWeaver role plays.

2 Process Definition, Execution and Verification

In Chapter 1 we reviewed the sequence of steps that one should go through when developing a process-centered environment (Figure 1.1). The main technical components of these steps can be summarizes as follows:

(a) graphically define the static process model —>
(b) develop the executable process specification —>
(c) build the process-centered environment —>
(d) execute, track and verify the process.

Chapter 2 now discusses issues associated with topics a, b, and d. The approach followed in this chapter is to develop a set of specific techniques as a means of gaining insight into process definition, execution and validation issues.Commercial technologies for building the environment (topic c) are the subject of Chapter 3.

After providing some background in Sections 2.1 and 2.2, Section 2.3 introduces ProNet [1], a process definition language, and illustrates how one can define processes using it (step 2 in Figure 1.1). Section 2.4 then shows how a defined process can be transformed into an executable representation that we call ProSim (steps 3 and 4 in Figure 1.1) and provides general mapping rules for this transformation. Section 2.4 also defines the process model (a document update process) that is used to evaluate the two commercial products as described in Chapter 3, and shows how this document update process can be implemented with ProSim. Thus Section 2.4 provides insights into the relationship between process definition, execution and some of the extensions needed to build a complete PCE. Finally, Section 2.5 shows how, using process-based metric data, the verification of an executed process can be performed using the constructs similar to those provided by ProSim (step 9 in Figure 1.1). Sections 2.4 and 2.5 are more technical, as they involve implementation details using the Prolog language [Bratko 86]. However, these sections can be understood in a broader sense by persons who do not have a familiarity with the language.

Other process modeling notations such as STATEMATE [Harel 90] or Petri Nets [Reisig 82] could have been used to define and execute (in a simulation sense) the process models used to support topics a and b above. However, ProNet and ProSim

---

1. ProNet stands for *Process Network*

have proved to be very flexible testbeds for investigating ideas in process definition, execution and verification. In particular, the concepts explored in verification could not have been performed with existing tools.

2.1 Underlying Concepts

Whether one wishes simply to understand a process, or to develop an executable model of the process, the process must first be defined. A variety of basic modeling approaches, emphasizing different aspects of process, is available. Some of these modeling approaches are graphical while some are textual. Graphical implementations often include or combine elements of three basic descriptive views:

Functional view. The functional view emphasizes the activities that are performed, along with the entities (artifacts, data etc.) that flow into and out of the activities. This view is often expressed through data flow diagrams [DeMarco 79]. An simple example of such a diagram is shown in Figure 2.1(a).

Behavioral view. The behavioral view emphasizes *when or under what conditions* activities are performed. Such models are often based on state transition diagrams [Harel 87]. When a process is in a particular state, an event may occur that allows the process to make a transition into another state. Behavioral models must consider decisions made, and the impact these decisions have on the direction of the process. There is often a close relationship between the states associated with state transition diagram and the activities associated with a data-flow diagram, although one state may correspond to multiple activities or one activity may occur over multiple states. An example of a state transition diagram is shown in Figure 2.1(b).

Structural view. The structural view expresses the relationships between the objects being manipulated or transformed by the process. These models are often based on entity-relation diagrams [Chen 83], and allow for aggregation (e.g., through the relationship *is-part-of*), inheritance (e.g., through the relationship *is-a*), and other relationships between entities. An example of an entity-relationship diagram is shown in Figure 2.1(c).

These views have been used to a great extent in tools and techniques that support software specification and design. However, there is much conceptual overlap between that field and the field of software process definition. Hence these tools and techniques have been "imported" in many cases to support software process definition. For example, the software specification tool STATEMATE from i-Logix Inc. [Harel 90] has been used successfully to define complex software development processes in a rigorous manner [Kellner 89] while the IDEF0 technique [Ross 85] has gained widespread popularity in defining process from a data flow perspective. A role-centered view of process that is gaining strength is the Role-Interaction Network (RIN) [Singh 92]. This view emphasizes the organizational aspects of process, and highlights how artifacts flow between the roles in the organization. RINs are ap-

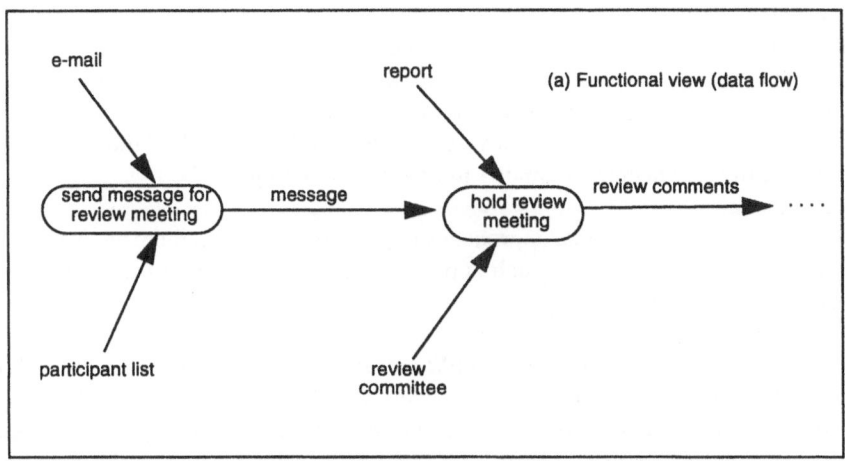

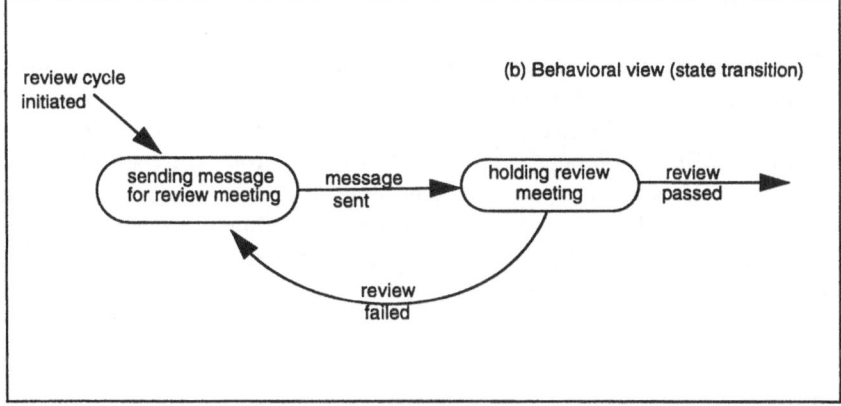

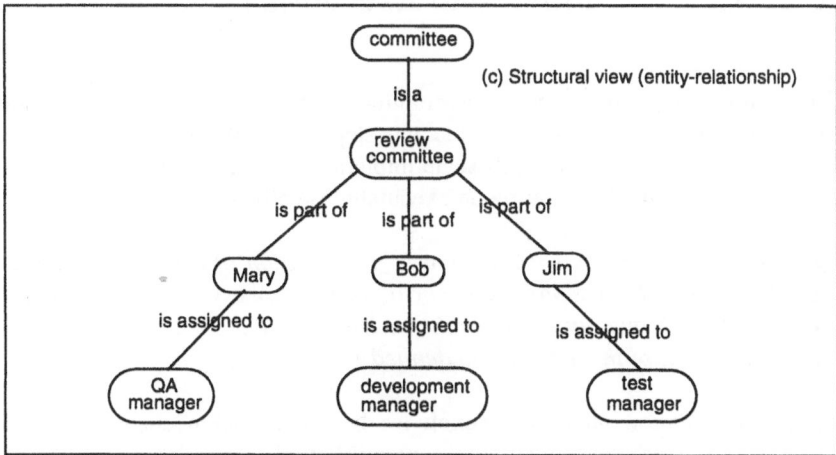

Fig. 2.1. Examples of three basic process modeling views

pealing since, as well as being highly descriptive in a graphical sense, have a formal underpinning that allows for their potential execution. A notation that has a similar role-oriented point of view, and has potential for execution is the Role Activity Diagram (RAD) [Huckville 93]. A taxonomy of available tools and techniques based on functional, behavioral, and data views is given in [Brandl 90]. Additional background on these concepts as applied to process modeling can be found in [Clough 93, Rumbaugh 91]

In addition to the graphical approaches to process definition, there are also textually oriented approaches. One such approach is ETVX. Quoting from [Radice 85], this approach provides:

> 1) a list of entry criteria that should be satisfied before beginning tasks, (2) a set of task descriptions that indicate what should be accomplished, (3) a validation procedure to verify the quality of the work items produced by the tasks, and (4) a checklist of exit criteria that should be satisfied before the activity is viewed as complete.

ETVX lacks the formal structures necessary to support process execution. However, for organizations who wish to documented processes with the aim of process improvement, ETVX may be an effective choice. A textual tool that does provide more formality is MSP (Minimally Structured Processes) from Software Design and Analysis Associates Inc. [Nejmeh 94]. This tool is based on forms that support textual descriptions of the process, but the format is more highly structured than with ETVX. This structure provides the kind of rigor necessary to support process execution.

2.2 Process Definition and Executable Specification

Let us now turn to the issue of developing executable processes specifications. As mentioned in Chapter 1, this intermediate step bridges the gap between the static definition of a process and the full-scale implementation of a process-centered environment. First, what is meant by an executable specification?

> An executable process specification is a simulation of a defined process accounting for a) the temporal sequencing of the process's activities and b) the major inputs to and outputs from the activities, while c) leaving the implementational details of the activities undefined.

Thus the specification intentionally excludes the lower-level mechanisms needed to implement, for example, human communication, tool invocation and artifact (object) management. Debugging of the essential process aspects of the process-centered environment can thus separated from the implementational detail. Some of the process definition tools described above have sufficiently powerful formalisms that may be used to develop executable process specifications (e.g., STATEMATE, MSP and RIN). In particular STATEMATE has a variety of built-in functions to analyze executable models in order to ascertain their correctness and completeness.

Why develop a graphical process notation with executable characteristics? Some reasons are listed below:

- developing an executable process is considerably easier if a graphical interface is used rather than a textual interface. It is the author's experience that the opportunities for introducing bugs while programming with a textual interface are considerably greater than when programming with a graphical interface.
- With the help of a graphical interface, a variety of different executable process alternatives can be quickly explored before the desired process is implemented. By supporting the executable process through a graphical notation, many of its behavioral characteristics can be more easily identified, modified, and improved before a commitment to the operational model is made. This has implications, not only for establishing the initial process but for process modification/ improvement.
- Both the graphical model and its executable form will provide insight on tool integration issues. The process model specifies the input and output data and control information (through the artifacts and conditions) thus providing a rational basis for communication between tools. (Of course, actual integration of the tools within a process support environment raises many implementation issues not addressed by the specification [Brown 92].)
- Process improvement can be supported through quantitative simulation. Such simulations, supported by estimated task times and manpower availability, can be run to generate predicted project durations, manpower loadings etc. [Kellner 91]. These can then be compared to the metrics generated from the actual process, and this comparison can be used to improve the effectiveness of the process.

There are also significant advantages to defining the process graphically, independent of enactability considerations:

- Graphical specification provides a means to communicate to developers, management and others what the "new" process will look like. This generates early feedback from those involved in future use of the process, thus encouraging its success.
- It provides a means for managers to sign-off on a defined process without the manager having to understand a complex symbolic notation.
- The graphical process model can also be used to accelerate training for persons new to the organization.

Most current process-centered environments are research-oriented and as such have tended to focus on the low-level constructs required to investigate process execution concepts rather than on ease of model development. Consequently, they have sacrificed process clarity. In particular, their programming languages are usually textual rather than graphical. While some PCEs (particularly Petri-net based systems) are moving towards defining process graphically, others are not. This may change with time when it is realized that the ability to define a static process model, develop its executable process specification, and build the process-centered environment through one unified framework is very advantageous.

2.3 The ProNet Graphical Modeling Language

One general definition of process is: *A set of partially ordered steps intended to reach a goal* [Feiler 92]. Given this definition, steps, which are called activities in ProNet, take a central position. An activity may only be started if certain entrance conditions are met or if certain artifacts become available. As a consequence of the activity, exit conditions may change from false to true (or vice versa) and certain artifacts may be generated. Hence termination of one activity changes the state of the system, generating and setting up necessary entrance conditions for other activities to initiate. ProNet can thus be viewed as a declarative model. Each activity and its entrance and exit conditions bear a strong relationship to the elements of a rule in a rule-based system, and it is because of this characteristic that its use in process execution is possible.

2.3.1   Entity Classes

This section provides a definition of the notation. ProNet diagrams are based on a modified Entity-Relationship model [Chen 83], in which the entities fall into one of seven classes, each of which has its own icon. The following list defines these entity classes and their icons:

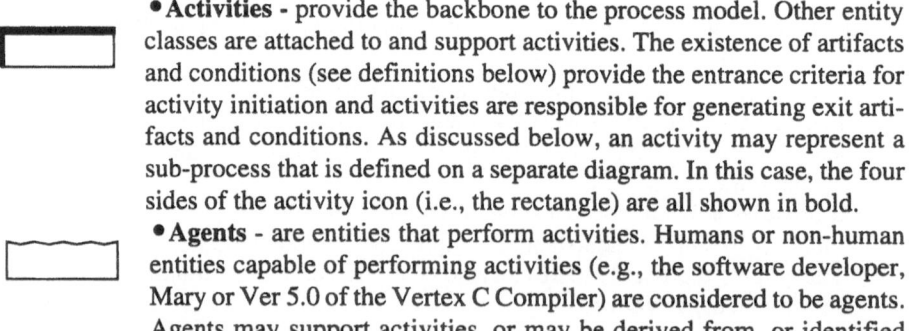

- **Activities** - provide the backbone to the process model. Other entity classes are attached to and support activities. The existence of artifacts and conditions (see definitions below) provide the entrance criteria for activity initiation and activities are responsible for generating exit artifacts and conditions. As discussed below, an activity may represent a sub-process that is defined on a separate diagram. In this case, the four sides of the activity icon (i.e., the rectangle) are all shown in bold.
- **Agents** - are entities that perform activities. Humans or non-human entities capable of performing activities (e.g., the software developer, Mary or Ver 5.0 of the Vertex C Compiler) are considered to be agents. Agents may support activities, or may be derived from, or identified by, activities.

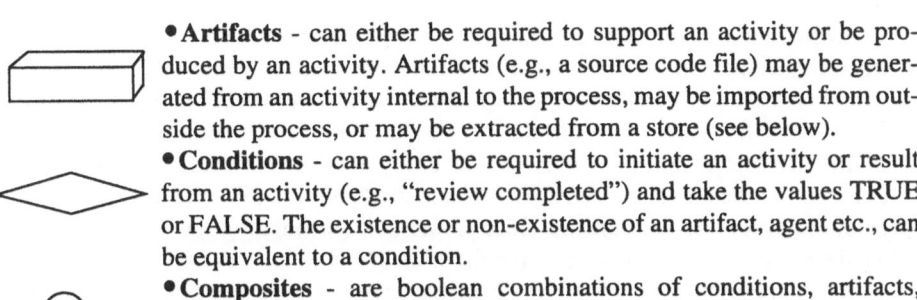

• **Artifacts** - can either be required to support an activity or be produced by an activity. Artifacts (e.g., a source code file) may be generated from an activity internal to the process, may be imported from outside the process, or may be extracted from a store (see below).

• **Conditions** - can either be required to initiate an activity or result from an activity (e.g., "review completed") and take the values TRUE or FALSE. The existence or non-existence of an artifact, agent etc., can be equivalent to a condition.

• **Composites** - are boolean combinations of conditions, artifacts, agents etc.

• **Stores** - allow for persistence of instantiated entities. Artifacts, condition values and even agents can be deposited in or retrieved from stores.

• **Constraints** - are policy restrictions imposed on an activity. Unlike conditions, these do not take on boolean values but may reflect guidance in how thinks are done (e.g., a quality assurance constraint such as on documenting written code).

Most relationships link the entities to the activities. As shown in Tables 2.1 and 2.2, relationships are of two types: *entrance* and *exit*. Entrance relationships identify those entities (artifacts, agents, etc.) necessary to perform the activity. On the other hand, exit relationships indicate those entities that are generated by an activity. Thus exit entities could be artifacts, conditions, or even agents (that are specified inside the activity).

Table 2.1.   Entrance Relationships

Entrance relationships	Inverse entrance relations
agent_A *is entrance agent for* activity_A	activity_A *has entrance agent* agent_A
artifact_A *is entrance artifact for* activity_A	activity_A *has entrance artifact* artifact_A
condition_A *is entrance condition for* activity_A	activity_A *has entrance condition* condition_A
composite_A *is entrance composite for* activity_A	activity_A *has entrance composite* composite_A
store_A *is entrance store for* activity_A	activity_A *has entrance store* store_A
constraint_A *is entrance constraint for* activity_A	activity_A *has entrance constraint* constraint_A

Table 2.2.   Exit Relationships

Exit relationships	Inverse exit relations
agent_A *is exit agent for* activity_A	activity_A *has exit agent* agent_A
artifact_A *is exit artifact for* activity_A	activity_A *has exit artifact* artifact_A
condition_A *is exit condition for* activity_A	activity_A *has exit condition* condition_A
composite_A *is exit composite for* activity_A	activity_A *has exit composite* composite_A
store_A *is exit store for* activity_A	activity_A *has exit store* store_A
constraint_A *is exit constraint for* activity_A	activity_A *has exit constraint* constraint_A

In the process diagrams, these relationships are all written in italics and the information they contain allows the reader to identify the class of entity that is linked to the activity. Also, if the relationship "artifact_A *is entrance artifact for* activity_A" holds, so does the inverse relationship "activity_A *has entrance artifact* artifact_A". In addition, a black dot is placed next to the entity at the end of the relationship. For example in the relationship "ABC *is entrance artifact for* XYZ", the dot would appear in the graphical relationship close to the box surrounding the activity XYZ. Thus the dot plays the same role as the tip of an arrow does in data-flow diagrams.

ProNet handles three other relationships types: *inheritance, aggregation* and *custom*. With respect to inheritance, there are two named relationships: *is instance of* and *is generalization of*, each of which is the inverse of the other. Unlike the relationships discussed earlier, these relationships link two arbitrary entities, so long as they are of the same class. With respect to aggregation, there are also two named relationships: *is part of* and *includes*, each of which is the inverse of the other. These also link arbitrary entities together, but there is no constraint that the joined entities be of the same class. Occasionally there is a need to define a non-standard relationship between two entities that does not fall into one of the predefined categories. ProNet allows definition of a "custom" relationship.[2] This feature allows creation of an arbitrary relationship (i.e., one not belonging to the pre-defined set) to link two entities. For example one might define the custom relationship *depends on* as in the example:

agent_A depends on resource_A

The inheritance, aggregation, and custom relations are not used in the executable implementation of ProNet (i.e., in ProSim). However, ProNet provides a second way of substructuring activities besides use of the *is part of* relationship, and this is used in executable models. While the *is part of* relationship allows the components of an entity to be displayed on the same graph as the entity itself, it is sometimes necessary to display the detailed structure of an activity as a sub-process on a separate graph. Most real-world process models have significant complexity, and this latter approach allows for multiple-levels of hierarchical decomposition of the process. In such a decomposition, the inputs and outputs at the higher level must match the inputs and outputs at the lower level. If a particular activity in a process diagram is expanded into a lower-level process, then its four sides are emphasized using bold lines. (As seen above, normal activities only have two sides in bold.)

In summary, ProNet is an entity-relationship diagram, that has a set of entity classes *activity, artifact, agent, condition, composite, constraint,* and *store* defined within the notation. A variety of predefined relationships bind instances of these classes together.

---

2. Because custom relationships are not defined within the standard set of relationships types, they weaken the formalism. This option thus cannot be used in an executable form of the model. However, from the point of view of describing process, as opposed to its execution, custom relationships can be useful if used with discretion

2.3.2   Basic ProNet Characteristics

In order to construct a ProNet model, there are various additional properties that need to be defined beyond the entity classes and relationships. These are described below.

A Minimal Process Construct: As previously stated, the notion of activity is central to ProNet models. Generally the goal of the software process is to produce software products (i.e., artifacts). Thus one outcome of activities is to produce artifacts. Another outcome of activities is to make decisions that are reflected in the values (e.g., true or false) of conditions. Also, in general, activities cannot begin unless certain artifacts and agents are available, and certain conditions are satisfied. This view can be represented as shown in Figure 2.2.

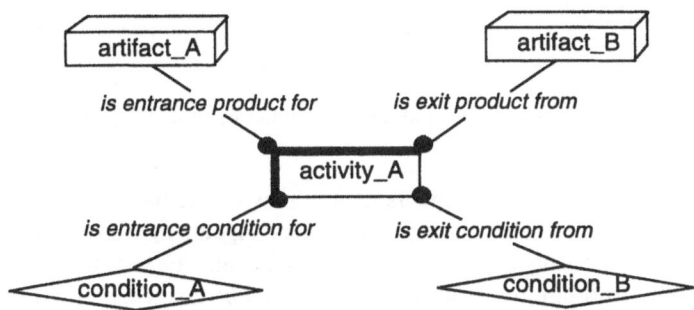

Fig. 2.2. Basic representation of a process element

Note the dots at the ends of the relationships in Figure 2.2. These dots signify the direction of the relationship between the entities and not temporal flow. Temporal flow is implied by the fact that when the preconditions for an activity are appropriate, then the activity can take place. Thus in Figure 2.2, if *actifact_A* exists, con*dition_A* is *true* and the *activity_A* has not yet been performed, then *activity_A* can be performed. On completion of *activity_A*, *actifact_B* is generated and *condition_B* is set to *true*. These latter entities may then initiate subsequent activities.

Entity Instantiation: A distinction must be made between entities that are instantiated at process definition time and entities that are instantiated at run time. For example, a process diagram may specify that the agent *developer* supports activity *develop_code*. The person who will take on this role is left unspecified at process definition time. However, to execute the process, a specific person (e.g., Jean) must be identified for the role at run time. In a similar way, artifacts, conditions etc., may be left uninstantiated in the process diagram. In order to distinguish between entities instantiated at definition time and run time, a "$" sign is placed in front of the entity whose value is specified at run time. This convention is also shown in Figure 2.3.

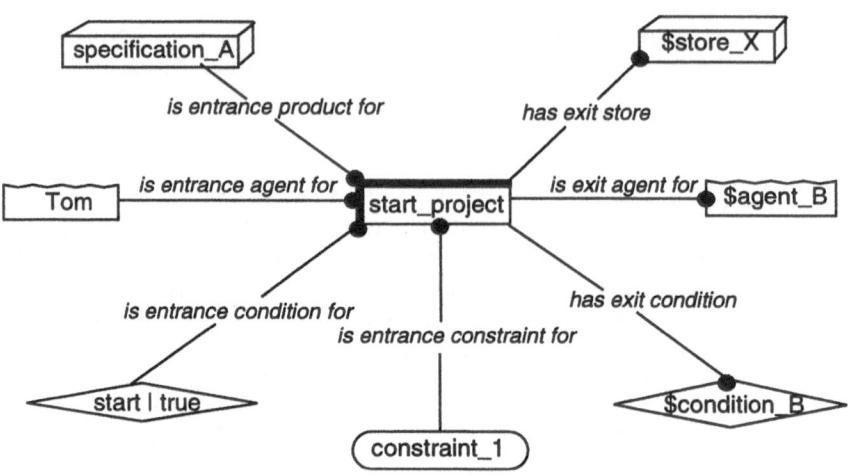

Fig. 2.3. Augmented representation of a process element

Some Properties of Agents: Agents may or may not be human. Examples of non-human agents are compilers and spell-checkers. Agents not only support activities (through the relationship *is entrance agent for*), but may be selected by, or generated by an activity (through the relationship *is exit agent for*). Generally human agents are selected (e.g., the consequence of Activity_X may be that Jean is selected to perform some subsequent activity). Non-human agents can be either selected or generated. An example of a generated exit agent is a software tool that is the product of a compiler. ProNet does not explicitly distinguish between human and non-human agents and, for both cases, the ProNet relationship is *is exit agent for*. However, for process execution the distinction may be important since automated agents may initiate activities without human intervention. The use of entrance and exit agents is shown in Figure 2.3. Note that the exit agent is still to be instantiated, indicating that the associated activity is responsible for the selection.

In general, entrance agents are required to support activities - someone or something is needed to perform the task. However, there are two cases where an agent may not be required. In the first case, the activity may be a high-level abstraction, that is, it can expanded into a lower-level process where the agents are defined. In the second situation, the activity may be automatically performed and agent identification is unnecessary. Whether the machine agent is defined or not is a question of judgement based on context. One example where an agent may be missed out is in the *put* and *get* operations associated with entity stores. (See the discussion on stores later in this section.)

Condition Types and Boolean Constructs: Conditions can be represented by two different approaches. In the first, a condition is defined to be true if it has been generated by an activity, while its absence implies it is false. Consider the example in Figure 2.2. If activity *activity_A* has been successfully completed, then condition *condition_B* exists (i.e., is true), otherwise, *condition_B* does not exist and is considered to be false. In the second approach, the truth or falsity of a condition is shown by explicitly appending the word *true* or *false* to the condition name. i.e., *condition_B* | *true* and *condition_B* | *false* These two representations may be called implicit and explicit respectively and will both be used in process models defined later in this chapter. An example of this latter approach is shown in Figure 2.3.

An important concept in the basic notation is the composite class. Composites allow boolean combinations of entities to be logically combined, either as input to an activity or as the output from an activity. There are four instances of the composite class: CA, CO, DA, and DO, where "C" stands for "convergent", "D" stands for "divergent", "A" stands for "AND" and "O" stands for "OR." Since convergent composites are always implemented prior to an activity they are called "entrance composites." Similarly, since divergent composites are always implemented after an activity they are called "exit composites." These are described below:

- CA: This stands for a "convergent AND" composite. In this kind of composite, an example of which is shown in Figure 2.4, several entities must all be present before the output from the composite is activated
- CO: This stands for a "convergent OR" composite, and is similar in structure to the CA composite. However in this case, only one branch of the inputs needs to be activated before the activity can be initiated.
- DA: This stands for a "divergent AND" composite. As a result of an activity, a conjunction of conditions, artifacts and agents may result.
- DO: This stands for a "divergent OR" composite, and is similar in structure to the DA composite. However in this case, only one branch of the outputs will be activated. Thus in Figure 2.5, either *artifact_A*, *artifact_B* or *condition_A* will activate.

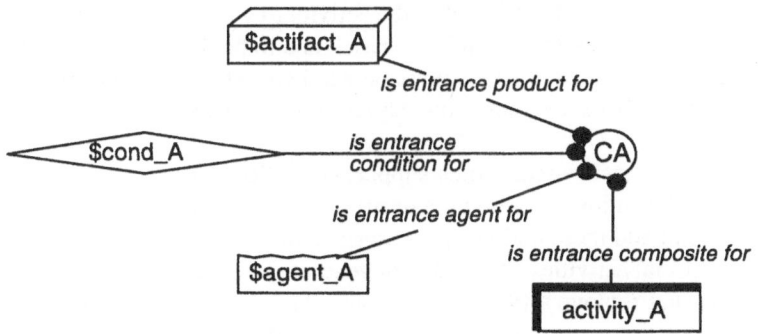

Fig. 2.4. Example of a *CA* composite

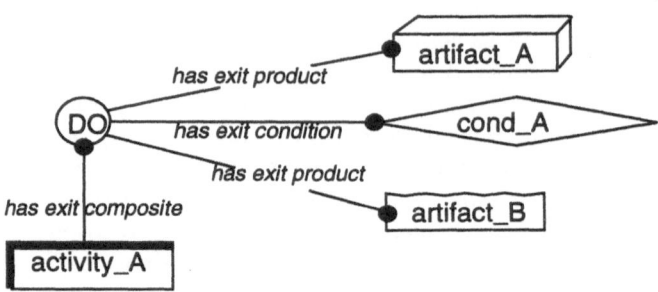

Fig. 2.5. Example of a *DO* composite

It should be noted that if multiple conditions and/or artifacts tie directly into an activity, then, by default, these are all assumed to be conjoined (i.e., no CA box is needed). The same rule applies for conditions/artifacts exiting an activity (i.e., no DA box is needed). This default can be seen in Figure 2.3. Finally Figure 2.6 illustrates a complex Boolean expression that serves as input to an activity that in turn generates an artifact and sets a condition.

Iteration and Version Management: Iteration is easily accommodated within the existing notation. Iteration is required, for example, when a artifact undergoes a series of revisions, each revision being different from the last. Figure 2.7 illustrates the approach. A change request (*CR*) is initially composed at which time the incrementing variable i is set to an initial value *(initializeCR | i=1)*. Each time the change request is updated, the variable is incremented (*updateCR | i++*). Versions of artifacts can be tagged with the variable i, and hence versions of the artifact are defined. Thus *revReq | i* represents the i-th version of the revision request. Nested loops can also be implemented using this notation.

When an integer variable is incremented through, for example, the expression $i++$, this action is performed at the end of the activity to which the expression is attached. Thus any i attached to exit entities is assumed to be the incremented value. If the expression $++i$ is used, then i is incremented before the activity begins. Similar reasoning holds for the decrementing expressions $i--$ and $--i$.

Stores and Entity Persistence: Stores support collections of artifacts and conditions values, and thus allow for modeling of persistency of generated entities. Since we must be able to add these entities to, or retrieve these entities from, a store, we introduce two special activities. These do not generate artifacts, conditions etc., but add artifacts to, and remove artifacts from stores. The activity types (*put, get*) are illustrated in Figure 2.8 and are added on to the front of the activity name as shown in the figure. Note that in the case of the *put* operation, there must always be an exit condition stating that the activity has taken place. Likewise, in the *get* operation, an entrance condition must be present in order that the operation can be initiated. En-

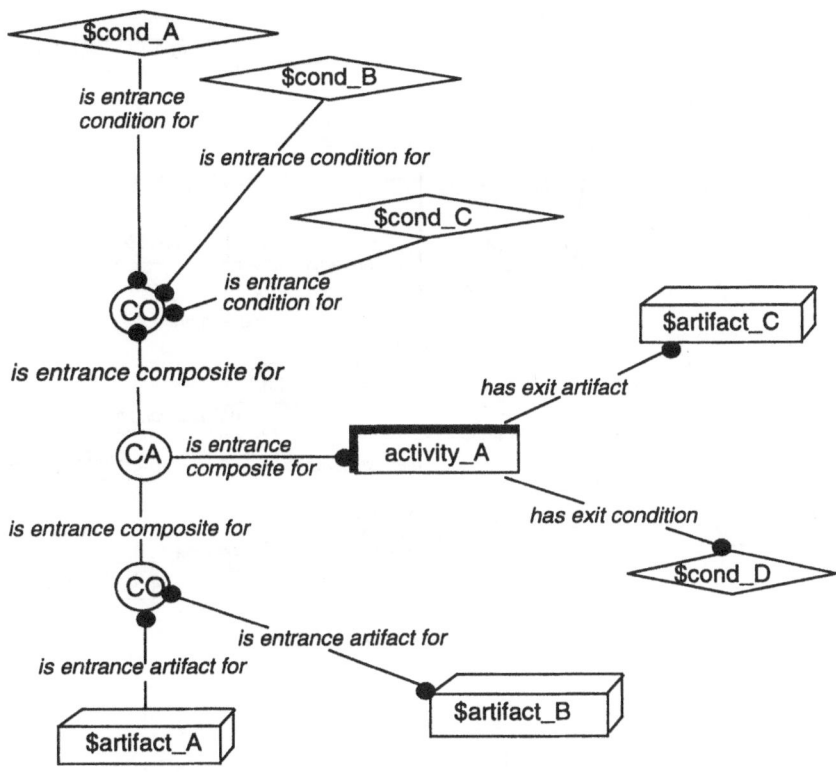

Fig. 2.6. An example of a complex Boolean composite

trance stores (as in Figure 2.8) are used with the *put* and *get* operations. Exit stores are analogous to exit agents - they allow for the identification of stores at run time (see Figure 2.3).[3]

Process model hierarchies: It frequently occurs that processes are too complex to be described in one diagram. In such cases it is necessary to expand an activity on one process diagram (the parent) into a lower-level process diagram (the child). Such activities are identified graphically by having the four sides of the rectangle that represent the parent activity in bold. The inputs to, and outputs from the parent activity must be consistent with the inputs to, and outputs from the expanded child process. Inputs to a child process intersect with the left-hand edge of the child process diagram while outputs intersect with the right-hand edge of the diagram. This convention can be seen in Figure 2.7

---

3. This convention differs from previous ProNet conventions [Christie 93a].

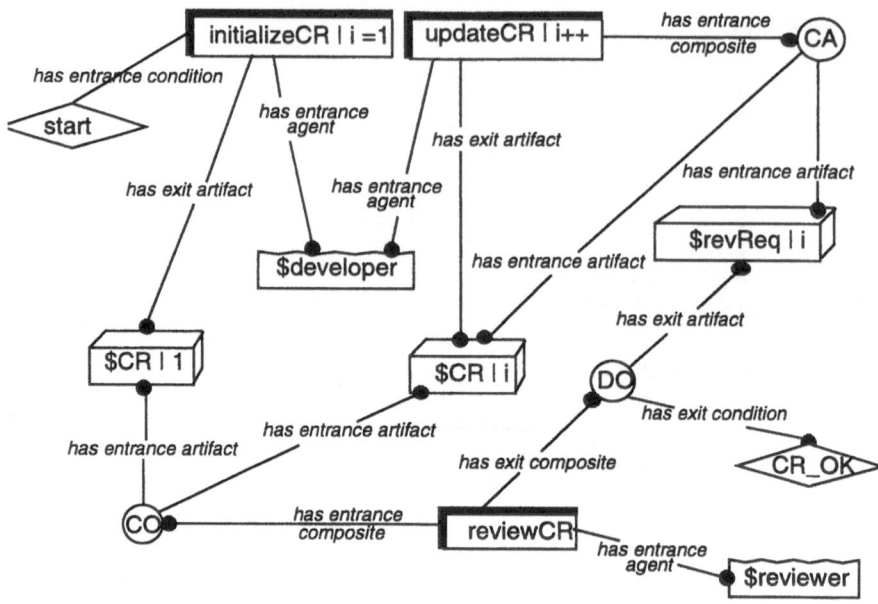

Fig. 2.7. An example of iteration

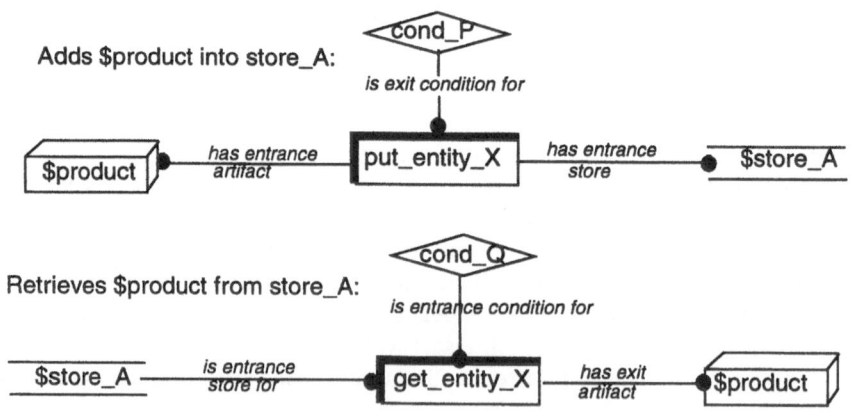

Fig. 2.8. Definition for the *store* entity

Suppression of relationship names. ProNet diagrams may become cluttered, in part because of the names of relationships that link entities together. Under mildly restrictive conditions, these names can be suppressed from the diagram without reducing the information conveyed. In order to do this one must consistently use either the relationship types *is entrance XXX for*, and *has exit XXX* or the relationships types *has entrance XXX* and *is exit XXX for*, where *XXX* can stand for *agent*, *artifact* etc. When either convention is used, the directional links together with the entity icons provide the relationship information. These two conventions are illustrated in the lower and upper process elements of Figure 2.8 respectively (although the relationship names have not been suppressed). Either one convention is used universally, or the other is used; they cannot be mixed. Some restrictions to this convention do apply. If the relationship type is *inheritance*, *aggregation*, or *custom* than the relationship name must be included, as the icons do not provide sufficient information.

2.3.3 A ProNet Example

To illustrate the modeling concepts discussed in ProNet, the following simple software development example is given. While this example is small, it illustrates many, but not all, of the concepts that may go into a ProNet model. For a large and detailed ProNet model of a real software maintenance process, [Slomer 92] should be consulted.

Figure 2.9 shows the model. In this figure, the major relationships (arcs) are shown with continuous lines, while supporting relationships are shown with dashed lines. This distinction is not essential for process definition but is required for process execution. This will be discussed further in Section 2.4. To initiate the process, entry artifacts or entry conditions are placed along the left-hand edge of the diagram. In this case the process starts with the condition *startCodeMod*. Similarly, the process terminates with exit artifacts or conditions placed along the right hand edge of the diagram. In this case there is one exit condition *sourceUpdated*. Thus the process can be followed by starting on the left of the diagram and working over to the right.

The condition *startCodeMod* initiates the activity *getSourceCode*. This activity is performed automatically and it does not have an associated human agent. Also the variable i is set to 1 at this point. As a result of the activity, two modules are extracted from the repository *sourceRepos*. In addition, the activity *getSourceCode* generates the condition *SourcesRetrieved | 1*. The modules *$codeModule1* and *$codeModule2* are then worked on by developers *$developer1* and *$developer2* respectively using *$changeRequest*. On completion of both modules, the tester then builds and tests an executable version of the code. If the test passes then the modules are placed back into the repository through the activity *putSourceCode*. If failure results, then the modules have to be updated again.

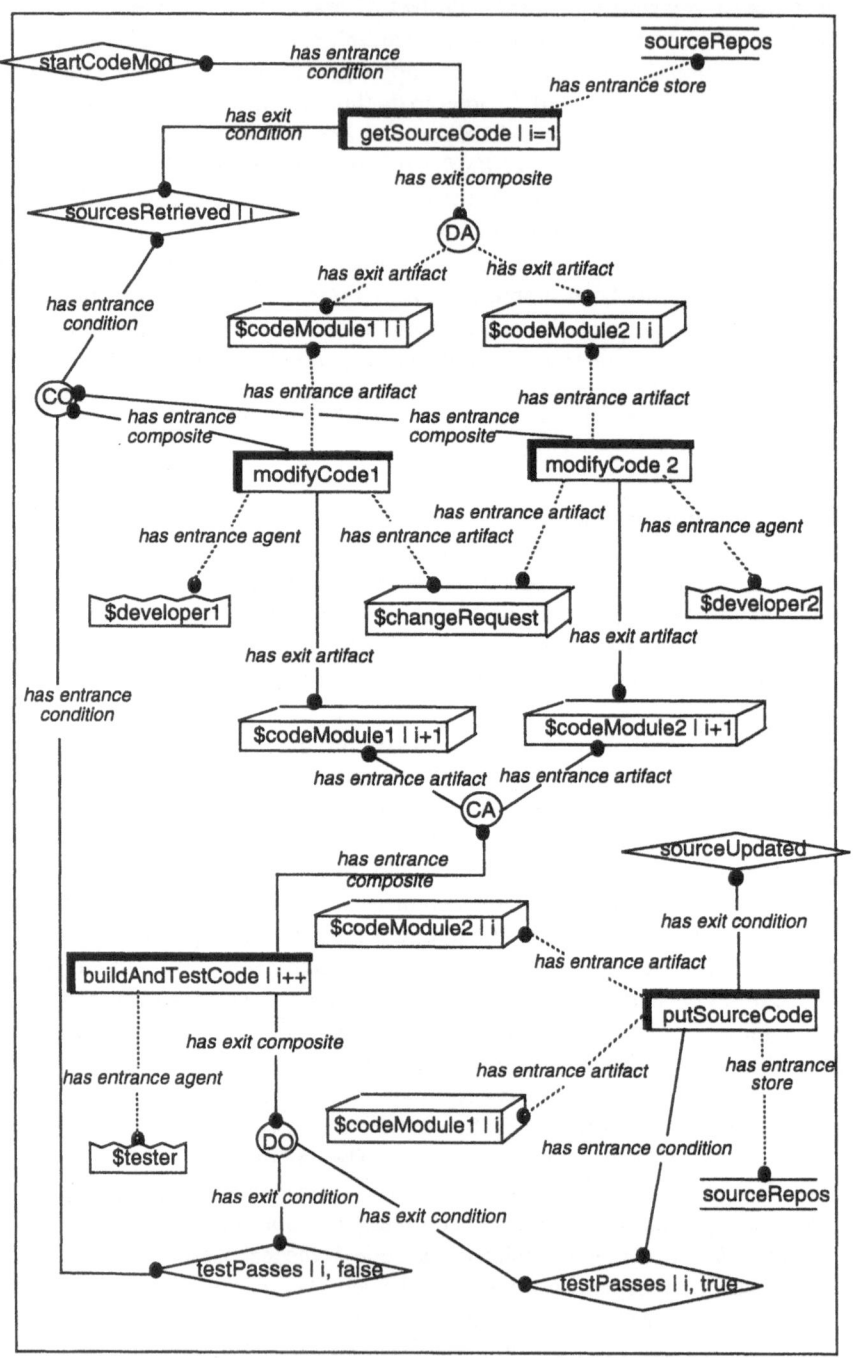

Fig. 2.9. Simple software development process model

2.3.4 Relationship to other Modeling Techniques

The approach to process modeling taken by ProNet has connections to other modeling notations. In particular, there are elements in common with entity-relationship models, state transition diagrams, data flow diagrams, and Petri Nets. ProNet can also be interpreted in a declarative rule-based sense. However, since this rule-based interpretation is discussed in some detail in Section 2.4, it is not dealt with here.

The connection between ProNet diagrams and entity-relationship (E-R) diagrams [Chen 83] is a fairly direct one. In one interpretation of E-R diagrams entities are connected by directed arcs, and names describe the relationships (i.e., arcs) between the entities. Entities may have attributes or properties and, in the database world, these can stored in tables. However, it is the concept of *relationship* that is of importance to ProNet rather that the concept of data structure.[4] While relationships in E-R diagrams can, in general, take on arbitrary values, in a ProNet model the relationships, such as *is exit condition for*, come from a predefined small typed set. (An exception to this rule is the *custom* relationship discussed in Section 2.2.1.)

State-transition networks [Harel 87], based on finite-state machines, can be used to model the dynamic (or behavioral) aspects of process. Such networks model *states* and *events* and the relationships between them. An event occurs (in theory) instantaneously, and represents control or stimulus information required to activate a new state. A state can represent a particular configuration of objects and may have implied activity associated with it. Through this activity, new events may be activated. In process modeling, the state-transition concept of *state* maps to the ProNet concept of *activity* while the concept of *event* maps loosely to the ProNet concept of *condition*. While an artifact may be interpreted as a physical object, its existence or lack of existence can also be interpreted as a condition.

ProNet has also much in common with data-flow (or functional) modeling techniques [DeMarco 79]. Data-flow diagrams define activities and the actifacts that flow between them. They also allow for stores in which artifacts, generated by the activities, are kept, or retrieved. They do not, however, consider the temporal sequence in which these activities occur and thus do not consider behavior. ProNet borrows several concepts from data-flow diagrams:

- activities play a central role,
- stores are used to contain entities,
- activities can be hierarchically nested,
- entities are explicitly generated by some activities and consumed by others.

Finally, ProNet has elements in common with Petri Nets [Reisig 82]. However, because Petri Nets are briefly discussed in Chapter 3 with respect to process execution paradigms, they will not be reviewed here.

Despite the influences of other modeling notations, ProNet has a combination of features that make it unique. These include:

---

4. See [Christie 93a] for a brief discussion of a data structure interpretation of ProNet.

- its constructs are designed specifically for process support, not software specification or other applications,
- its graphical notation is easy to understand by non-technical people,
- it provides for version management within a process definition/enactment context and provides for persistency of entities generated during enactment,
- its notation has direct extensions into process execution (as will be seen in Section 2.4) and verification (as will be seen in Section 2.5),
- its notation is precise and unambiguous (because of enactability).

2.4 Developing an Approach to Process Execution

This section describes how the ProNet language defined in Section 2.3 can be used as a basis to generate an executable model (see step 3 in Figure 1.1). The executable implementation of ProNet is called ProSim[5] and is written in the Prolog language [Bratko 86]. Prolog has previously been used by various researchers [Heimbigner 90, Lee 91, Emmerich 91], and appears to be an effective one for capturing process data and executing process models. Prolog's declarative characteristics allow for a straightforward mapping between the graphic form of the process and an equivalent set of textual rules through which the process can be executed. The identification of one activity with one Prolog rule is an appealing way to modularize the process model. This allows for easy modification of the Prolog-based executable model when changes are made to the graphical process model. However, for large hierarchical process models, one needs to add explicit information to the rules to reflect the structure of the model. Otherwise these rules will become unmanageable. A final advantage of basing the executable model on Prolog is that the "compiled" process model (being written in Prolog) is humanly readable and modifiable.

2.4.1   Mapping Activities to Rules

The sequence of steps we will now take are to:

- identify how Prolog rules can be derived from graphical process building blocks,
- illustrate how this derivation procedure can be used to generate Prolog rules from the example process shown in Figure 2.9, and
- generalize the derivation procedure.

This exercise is performed manually. While a means to "machine-compile" the diagrams into Prolog has not been implemented, such compilation would not appear to require any major conceptual challenges.

---

5. ProSim stands for *Process Sim*ulation

For an activity to be a candidate for execution, two elements must be satisfied. First, the activity's entrance conditions must be true and entrance artifacts must exist. For example, in order to save the code to the repository, consider the activity *putSourceCode* in Figure 2.9. The condition *testPasses* must be true for some version *i* of the code. Second, the exit conditions must be false and generated actifacts must not exist. Thus to initiate the activity *putSourceCode*, the condition *sourceUpdated* must be false (i.e., it does not exist). During process execution, a sequence of statements (called *log* statements) is generated. These leave a trace of what activities have been performed, and are required to assure that, once activities have been completed, they are not performed again. On completion of each activity, a *log* statement is generated and saved, thus indicating that the activity has been completed. A *log* statement contains information on which activity has been completed, what inputs were consumed and what outputs were generated. As will be discussed in Section 2.5, the trace generated by the *log* statements is also useful in supporting the audit trail required for process verification.

The above discussion gives a flavor for the basis of the ProSim approach. It is a declarative model in which each activity forms the core of a rule. There is a variety of techniques for executing the rules. Two of these are the production system OPS5 [Brownston 85] or Prolog [Bratko 86]. Prolog was chosen since an implementation was readily available and the language is very appropriate to this type of problem. A knowledge of Prolog will be useful in the discussions below. We now look at the central process building blocks for:

- the basic activity,
- activities with conjoined inputs,
- activities with disjoined inputs,
- activities with conjoined outputs,
- activities with disjoined outputs,
- adding an artifact to a store,
- retrieving an artifact from a store, and
- iteration and version management.

In the following figures (2.10 through 2.16), artifacts and conditions are for the most part interchangeable as far as the Prolog structures are concerned. Also note that, in defining these building blocks, we will not consider the agents who perform the activities, nor will we consider the tracking of artifact versions. These issues will be covered when we look at the Prolog implementation of the example in Figure 2.9.

We start off with the simplest graphical process element and translate it into a Prolog clause. This is shown in Figure 2.10. The first issue that must be addressed is that Prolog will not accept the ProNet notation for variables, that is, the "$" prefix on the variable name. Variables must be converted into an appropriate Prolog notation and this is done in the following way. Variables in Prolog start with upper case letters. Thus, for example, we substitute the ProNet variable *$artifact* with the Prolog expression *artifact (Artifact)*. At execution time we need to specify what the variable *Artifact* is, and we do this by adding, for example, the clause

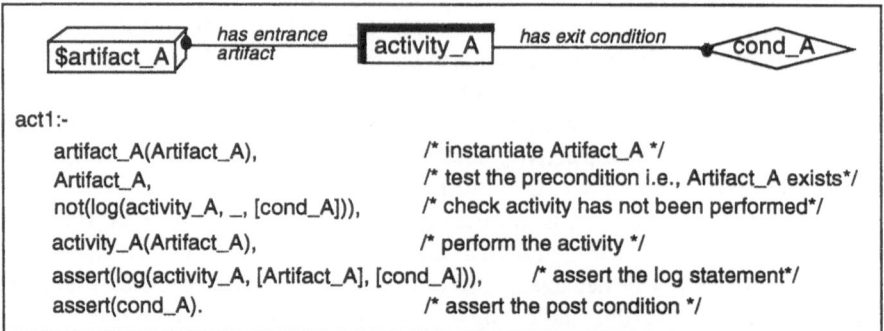

Fig. 2.10. A process element and its Prolog expression

artifact(reviewDoc). Prolog then "unifies" the clause *artifact(Artifact)* with the clause *artifact(reviewDoc),* thus instantiating the variable *Artifact* with the value *reviewDoc.* The activity *activity_A* requires artifact *$artifact_A* as input. Since the exit condition *cond_A* is, in this case, a known string value, it does not need to be explicitly generated by *activity_A,* but simply acts to indicate that the activity has been completed.

The equivalent Prolog statement, shown below the diagram, indicates that:

- *artifact(Artifact_A)* must exist in the Prolog database prior to performing the activity, and that
- the activity *activity_A* has yet not been performed (as determined through the truth of the *not (log (activity_A, _,[cond_A]))* statement).

With those two conditions met, the activity itself can be performed. The actual details of the activity are not of concern here. Once the activity has been completed, the statement *(log (activity_A, [Artifact_A], [cond_A]))* is added to the Prolog database through the *assert* function. This documents that the activity has now been performed and, as a result, the output condition *cond_A* can be added to the database. In general, a *log* statement defines the activity name, a list of the entrance entities, followed by a list of the exit entities. The square brackets around the entities indicate lists in Prolog (albeit, in the above cases, one element lists).

The above example illustrates how each activity can be treated as a separate chunk of knowledge, and is not explicitly coupled to any other activity. This allows for incremental growth of the model. The assertion of outputs from the activity (e.g., *cond_A*) then allows other activities to be initiated. In order that an activity be initiated, not only must the entrance conditions be satisfied, but a check must be made to assure that the activity has not already taken place.

Figure 2.11 shows how an activity can be initiated through one of two (or possibly more) artifacts being present, and in this case the activity generates an exit artifact. (Recall that *CO* stands for *Convergent OR.*) The fourth statement of the Prolog clause indicates that *X* can take on the value of either the first artifact variable *Artifact_B,* or the second artifact variable *Artifact_C.* Note that, as implemented above, the CO is an exclusive OR.

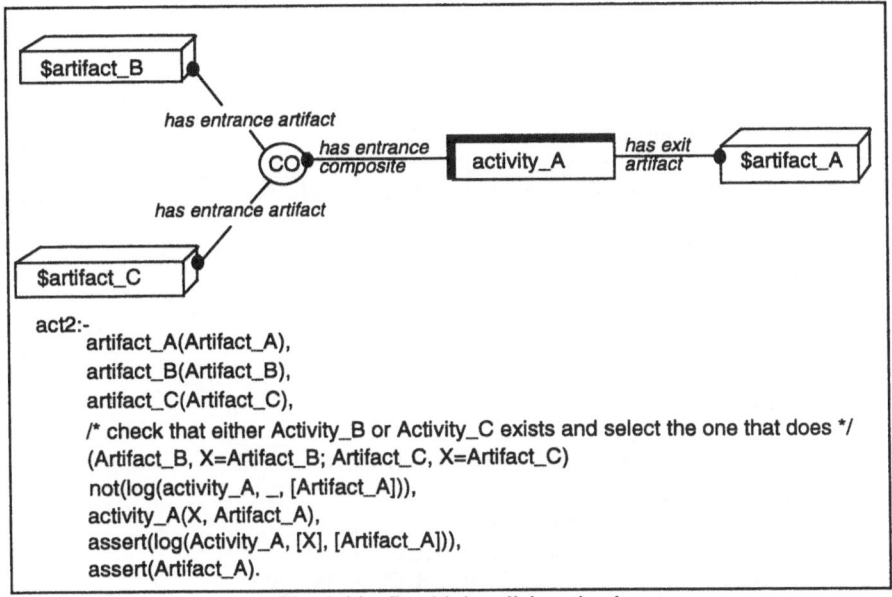

act2:-
    artifact_A(Artifact_A),
    artifact_B(Artifact_B),
    artifact_C(Artifact_C),
    /* check that either Activity_B or Activity_C exists and select the one that does */
    (Artifact_B, X=Artifact_B; Artifact_C, X=Artifact_C)
    not(log(activity_A, _, [Artifact_A])),
    activity_A(X, Artifact_A),
    assert(log(Activity_A, [X], [Artifact_A])),
    assert(Artifact_A).

Fig. 2.11. Combining disjunctive inputs

Figure 2.12 has a very similar structure to that of Figure 2.11. However, because this case is a *Convergent AND*, both entrance artifacts $artifact_B and $artifact_C need to be present as a condition for satisfying the execution of the Prolog clause.

The case where one of two possible outcomes is possible (a *Divergent OR*) is shown in Figure 2.13. Here the possibility of either outcome having previously occurred (*$artifact_B* or *$artifact_C*), along with the existence of the entrance artifact *$artifact_A* must be tested for. In addition, the body of the activity must contain some means of deciding which outcome is appropriate. In the Prolog clause, this is represented by the statement *activity_A(Artifact_A, Artifact)*. *Artifact* will take on the value of either *Artifact_B or Artifact_C* depending on the actions of *activity_A*. These actions are not considered to be part of the model at this level. The case for conjunctive outputs (the *Divergent AND*) is straightforward and is shown in Figure 2.14.

Stores are repositories that provide for the persistence of entities. The next two structures deal with the insertion of entities into, and removal of entities from such stores. In order to enter an entity (artifact, condition, etc.) into a store, an activity with the prefix *put* is used. This is shown in Figure 2.15. The function *put_ent* is used to store the entrance entity (e.g., $artifact_A) into the store (e.g., $store_A). A condition is generated to indicate that the store operation is completed. The store is implemented as a Prolog list of names of the entities in the store. These names may be the identifiers of files in which the contents are actually kept. They could even be the names of agents who are associated with the process.

Finally Figure 2.16, illustrates the *get* operation through which entities are retrieved from a store. The *get* operation checks to see if the entity is in the store, and

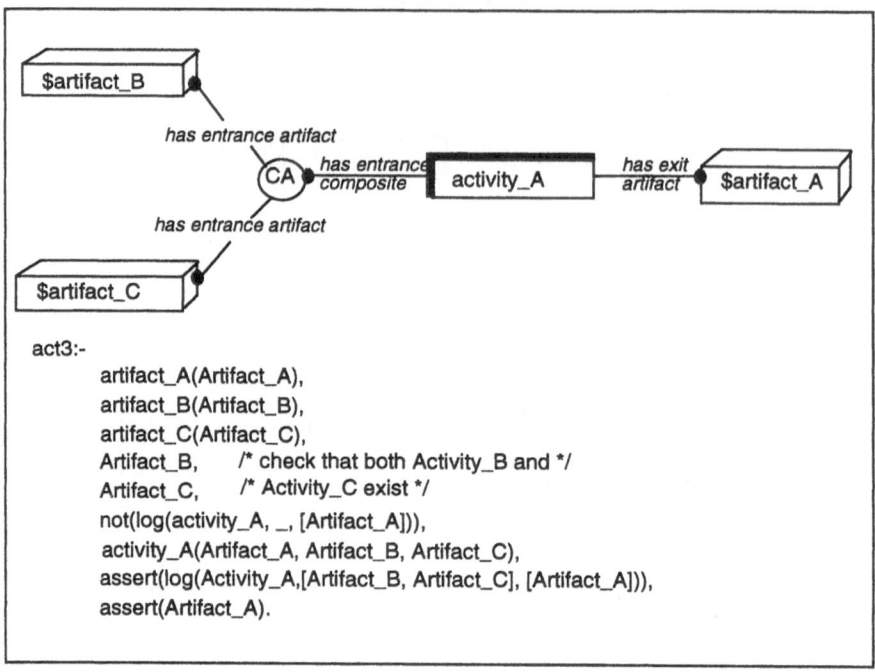

```
act3:-
        artifact_A(Artifact_A),
        artifact_B(Artifact_B),
        artifact_C(Artifact_C),
        Artifact_B,      /* check that both Activity_B and */
        Artifact_C,      /* Activity_C exist */
        not(log(activity_A, _, [Artifact_A])),
        activity_A(Artifact_A, Artifact_B, Artifact_C),
        assert(log(Activity_A,[Artifact_B, Artifact_C], [Artifact_A])),
        assert(Artifact_A).
```

Fig. 2.12. Combining conjunctive inputs

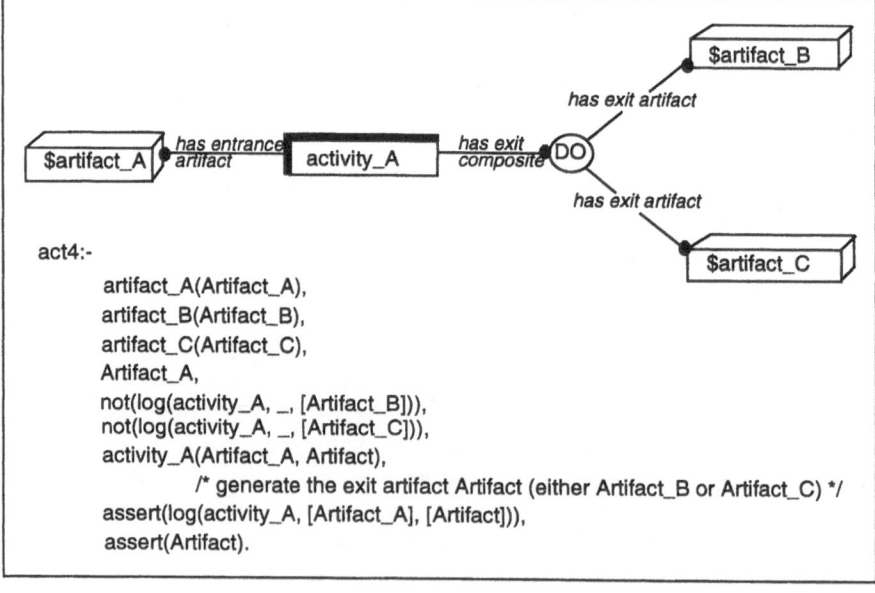

```
act4:-
        artifact_A(Artifact_A),
        artifact_B(Artifact_B),
        artifact_C(Artifact_C),
        Artifact_A,
        not(log(activity_A, _, [Artifact_B])),
        not(log(activity_A, _, [Artifact_C])),
        activity_A(Artifact_A, Artifact),
                /* generate the exit artifact Artifact (either Artifact_B or Artifact_C) */
        assert(log(activity_A, [Artifact_A], [Artifact])),
        assert(Artifact).
```

Fig. 2.13. Generating disjunctive outputs

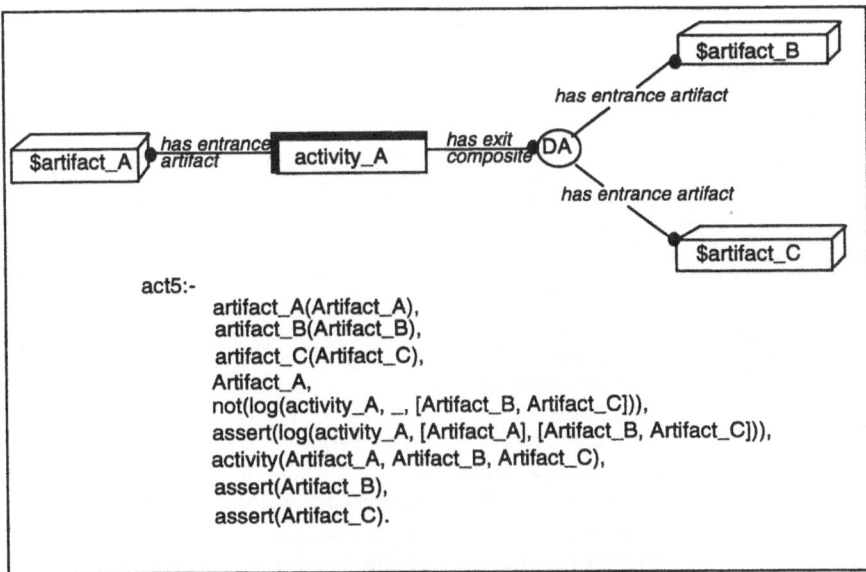

Fig. 2.14. Generating conjunctive outputs

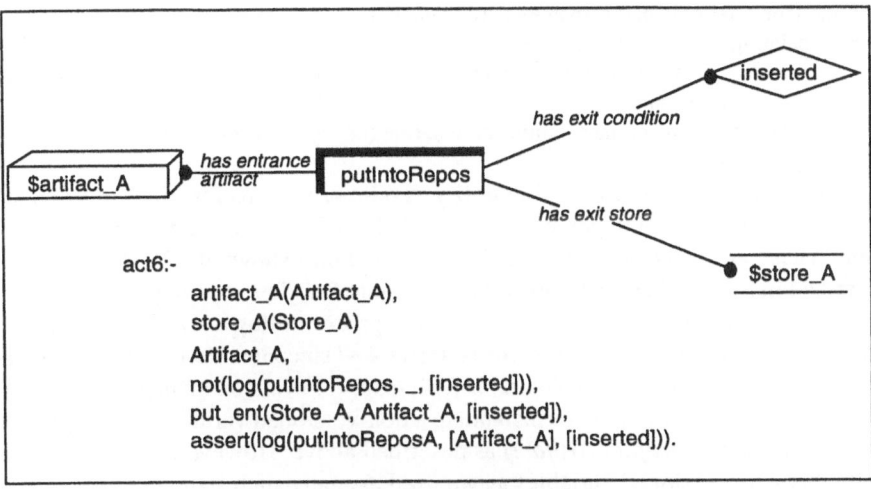

Fig. 2.15. Inserting an artifact into a store

asserts the name of the entity through the Prolog expression *assert(X)* where, in Figure 2.16, *X* is equivalent to *Artifact_A*.

There are various miscellaneous items that have to be reviewed before the rule definition can be considered complete. These items are:

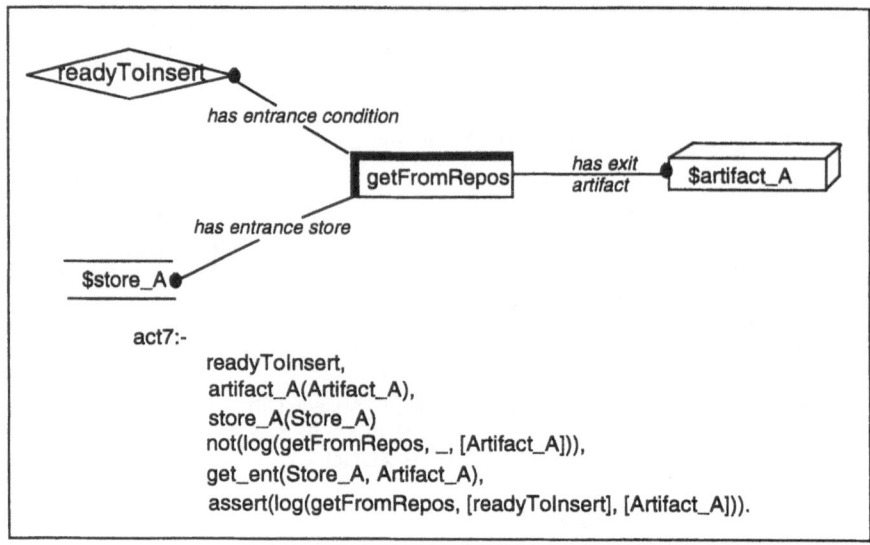

Fig. 2.16. Retrieving an artifact from a store

- modeling iteration and managing entity versions,
- associating agents with activities,
- preventing a premature abort when an attempt is made to instantiate an item not in the Prolog database, and
- controlling which entrance entities initiate rule (i.e., activity) execution.

Modeling iteration and managing entity versions: Various functions must be included to manage the integer variables needed for iteration and version management. These are listed in Table 2.3. The first column shows the ProNet notation described in Section 2.3.2 and illustrated in Figure 2.7. The second column defines the equivalent Prolog functions. (These are not part of Prolog but are built using the Prolog language.) *inc* is used both for *i++* and *++i* since its interpretation depends on its placement within the Prolog rule. With respect to version management, an additional function is required. To instantiate a non-versioned variable, we simply use statements such as *artifact(Artifact)* as described above. However, it is impractical to do this with versioned variables as we need as many such statements (e.g., *artifact(Artifact,5)*) as there were versions of a entity. Thus we provide a function *instantiate* that allows us to instantiate an arbitrary version of an entity. This is used in the following way for (say) the 5th version of the entity *artifact*. The expression *instantiate(artifact(5), Artifact)* will instantiate *Artifact* with *document(5)* if we have initially defined *artifact(document)* in our Prolog database.

Table 2.3.   Prolog Equivalents to ProNet Notations

ProNet Notation	Prolog Function	Comments
l i=1	set(i,1)	Sets the variable i to the value 1
l i	ver(i,I)	Instantiates I with the value of i
l i++ or l ++i	inc(i)	Increments the variable i by 1
l i-- or l --i	dec(i)	Decrements the variable i by 1

Associating agents with activities: Agents may be identified at model definition time, at the start, or even during process execution. Agents are treated in the same manner as any other variable in that, if they are not known at model definition time, the name is prefixed with a "$" sign. In this case an agent's name is instantiated through a statement, such as *agent(tom)*, that has been placed in the Prolog database. Thus if *agent(Agent_A)* is placed inside a rule, *Agent_A* will be instantiated with *tom*. This agent will be needed inside the function that actually performs the activity. Thus the rule in Figure 2.10 would be modified to read:

```
act1:-
        artifact_A(Artifact_A)
        Artifact_A,
        not(log(activity_A, _, [cond_A])),
        agent(Agent_A), /**** new line ****/
        activity_A(Artifact_A, Agent_A), /**** modified line****/
        assert(log(activity_A, [Artifact_A], [cond_A])),
        assert(cond_A).
```

Preventing a premature abort when an attempt is made to instantiate an item not in the Prolog database: If an attempt is made to test for a clause that does exist not in the Prolog database, Prolog will abort; an undesirable occurrence. However, with due precaution, this can be avoided. For example if we are testing to see if the condition *readyToInsert* is true, but the statement has not yet been *assert*ed into the database, then Prolog will generate an abort error. To prevent this from happening, a "?" can be added to the front of the test (i.e., *?(readyToInsert)*). With this modification, the test only "fails" (in the Prolog sense), that is, the test does not succeed, but the program does not abort.

Parallel testing to identify all currently valid activities: As each of the rules in Figures 2.10 through 2.16 is structured, the preconditions form an integral part of the rule. Hence the associated activity will be performed as soon as the rule preconditions are validated. Other rules, that have an equal right to execute at that time, will consequently have their execution delayed. Thus the rules need to be restructured in order that we can identify all the candidates for execution prior to that execution. To do this, each rule is split into two: a *test* component and an *act* component. Prior to rule execution, all rules are tested, and those that are current candidates are identified. To illustrate this splitting of a rule, Figure 2.17 separates the rule show in Figure 2.16 into *test* and *act* components. If this *test* succeeds, it places *act7* on the candidate list of activities that may be performed. The actual mechanics of this procedure will be described in Section 2.4.3. Note also that the rule has been modified to prevent non-existence of *readyToInsert* from aborting the process through the use of the "?".

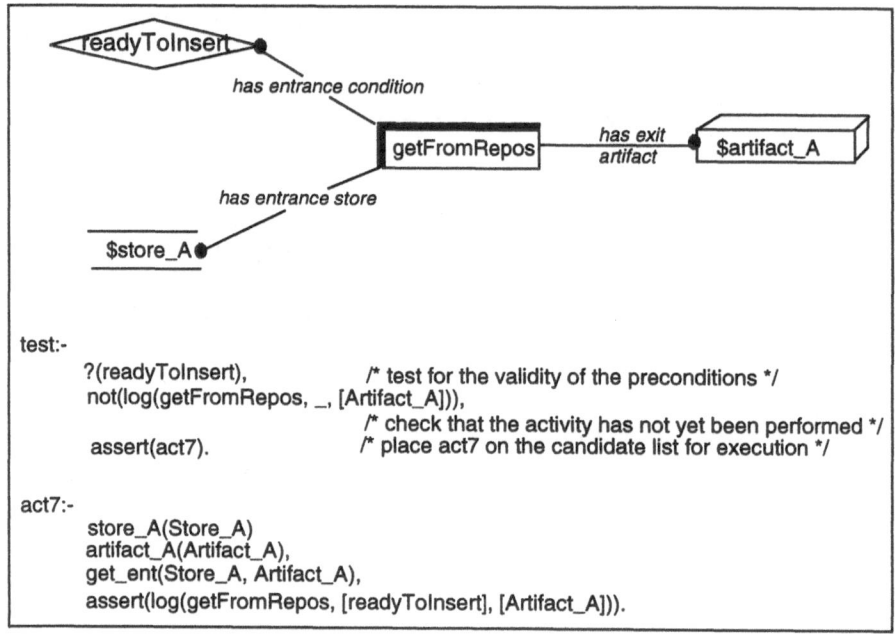

Fig. 2.17. Separating a rule into *test* and *act* components

Controlling which entrance entities initiate rule (i.e., activity) execution: If we look back at Figure 2.9, we will see that some of the arcs are solid while some are dashed. The solid lines reflect connections to those entities that are 1) associated with pre- or post-conditions on the Prolog clause for that activity and 2) are captured in the *log* statement. Thus solid lines reflect the critical input and output relationships that determine activity execution. The other relationships shown as dashed lines (such as who performs the activity) are important but may not affect the execution sequence. Which entities are considered to be the critical is at the discretion of the process designer. In Figure 2.10, the arcs associated with both the input and output relationships are represented with solid lines and hence the associated entities are part of the *log* statement and the pre-, post-conditions.

2.4.2   Generalizing the Rules

Figures 2.10 through 2.16 provide insights into how to define the graphics-to-symbolic mapping. Table 2.4 summarizes the general rules for performing this mapping. The table can either be used as a basis for manually mapping a graphically defined ProNet process or as a mechanism for developing an computer-based approach. The latter has not, to date, been done. This procedure is applied to each activity and the entities (i.e., artifacts and conditions) upon which the activity is dependent. Table 2.4 has three columns. The first column lists the item number. Note that in Table 2.4, the only functions defined within the Prolog language are *not* and *assert*. All other statements and functions (e.g., *instantiate and put_ent*) are defined as part of the executable ProNet model.

Using Table 2.4, the rules that define the process can be generated. However, in order to make the process executable, a rule-driver is required. While the rules themselves are dependent on the process being defined, the rule driver is process independent and controls the order in which rules are fired as the process is enacted. The rule driver is discussed immediately below.

Table 2.4.   Mapping ProNet Model to its Enactable Form

#	Mapping Task	Example Statements
	Assert entrance entities	
1	Convergent AND (CA) (Artifact_B defined at execution time)	artifact_A, artifact_B(Artifact_B), Artifact_B,...
2	Convergent OR (CO) (Artifact_B defined at execution time)	artifact_B(Artifact_B), (artifact_A, X=artifact_A; Artifact_B, X=Artifact_B),
3	Assert entity, version I. (Artifact_A(I) defined at execution time)	instantiate(artifact_A(I), Artifact_A), Artifact_A,...
	Managing incrementing variables	
4	Instantiate integer values	ver(i, I),...
5	Initialize integer	set(i,1),...
6	Increment integer	inc(i),...
7	Decrement integer	dec(i),...
8	Add temporary increment statements	I1 is I + 1,...
9	Tests on integer variables	I =:= 2,... J =\= 2,... K>2,...

Table 2.4.   Mapping ProNet Model to its Enactable Form (Continued)

#	Mapping Task	Example Statements
	Test for existence of *log* statements:	
10	Test on a divergent AND (DA)	not (log (activity_A, _, [Artifact_A, Artifact_B, cond_C])),...
11	Test on a divergent OR (DO)	not (log (activity_A, _, [Artifact_A])), not (log (activity_A, _, [Artifact_B])), not (log (activity_A, _, [cond_C])),...
	Assert *log* statements:	
12	convergent AND (CA), divergent AND (DA)	assert(log(activity_A, [Artifact_A, Artifact_B, cond_C], [Artifact_X, cond_Y])),...
13	convergent AND (CA), divergent OR (DO)	activity_A (Artifact_X, Y), assert (log (activity_A, [Artifact_X], [Y])),... --- "Y" may take different values depending on the outcome of Activity_A
14	convergent OR (CO), divergent AND (CA)	assert (log (activity_A, X, [Artifact_X, cond_Y])),... --- (X as in 2 above)
15	convergent OR (CO) divergent OR (DO)	activity_A (Artifact_A, Y), assert (log (activity_A, X, Y)),... --- (X as in 2 above)
	Database operations	
16	Add item to database (*put_*...)	put_ent (store_A, Artifact_A, [a_added]),...
17	Remove item from database (*get_*...)	get_ent (store_A, Artifact_X),...
	Assert exit entities:	
18	divergent AND (DA)	assert (Artifact_X), assert (cond_Y),...
19	divergent OR (DO)	activity(Artifact_A, X), assert (X),...

2.4.3   Managing Execution of the Rules

Let us first look at how a user would interact with our simple ProSim executable process model and then address the issue of managing the rule base. We have referred above to the *rule driver*, that is, the part of the system that selects and displays appropriate information (e.g., current activities) to the user. From an implementation point of view, the name *rule driver* is appropriate, but from the perspective of a user of the process, it is not. In this section it is more appropriate to rename it as the *process controller*.

The structure of the ProSim process controller is shown in Figure 2.18. It is (of course) defined in ProNet notation.[6] On initiation of the project, a list of all the activities that can start the process is generated (see #1 and #2 in Figure 2.18). The activities in this list are identified using the *test* clauses, an example of which is shown in Figure 2.17. Appropriate information is then sent to the agents in order that they can perform the activities (see #3). The information on the details of the activities execution are embedded inside a function such as *activity(ArtifactA, Artifact_B, Artifact_C)* shown in Figure 2.14. On completion any of these activities, a new list of activities is generated that includes both currently executing activities and any activities that can now be performed as a result of the termination of the completed activity (see #4 and #5). Any currently executing activities are then removed from this list and the resulting list contains only new activities (see #6 and #7). If this list is empty then the process is considered complete. The process controller continues to cycle round the tests defined in the rule-base and on each cycle initiates a number of activities. Cycling continues until the activity list is empty

This procedure of generating a list that contains both the executing and new activities may seem a little devious. Why not directly generate a list of new activities? The answer lies in the fact that, from an implementational point of view, generating a list that includes both the executing and new activities is easier than generating the list of only-new activities (since the *test* clause identifies both).

Thus the controller acts like an rule-based production system [Brownston 85]. From the above discussion and Figure 2.18, it should now be clear why the entrance conditions (the tests) are separated from the actual activities. All entrance conditions must be checked in order to generate the current activity list prior to activity execution. While the process is being executed, artifacts and conditions are generated, artifact versions are being added to and removed from stores, and a history of the user-defined process path is being captured.

Appendix A provides the Prolog listing of the process controller implementation.

---

6. It is tempting to think that the controller, being defined in ProNet notation could itself be automatically generated as a rule-base. However, given the exploratory nature of this implementation, the controller was developed using a more conventional approach.

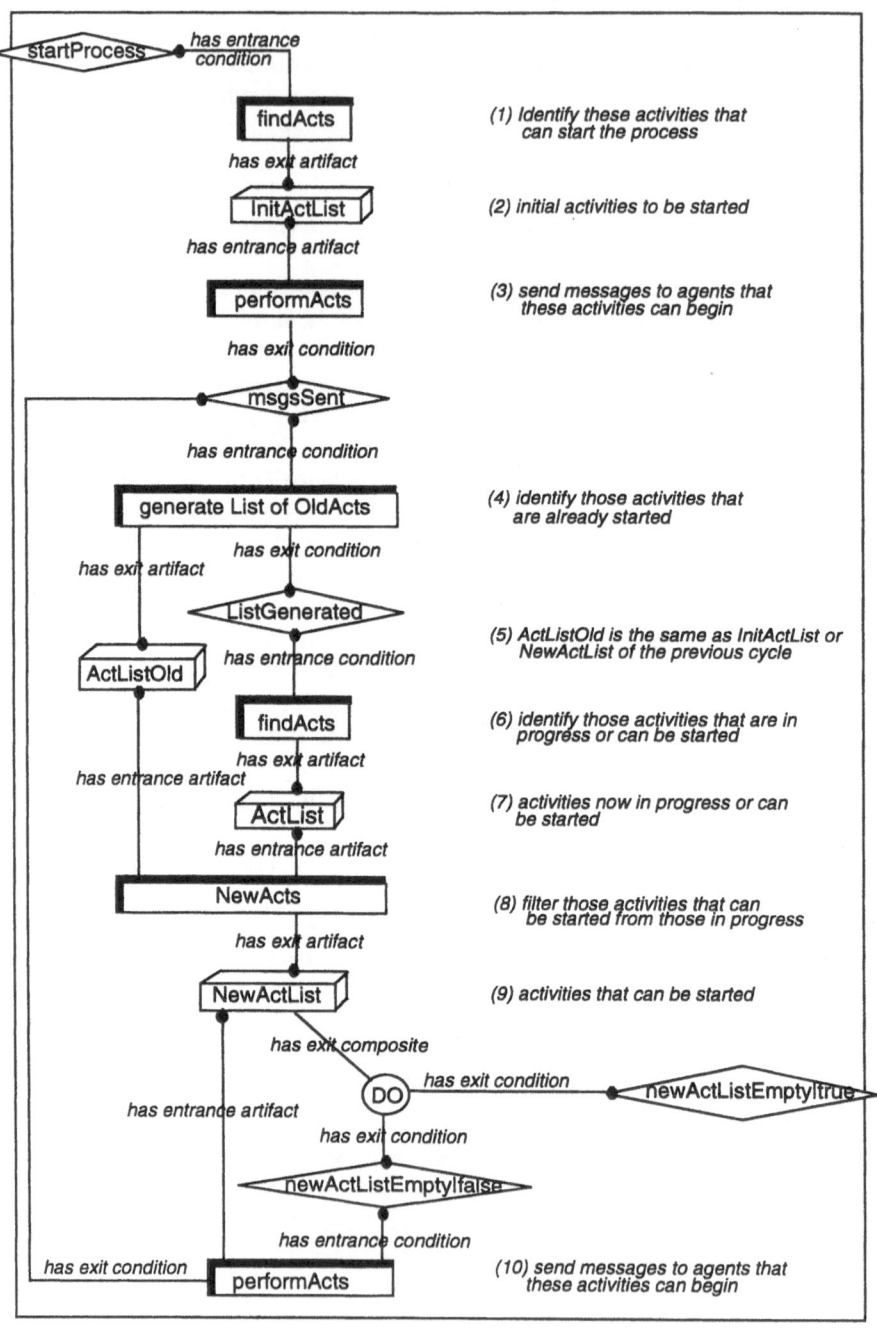

Fig. 2.18. Process controller for ProSim

2.5 Two Examples of Process Execution

We will now illustrate the concepts developed in the previous sections by implementing executable models of two processes. The first model we have already seen;
it is the simplified software development process defined in Figure 2.9. The second
is a more complex model of a document update process. This latter model addresses
two additional issues: modeling process hierarchies and implementing the functionality needed to perform activities. The document update process will also be used as
the basis for investigating the characteristics of executable models in SynerVision
and ProcessWeaver. This investigation is the subject of Chapter 3.

   Appendix A provides Prolog listings of both these executable models. The process controller functions are listed separately in this appendix since they are application independent. While excerpts from these listings are provided below, the
listings should be examined to understand the interaction of the various process elements.

2.5.1   The Software Development Process

In this section, we will illustrate the mapping of one of the graphically-defined activities in the software development model, shown in Figure 2.9, to its Prolog equivalent. This mapping is performed with the aid of Table 2.4. The activity selected
(*getSourceCode*) is shown in Figure 2.19, and corresponds to the first activity in
Figure 2.9. This figure also shows the corresponding Prolog clauses. In order to
compare the other graphical model elements to their Prolog equivalents, Figure 2.9
should be compared to the Prolog listing provided in Appendix A.

   Like all activities, this activity is composed of several elements. These are shown
in Figure 2.19 with circled numbers that correspond to the item numbers in Table
2.4. The reason for each of these is summarized below:

   - 1: entrance condition needed to start the activity.
   - 3: instantiation of versioned artifacts,
   - 5: initiation of an integer variable,
   - 10: test (*not(log(...)*)) that this activity has not been performed,
   - 12: assertion (*assertz(log(...)*)) of this activity into the Prolog database,
   - 16: specification of artifact store.
   - 18 assertion of exit condition,

Note that arcs that are in bold define the entrance and exit conditions. While *code-
Module1* and *codeModule2* are artifacts generated by the activity, they are not required to initiate the next activity.

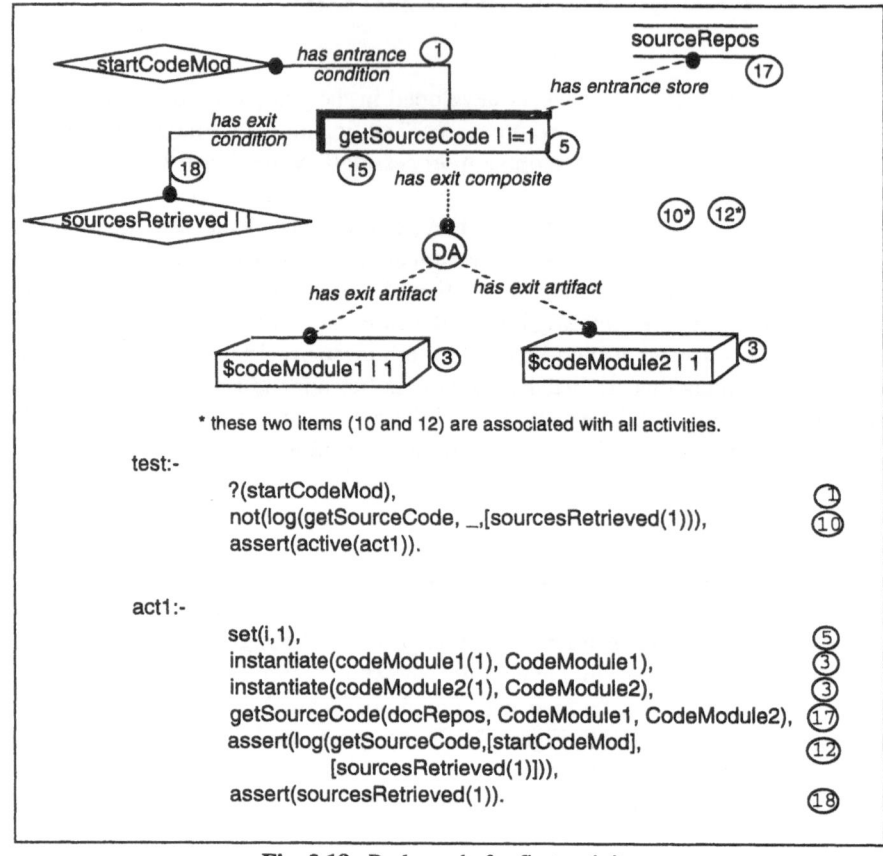

Fig. 2.19. Prolog rule for first activity

2.5.2   The Document Update Process

The document update process, while still too simple for real use, is more complex than the software development process. As noted above, this process is being introduced for two reasons. First, it illustrates additional functionality needed for real-world modeling, and second it forms the basis of examining the two commercial products reviewed in the next chapter. The document update process has three activities in the top-level process diagram. These are:

1. accepting a change request,
2. selecting the agents who will perform the updated task, and,
3. performing the update itself.

Activity 1 is a simple task with no underlying process diagram, activity 2 exercises notions of communication between the agents, while activity 3 invokes the tools necessary to perform the editing. The top-level process is shown in Figure 2.20

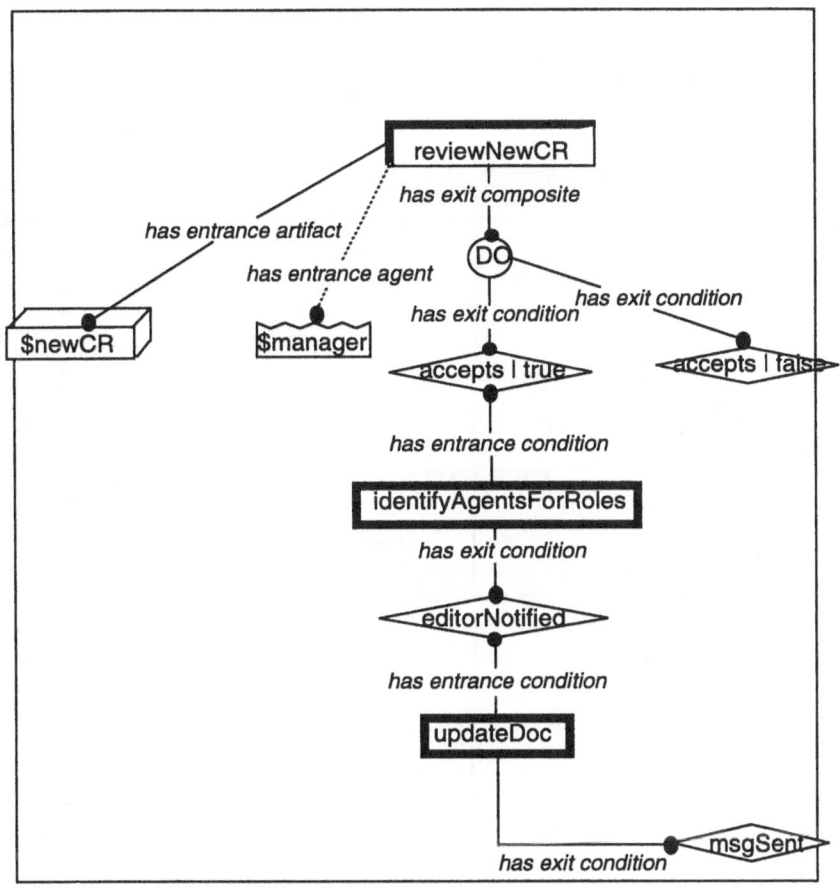

Fig. 2.20. The *document update* process

while the processes for activities 2 and 3 are shown respectively in Figure 2.21 and 2.22.

Note that the inputs and outputs between the activities in these diagrams are all consistent. For example, the input *(accepts | true)* and output *(editorNotified)* from the activity *identifyAgentsForRoles* in Figure 2.20 are consistent with the input and output to the process diagram for that activity (Figure 2.21). Information generated in one activity can be propagated to another sub-activity by two other means. The first means is through the use of stores. Entities inserted into a store during one activity can be retrieved from that store during a second activity. The second means of communicating information is through the instantiation of a variable entity in one activity and its subsequent use in a second activity. Both these approaches are used in the document update process.

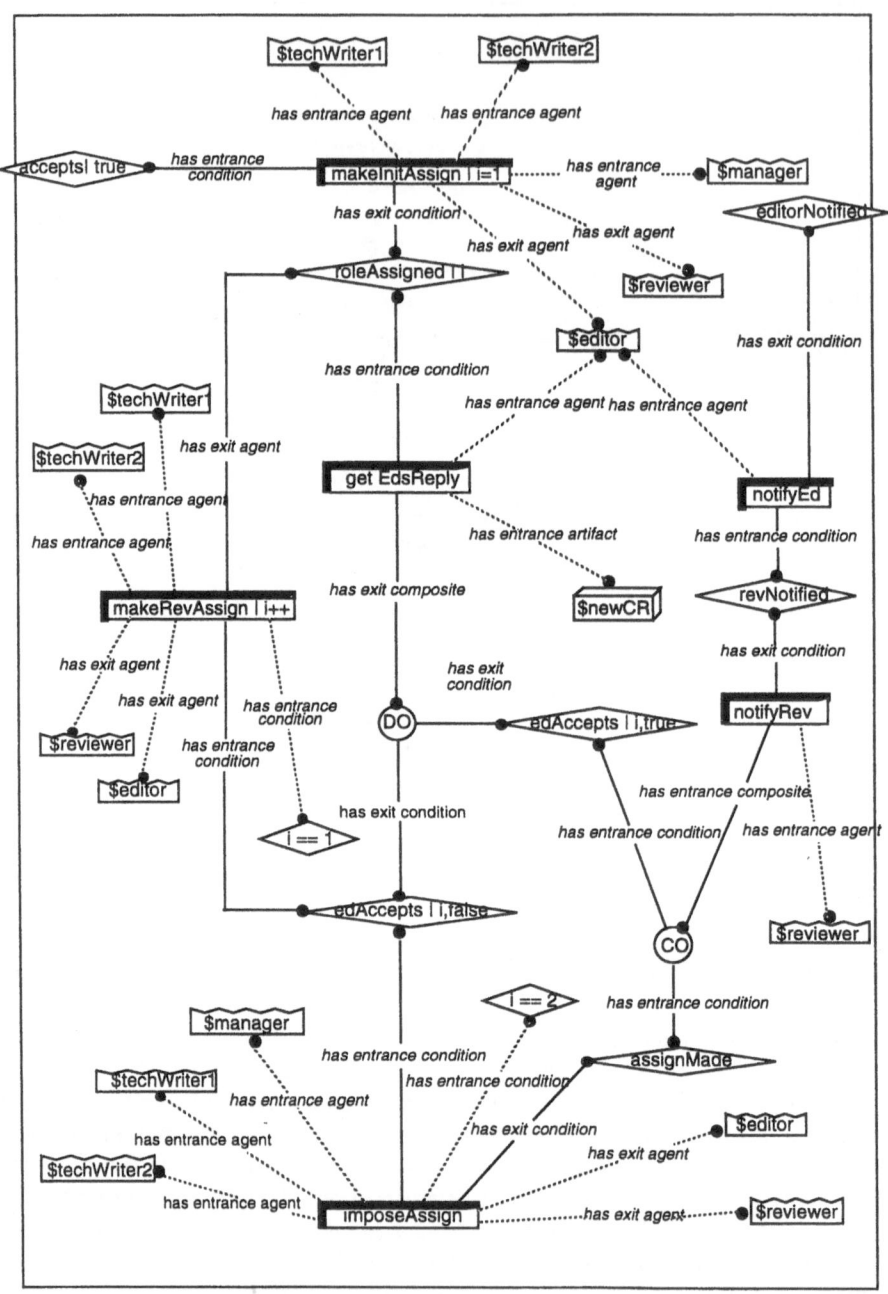

Fig. 2.21. The *identify agents for roles* process

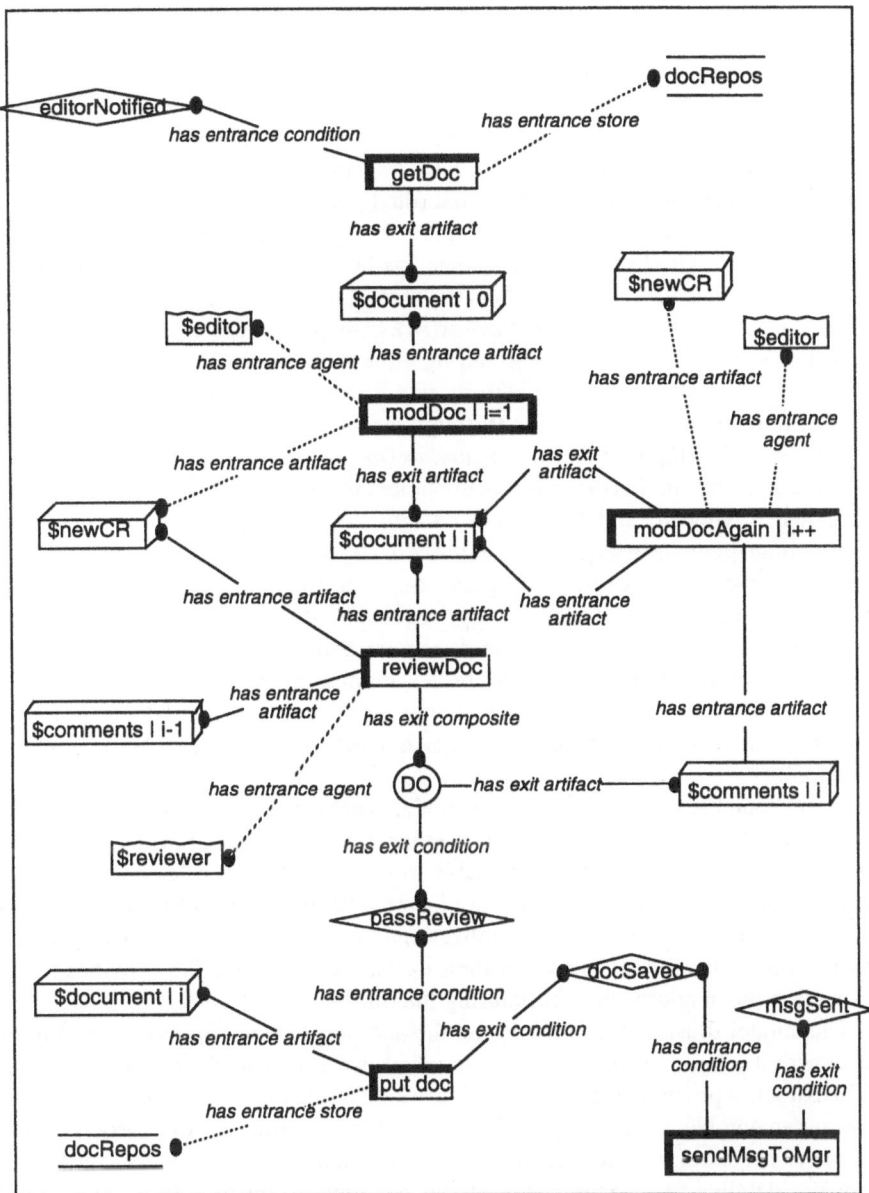

Fig. 2.22. The *modify document* process

The group that performs the document modifications consists of a manager and two technical writers. Following the process flow, shown in Figure 2.20, the manager receives a change request (CR) from outside and determines through the activity *reviewNewCR*, if it is appropriate for processing. If it is, then there is a selection process, *identifyAgentsForRoles*, that determines which technical writer will perform the editing function and which will perform the review function. Finally there is the update process, *updateDoc*, in which the changes are actually made.

The *identifyAgentsForRoles* process, shown in Figure 2.21, contains elements to exercise communication between the human agents. The manager makes an initial assignment of the editor and reviewer roles (*makeInitAssign*). The person assigned to the editor role can accept or reject that role (*getEdsReply*). If the reply results in the condition *edAccepts| i,true*, then the other person is automatically notified through the *notifyRev* activity that he/she has been given the reviewer role. If the first person rejects the editor role, then the second person is automatically requested to take on the editor's role (*makeRevAssign*). This person can also accept or reject the editor's role. If the role is rejected then the manager is notified and a manual assignment is made through the activity *imposeAssign*. In this case the writers are notified of the manager's decision (through the *notifyEd* and *notifyRev* activities).

The remaining high level process, *updateDoc,* is shown in Figure 2.22. To perform the activities in this process, the document is removed from a simple repository, edited, reviewed, and then replaced into the repository. Thus some simple version management is required. The process starts with the system extracting the document from the repository and presenting it to the editor (*getDoc*). The editor then revises it as described in the change request (*modDoc*). After the modified text has been reviewed (*reviewDoc*), the document is then either approved by the reviewer or sent back to the editor with review comments for further modification together (*modDocAgain*). If the reviewer approves the changes, the document is put back into the repository and the manager is notified that the process is complete (*putDoc*).

The executable form of this process model is provided in Appendix A. While the hierarchy of activities/processes is very evident in the graphical formulation of the model, it is not evident in the executable model. That is, the rules do not indicate where in the process hierarchy they are located. While this is not important for execution of the rules, it does have implications for both the organizational clarity of the rules and also the efficiency of their execution. Section 2.7.5 provides further discussion on an approach to structuring the rule-base.

This model illustrates another issue: the addition of functionality to the lowest-level activities (the "leaf" activities) in which work is actually performed. Figure 2.23 extracts a process element from Figure 2.22 while Figure 2.24 provides its Prolog equivalent. Note that in Figure 2.24, there are now three clauses associated with an activity. As before, there is the *test* and *act* clauses. However, the third clause provides detailed functionality that allows the agent to meaningfully interact with the process. While full information defining the test and act clauses can be extracted from the ProNet diagram, the internal behavior of the activity cannot. Although some automation of this behavior may be possible, a greater degree of hand customization is to be expected. The implementation of this functionality will be more machine dependent (or environment dependent) since it has to deal with issues related to communication protocols,[7] window management, and tool integration mecha-

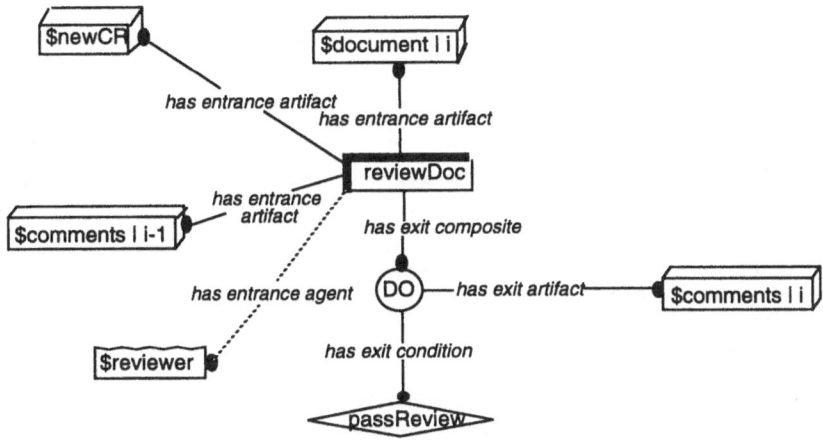

Fig. 2.23. Process element from *modify document*

nisms. Figure 2.24 only illustrates some simple window management functions for this Macintosh version of Prolog[8]. It does not address communications or tool support issues.

2.6 Software Process Verification

This section of the paper presents an approach to assuring that any software product either meets the requirements of the defined process, or alternatively, identifies deviations from the defined process [Stanley 92, Cook 94]. Process verification, as defined here, is a post-analysis of process data gathered during product development (down to an appropriate level of granularity). The act of verification will identify where deviations from the agreed-to process occurred, and allow a determination of the severity of those deviations. (See step 9 in Figure 1.1.)

Deviations need not invalidate a non-conforming process path. Indeed, they could be benign or even beneficial. Some process changes may be due to unforeseen circumstances such as accounting for the replacement of an assigned developer by another developer in the execution of certain tasks. Others may be made to allow for creative improvements such as the replacement of a specified compiler by a more efficient one. Whatever deviations are made, a post-project evaluation can be performed to assess their impact on the resulting software quality, provided that the en-

7.   This including human-to-human, human-to-machine, machine-to-human, and machine-to-machine communications.
8.   Advanced AI Systems Prolog [AAIS 91].

```
test:-
        ver(i,l),
        instantiate(document(l),Document),
        ?(Document),
        instantiate(comments(l),Comments),
        not(log(reviewDoc,_,[passReview])),
        not(log(reviewDoc,_,[Comments])),
        asserta(active(act10)).

act10:-
        ver(i,l),
        instantiate(document(l), Document),
        instantiate(comments(l), Comments),
        newCR(NewCR),
        reviewer(Reviewer),
        reviewDoc(Reviewer, Document, NewCR, Comments, PassCom),
        assertz(log(reviewDoc, [Document, Comments, NewCR], [PassCom])),
        assert(PassCom).

reviewDoc(Reviewer, Document, NewCR, Comments, PassCom):-
        write(Reviewer), write(', please review the document as per the change request'), nl,
        write('Add any comments to the comments window'), nl,
        create(file_edit_window, FEW1, [200,50, 400,550], NewCR, true),
        stripParen(Comments, Com),
        stripParen(Document,Doc),
        fopen('temp', "w+", _),
        create(file_edit_window,FEW2,[400,50, 600,550],'temp',false),
        create(file_edit_window,FEW3,[600,50, 800,550],Doc,true),
        write('Press y if review is OK, n if not OK: '),read(Pass),nl,
        (Pass='y',PassCom='passReview';
                    PassCom=Comments,save_window(FEW2, Com)),
        close('temp'),
        destroy(FEW1),
        destroy(FEW2),
        destroy(FEW3),
write('~~~~~~~~~~~~~~~~~~~~~~~~~~~~~~~~~~~~~~~~~~~~~~~~~~~~'), nl.
```

Fig. 2.24. The Prolog implementation of *ReviewDoc*

acted process is tracked. The approach to verification is the following. Throughout a project, the artifacts that are produced by the developers are automatically recorded, along with who produced them and how they were produced. On project completion, the manner in which these artifacts were produced, who produced them etc., can then compared with the requirements of the defined process.

The approach implemented here taken rests on the Prolog-based process modeling concepts described in previous sections. In particular, the *log* statements used to record process history are used to verify the correctness of the as-performed process. If the process has been followed exactly as specified in the enactment model, then a set of *log* statements, consistent with the defined and implemented process, must exist. However, if the process has been modified during execution, the sequence of activities, inputs to, or outputs from the activities will not match the agreed-to process. This information will be captured in the *log* statements. Note that the *log* data structure is appropriate for this Prolog implementation. However, if the same data were collected using a commercially available process-centered environment, then the same type of analysis could be performed - even if the process data is captured in a different format.

Process verification has an impact on several areas. First, the tools used to develop the software have to be instrumented to record what is being performed. Second, there are implications for metrics tools, since process data have to be recorded. Third, consistency of intermediate product versions is essential to assure final product quality. Hence, there are implications for configuration management. Finally, there are of course implications for process, process specification, and process modeling.

It should be noted that process verification can form a basis for process certification. In this context, "process-certified" software implies that either the end products are guaranteed to have been generated using an agreed upon process, or non-conformances are identified and justified. This does not of course guarantee that the software performs to specification, but certification may be regarded as a necessary if not sufficient guarantor of software quality. Such certification may be of interest to any organization that subcontracts out software development.

2.6.1   The Basis for Process Verification

The basis for verification has already been laid through the ProNet notation presented in Section 2.3 and the subsequent discussion on process execution in Section 2.4. The verification process is the inverse of the enactment process. During execution, activities follow the forward flow of time and the events are recorded (through the *log* data entities as described Section 2.4). However, verification takes place by starting with the end product, applying the *log* statements generated during process enactment, and working backwards. The object here is to prove that the implemented process, as defined through the *log* statements, is consistent with the defined process as reflected through the process model. The end product establishes the "initial conditions" for verification, and one *log* statement is consumed as the corresponding activity joins those in the set of verified activities. While this approach is not as formal as proof of correctness of programs [Greis 81], it is interesting to note that both perform their verification proofs in this backward manner.

Summarizing, the following sequence of activities is performed for process verification:

- Prior to initiation of the software project, the software development process is established using an appropriate process modeling technique such as ProNet. The level of process detail should be such that important entities (artifacts, conditions agents) can be tracked.

- During the project, all critical activities are instrumented such that their input and output artifacts and conditions (and their version identifiers) are recorded. Conditions must be tracked, since these are important process indicators.
- When the end product has been generated, comparison is made between the agreed-to process model and the *log* statements generated during project execution. For verification of the end product, there must be complete consistency between a subset of the intermediate artifacts produced and those expected by the process model.

It should be noted that the above sequence need not only be applied to a complete project. If the project is sufficiently large, then intermediate products from sub-projects can be individually verified using the appropriate sub-process. These intermediate products then contribute to the verification of products at a higher level in the overall project.

2.6.2   Implementing the Approach

In the implementation of process verification, the goal is to prove that at least one subset of the collected *log* data statements is consistent with the defined process. Figure 2.25 illustrates the elements of this theorem proving approach. The diagram in Figure 2.25 shows a process model element in which artifacts *prod1* and *prod2* support activities *act1* and *act2*, these activities generating artifacts *prod3* and *prod4*. This process is defined by the two *verify* statements also shown. The *log* statements represent the historical data gathered during execution of the process. The first *log* statement, for *act1*, uses versions v1 for both input artifacts *prod1* and *prod2*. The resulting version of artifact *prod3* is also version v1. As with the enactment model, the verification model is written in Prolog notation. In fact, as will be seen later, the implementation of the verification procedure is very similar to that of the process enactment procedure.

Let us now compare the process model data (the *verify* statements) with the tracking data (the *log* statements). The first *verify* statement asserts:

> **IF**
>> *prod4, version K* exists,
>
> **AND**
>> activity *act2* generates *prod4, version K* as output and uses *prod 2, version L* and *prod3, version M* as input,
>
> **THEN**
>> delete the *log* statement,
>> add *prod3, version M* and *prod2, version L* to the database,
>> delete *prod4, version K* from the database,
>> find the next applicable *verify* statement to execute.

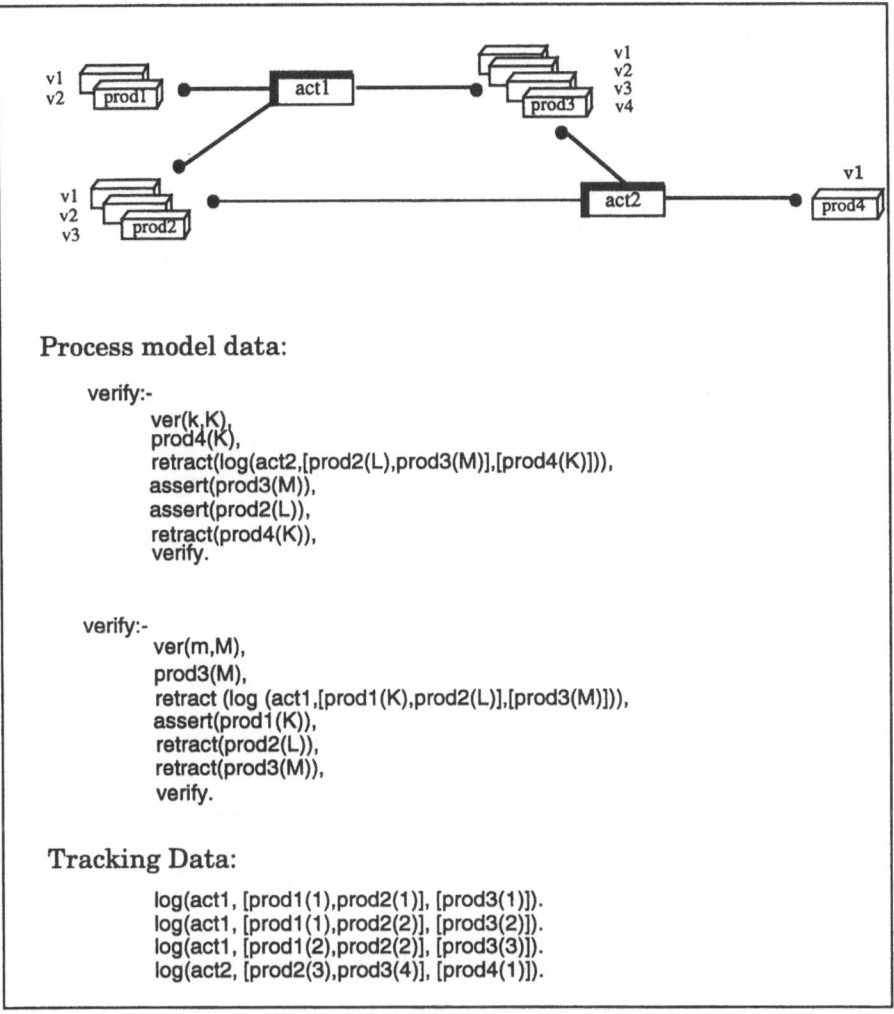

Fig. 2.25. A simple process model with process data

The initial *ver* statement in the verify rule simply identifies the current value K of the version number k. The second *verify* statement in Figure 2.25 has a construction very similar to the first. The values L and M of version numbers l and m, are determined when the appropriate *log* statement is instantiated. In this example, *prod4* takes on the version value 1, thus forcing (through the *log* statement for *act2*), the version numbers l and m to take values of 3 and 4 respectively. Hence *prod2, version 3* and *prod3, version 4* are added to the database. Since *prod3* is now in the data base the second verify rule is now activated. However, there is no *log* statement that has *prod3, version 4* in its output list. Hence there is a disconnect in the process, and the verification fails.

This simple example also illustrates how the process verification procedure does not care what activities have been performed (e.g., there may be many redundant *log* activities), so long as there is a core set that can be threaded together consistently, as defined by the process model.

2.6.3   A Simplified Verification Program

As with process execution, process verification is implemented through a rule-based, forward chaining production system. However, unlike the execution program, verification is not, and does not need to be interactive. The "initial conditions" for verification are the name (and version) of the end product and the *log* statements generated during execution of the project. As verification takes place, intermediate products appear and disappear and log statements are consumed, as the valid paths extend further backwards in time. At the end of the verification procedure (assuming the process is verified), all the *log* statements associated with the verified paths will have been be consumed and the entry artifacts/conditions for the process will be generated. The symmetry between process enactment and verification is shown in Figure 2.26.

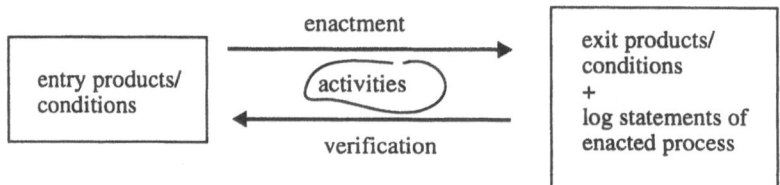

Fig. 2.26. Symmetry between enactment and verification

The *verify* program is listed in Appendix B. This program consists of:

- a set of clauses to drive the verification procedure,
- a set of clauses that define the verification rules, each rule being associated with an activity in the defined process,
- a set of *log* statements that were previously generated during process enactment.

The process used in verification is identical to that defined in Figure 2.9 (the simple software development process), and the *log* statements were physically removed from the output of an execution simulation. Thus there is complete consistency between the enactment model and the verification model. It should be noted that, while we have not discussed automated generation of the rules for a verification model from the graphical process model, such automation could be performed using a mapping quite similar to that shown in Table 2.4.

2.6.4   Implications for Verification

The exploratory work described above has some significant implications. These fall under the main headings of software quality and process certification, user interaction, and finally, metrics and process improvement. These are briefly discussed below.

- Software quality and process certification. On completion of a project, a verification analysis can formally be made to assure that all steps have been completed and that they have been completed in the right order. Such formal verification may have implications for contractor process certification and the ISO 9000-3 standard [ISO 91].
- User interaction. A major concern in enforcing effective process is the imposed restrictions that software developers feel, either from a supervisor, or from an automated environment. (This is discussed at length in Chapter 4.) The approach to verification in no way restricts the manner in which work is accomplished in terms of detailed oversight. It only requires that, when the project is completed, at least one consistent path through the agreed upon process has been taken, or if deviations from the defined path have been taken, they can be justified.
- Process improvement and metrics. Throughout a project that uses process verification, significant quantities of historical data will be gathered. This data can be used, along with like data from other projects, for long-term process improvement. Data from each project can be analyzed to see, for example, where bottlenecks occur, estimates are wrong, and process inefficiencies occur. By having formally defined process models and data from their enactment, considerable insight can be thus obtained. This provides all the needed ingredients for both qualitative and quantitative process improvement.

2.7 Miscellaneous Issues

There are several issues that arise from the design and implementation of the process modeling and language and its extensions into execution. These issues are discussed below.

2.7.1   Process Workahead

In practice, there are many cases when preliminary work can be performed on an activity prior to the time when all the specified entrance conditions are satisfied. This informal initiation of future activities is sometimes called *workahead*. For example, one might wish to start reviewing a document prior to the time when review authorization is given. Inability to allow for workahead is unfortunately exhibited by some current process-centered environments and is also exhibited by the above ProNet approach. However, within the ProNet formalism, the problem can conceptually be overcome in the following straightforward way. An activity is allowed to begin at any time; however it cannot considered complete until all its inputs are available. Thus the activity cannot release its exit artifacts etc., until all the inputs are accounted for. While the current ProNet approach maybe considered overly restrictive, the suggested modification may be considered too relaxed - we may still wish to constrain activity initiation until some important artifacts are available or conditions are met. Using a mixed approach allows the best of both worlds. For this, the process programming language should have the capability to prohibit the initiation of an activity if certain artifacts are unavailable while allowing initiation if other artifacts are unavailable. An activity cannot, however, be considered terminated until all its inputs have become available (as well, of course, as generating its outputs). This approach to activity initiation should be adaptable to most process automation techniques.

2.7.2   Process Rollback

A process-centered environment should account for the fact that mistakes will be made during the execution of the process. Even the simple clicking of an inappropriate button may take the process off in a wrong direction. It may then be impossible to correct for this unless recovery mechanisms are built in. Mistakes may be of two kinds. The first is as described: the immediate realization that a wrong button has been clicked on. The second is the realization, long after the fact, that a mistake was made (e.g., a wrong file version was used). The first type of error will be the most common and the easier of the two to implement corrective mechanisms for. The latter may involve complex transactions, and unless a detailed history of the process has been kept, they may be impossible to fix. The approach to process execution described above contains the elements of a possible solution. The process is recorded through the use of the *log* statements. If such statements are generated, and, in addition, a complete track of all file versions is maintained, then it would be possible, in principle, to backtrack to any earlier point in the process and from there to restart.

2.7.3   Process Backtracking

Another restriction on the current model is that the process driver only accounts for forward chaining, and not backward chaining. Forward chaining implies that activities are performed only when their entrance conditions are met (as described in the previous paragraph). However, it could be that an agent wishes to perform an activity, some of whose entrance conditions are not met. The agent may wish to satisfy that constraint by "backtracking" through the sequence of, as yet, unperformed activities in order to generate the unsatisfied entrance condition [Kaiser 87].

Figure 2.27 provides a simple example. Assume that *activity A*, *activity E*, and *activity F* have been completed. The agent next wants to start on *activity G*. However, *prod 3* is not yet available. To generate *prod 3*, *activity C* must be performed. This in turn requires *activity B* be performed. Hence to satisfy the entrance conditions to *activity G*, one option is to "backtrack" through these unperformed activities necessary to support *prod 3*. This control scheme is tighter than the one required for workahead, in that it still requires all input entities to be available before an activity can be started. However, it does allow an agent to start an arbitrary activity at any time; the system will then guide the user to perform the necessary precursor activities.

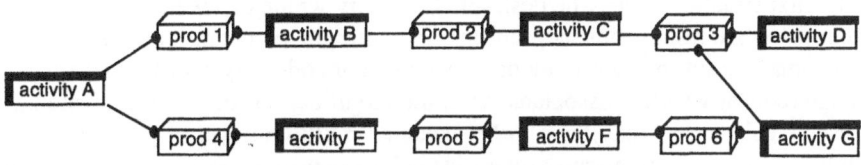

Fig. 2.27. Backtracking to define activity inputs

2.7.4   Process Visibility

A limitation of process execution, as it has been described, is related to the manner in which activities are displayed to the user. The simple user-interaction model initiates activities to be performed (see Appendix A), but provides little process context to the user. A significantly improved interface would show the graphical process model, driven by real-time execution data, and indicating project status [Mi 1992]. Color, or symbolic coding of the degree of activity completion, ownership of activities, would provide instant information on and control of the project. By clicking on an activity, the agent would thus open that task for development. Such a presentation capability would be particularly appealing to management by providing a rapid overview of project status.

2.7.5   Rule Hierarchies

As noted above, the graphical ProNet model of the document update process reflects a hierarchy of process, with higher level processes calling on lower-level processes. However, the equivalent rule base does not exhibit any structure - all rules are on the same level. For the size of models discussed in this chapter, this is not critical.

However, for large processes in which there are multiple process levels, modifying or maintaining a set of unstructured rules could become a burden. In addition, in an unstructured rule set, all rules are checked every process cycle, and thus the computational load significantly increases. To overcome these problems, a mechanism is needed to allow rules to be locally grouped. This could be implemented by appending a sub-process identifier to the head of each of the *test* clauses (such as in Figure 2.17) associated with that sub-process. Thus for a sub-process "A", all the tests associated with its activities would be named *test_A*. However, this has not been implemented.

2.7.6   Process Specification at Run Time

There are two situations where run-time binding of sub-processes may be desirable. In the first situation, it may be desirable to specify which of several alternate ways of performing a task is most appropriate only after the parent task has been started. For example, a sub-process to modify a segment of code may depend on the type of change request which is associated with the modification. In the second situation, the same subprocess may have to be executed multiple times in parallel, but the number of instances of the sub-process is not known prior to process execution. This situation can occur, for example, when multiple components of a software system are worked on simultaneously prior to integration.

Currently ProNet does not include mechanisms for modeling these situations, although extensions could be defined. As yet, these issues have not been adequately addressed in commercial process-centered environments.

2.7.7   Adapting the Process "On the Fly"

Not only must process models be sufficiently flexible to account for a wide variety of scenarios, but they must also allow for the adaptation of existing scenarios. Processes modification can take place in at least in two ways: as part of a process improvement effort, and "on the fly" while in the middle of a project. The former is based on a long-term strategy, supported by metrics gathering and analysis, and implemented through process redesign and verification. While this is challenging, with sufficient lead-time the inherent risks can be minimized. However, real-time modifications to an on-going process contain significant risk. Nevertheless such changes may have to be made for a variety of reasons. For example, the process may not be performing as expected (i.e. it was not adequately debugged), or circumstances such as new schedule constraints may force process changes. With a manually implemented process, changes can be made on an informal basis. However, if the process is automated, the ability to adapt the process may be significantly restricted. Like all knowledge-based computer models, process programs rely on reasoning (for example, rule based or state transition based) that explicitly takes into account only specified and understood changes in the system behavior. While a well regulated process will have a significant degree of predictability there may be instances when unaccounted for circumstances occur. These are much more difficult to handle within an automated environment.

The question of what mental models humans apply to situations where corrective action is needed has been addressed by the Danish industrial psychologist Jens Rasmussen [Rasmussen 79]. He perceives three levels of cognitive abstraction. At the lowest level there is the reflexive "if this happens...then do that" that is applied under normal conditions. This he calls the "skill" level. Computer modeling this level has shown significant success using, for example, expert systems. At a second level, the expert may have to rely on past experiences to reason about a condition that is not normally encountered and from these, formulate a plan. An example might be how to modify the process if a hard deadline is approaching. This he calls the "rule" level, and while amenable to computer analysis, is more challenging then in the skill-based regime. Finally the expert may encounter an altogether new situation where he/she has to reason from first principles. Examples of this might be loss of critical project data through natural disaster or having to deal with a virus-infected repository. This he calls the "knowledge" level and probably requires complete human intervention.

These examples indicate how human experts adapt their reasoning depending on the complexity and novelty of the situation. It is this kind of flexibility in reasoning that is difficult to build into a software system. To help in process adaption on the fly, PCEs need a variety of capabilities. Features to support such needs as graphical process definition, automatic translation of graphically defined process to enactable form, verification of the completeness and correctness of the process model, or part of it, and process simulation capability will be very useful in this regard. Also needed for modifying an executing process is the ability to assure that the end-state of the non-modified executing process is compatible with the start-state of the modified process. Finally, there may be severe disruptions from which it is not possible to revert to an automated process. For such circumstances, it may be necessary to incorporate features so that a process can taken off-line and operated in a manual mode. Because these activities have the potential to introduce erroneous process behavior from which it may be very difficult to backtrack, such modifications can have potential danger and must be managed very carefully.

2.7.8   Configuration Management, Conflict, and Cooperation

In any practical PCE, the ability to handle products within a cooperative group environment could be important, particularly at the software development level. Currently configuration management tools do support cooperative development. For example, tools such as SHAPE, SMS and NSE provide isolated workspaces, and the ability to resolve conflicts when merges are made between workspace product versions and the public repository [Dart 91]. In particular, NSE [Feiler 90] provides for multiple workspaces. Each workspace can have a virtual copy of the original parent environment, and only when a file is checked out in the workspace is a physical copy of it made. If files in the parent environment have been updated by one developer, then modifications from another developer (who also removed a copy of the unmodified parent) cannot be merged into the environment. The second developer must perform a local merge of the files and debug the two set of changes before updating the parent environment.

The above approach to parallel development does relax the constraint that development is strictly serial. However, it still does not support close cooperative development. For example, two persons may not be able to work in an interactive way on a section of code. As stated in [Bargouti 90],

> *"Having the development process explicitly encoded does not alone solve the problem of supporting multiple users, a requirement for any large-scale software development effort. The basic problem is the inability to allow concurrent access to project components while still maintaining the consistency of these components."*

Work that investigates graphical modeling in these areas is however discussed by [Singh 92] using a role-centric approach supported by Petri Nets. Such work might help illuminate some of the problems associated with developing enactable PCE specifications when, for example, close developer cooperation is required.

2.8 Summary

This chapter has explored a variety of issues at the intersection of process definition, process enactment, and process verification. The central focus has been to describe a unified approach to these topics. It was suggested that construction of a process-centered environment can be facilitated through the development of a graphically-based specification of the process to be automated. This specification should allow for automatic compilation into an executable form, and can be of significant help in establishing a behaviorally correct process model.

The ProNet graphical process notation was first introduced (Section 2.3). This exhibits many of the needed characteristics for process definition, and accounts for:

- agents, artifacts, and activities,
- control flows,
- artifact version management, and
- hierarchical nesting of processes.

To investigate issues associated with enactment, the ProNet notation was used. Fortunately, as shown in Section 2.4, this graphical notation is appropriately structured for translation to an executable form. Examples of how different graphical process elements can be mapped to corresponding symbolic forms was provided in Section 2.5. This mapping was done by hand and used the example of a change request process. However, as was shown in Section 2.4, there exists a well-defined set of rules whereby the mapping could be automated. The symbolic form is declarative and is implemented in Prolog. It results in a production system in which each of the activities in the process model translates into a rule. These rules are managed by a process controller that allows for process interaction with the user. The actual program is listed in Appendix A.

Process verification, as defined here, is a post-analysis of process data gathered during project execution (down to an appropriate level of granularity). This was discussed in Section 2.6. The object of verification is to determine if a subset of all the activities that have been performed, and products that have been produced conform to the prescribed process. With process automation in place, gathering process data is essential (otherwise the system would not be smart enough to know what needs to be performed next). Thus the data needed for verification comes at little extra cost. If a project strictly adheres to the defined process during process execution, then the data should be valid, by definition. However, in real situations, there are likely to be manual interventions that may compromise strict adherence to the defined process. Thus the verification procedure provides a final assurance that any deviations are acceptable. It was found that there is a symmetry between process enactment and verification. While enactment moves forwards in time and generates a trace of the process history, verification starts at the end and works backwards in time, consuming the trace generated by the enactment activity. The program with which process verification was investigated is provided in Appendix B.

Finally, in Section 2.7, we reviewed some modeling issues that have a bearing on the design of executable systems. Potential solutions or insights into these issues were reviewed.

Information on obtaining a commercial implementation of ProNet is provided at the back of the book

3 An Investigation into Process-Centered Environments

To better understand process-centered environments, we will first provide some background context with respect to implementation methods and related technologies. The remainder and larger fraction of the chapter will then be devoted to a detailed examination of two commercial products. These products are ProcessWeaver, developed by Cap Gemini [ProcessWeaver 92], and SynerVision, developed by Hewlett-Packard [SynerVision 93a, SynerVision 93b]. They were selected because they represent major products in the new field of software process automation. This examination is intended to provide a feel for technology and its status. Currently, a rapidly growing number of such PCEs is becoming available in the market and vendor information for some of these can be found in Appendix C.

3.1 Setting a Context for PCEs

Commercial process-centered environments have not evolved in a vacuum, but have resulted from a significant amount of research into the nature of process and its execution. In addition, there is a variety of fields that have either influenced the design and functionality of PCEs or are, in some ways, related. The following two subsections provide some perspective on these issues.

3.1.1 Process-Execution Paradigms

There are several process-execution paradigms on which process-centered environments can be constructed. These different paradigms have been developed in the research community and from these origins many (but not all) the commercial offerings have originated. While it is difficult to cleanly separate the basic approaches, three major paradigms, described briefly below, are evident [Conradi 92]. These paradigms are based on network concepts, production rule concepts, and process programming concepts.

In the network paradigm, Petri Nets [Reisig 82] play a dominant role. Petri Nets were initially developed to model synchronous and asynchronous events in communication systems. These nets consist of three types of elements that can be displayed graphically: *places* (denoted by circles), *transitions* (denoted by squares) and *directed arcs*. Arcs connect places to transitions and transitions to places. In addition, the concept of *tokens* (that are inserted into places) are used for process execution to mark a place that has been asserted in some way (e.g., is made "true"). If a token is in a place, then all the arcs emanating from that place are said to be *loaded*, and if all the places leading to a transition have tokens, then the transition is said to be *enabled*. Within this process context, transitions represent state changes while places represent states. Thus, when a condition is satisfied, and the associated action taken, the process can transition from one state to the next. The Petri Net concept of *place* is a generalization of the ProNet concepts of *conditions*, *artifacts* or even *agents*. The Petri Net transition is comparable to the proNet concept of *activity*. In Petri Nets, transitions are never connected directly to transitions. In the same way, ProNet activities are not usually connected to other activities. (The exceptions being through inheritance aggregation and custom relationships.)

Petri Nets are used as the basis for FUNSOFT nets [Gruhn 92]. FUNSOFT nets use the descriptive power of Petri Nets with extensions to allow process execution concepts to be more easily articulated. The FUNSOFT notation forms the basis of MELMAC, a process-centered environment for the management of real-time processes. Another Petri Net-based process execution language is DesignNet [Liu 89]. This forms the basis of DesignPlan which adds functionality on top of DesignNet (such as object management) in order to provide a more complete environment. Finally ProcessWeaver, which has origins in the Eureaka Software Factory [Fernstrom 91] project, is a Petri Net based system.

Because of its graphical basis, the network approach lends itself well to process definition. On the other hand, rule-based approaches are predominantly process-execution oriented and are generally implemented using a textual programming approach. Rules are well suited to defining processes as sequences of activities, since each activity in the process maps to a rule in the rule base. In many cases, logic programming (often Prolog based) is used for implementation. In such systems there is generally a set of preconditions that must be satisfied before an activity can begin, the activity itself, and a set of post conditions that determine the completion of the activity and allow for the initiation of subsequent activities. Specific research-oriented systems that have used this approach are Marvel [Kaiser 90], Merlin [Emmerich 91], Oikos [Ambriola 90], ESP [Ciancarini 93], and SLX [Lee 91]. Details of many PCE systems are provided in [Finkelstein 94].

In the final paradigm, process programming, a procedural approach to executing processes is followed. A strictly procedural approach to process execution would probably be too deterministic to easily account for the complexity of real processes. However, often the procedural paradigm is augmented by triggers that allow activities to be initiated in a manner more closely related to the rule-based approach. Systems that use the process programming approach are APPL/A [Sutton 90] and SynerVision [SynerVision 93a].

The three paradigms identified above are all explored, in one way or another, elsewhere in the book. As a process definition language ProNet, described in Chapter 2, falls into the network paradigm. While it is not derived from the Petri Net formalism, it has features in common with Petri Nets. With respect to process execution, ProSim, also described in Chapter 2, borrows from the rule-based paradigm rather than the Petri Net paradigm. ProcessWeaver [Fernstrom 91], the Petri Net based system described later in this chapter, modifies these nets to account for functionality needed to support the process concepts. Finally SynerVision, while influenced by research work, originated within Hewlett Packard and falls into the process programming category. SynerVision is also described later in this chapter.

3.1.2   The Relation of PCEs to Other Technologies

Process-centered environments can be viewed together as one instance in a class of environments that may be called computer support environments. Computer support environments are defined as environments that aid in the development of computer-based product, *but do not directly produce anything.* They are analogous to conveyor belts in a mass production factory in that they improve productivity but only indirectly affect the product. The major classes of computer support environments are:

- configuration management systems
- groupware products
- process centered environments
- software engineering environments
- workflow products
- workgroup products

In order to differentiate between the classes of computer support environments, we will describe them in terms of the attributes: data management, process support, tool integration and human communications. The description of each class of product is followed by a summary table of the importance of the attributes to that class, on a scale zero, low, medium and high.

Configuration management systems: With complex software products, the ability to manage versions and their components is essential, during both the development phase and maintenance phase. Thus configuration management is strong in modeling data entities, their versions and how these versions are combined into configurations. CM products, such as RCS [Tichy 85] may allow for the simple control of file versions, while others may provide broader functionality to support CM [Dart 91]. Recently some CM systems have emerged that are more process-oriented and allow end-users to defined their own CM lifecycles [CaseWare 92]. CM products do not generally emphasize either tool integration or human communications.

Table 3.1. Configuration management ratings

data management	process management	tool integration	human communications
high	low to high	low	low

Groupware products: There are several subcategories under the groupware heading. These are usually defined to be: communications (e.g., e-mail, group communications), collaboration (e.g., group document editing, document peer review) and coordination (e.g., schedule management). Thus groupware products may have to manage documents (in the collaboration area), but this facility is not central. Interaction between individuals using groupware products is usually ad hoc and thus little formal process is involved. To some extent invocation of tools is required. For example a group word processor maybe involved, and in fact may be the entire groupware product. (This case is the exception to the rule that computer support products do not generate product). Human communication is the most significant theme running through groupware products. Groupware products include Flecse [Dewan 93] and ConversationBuilder [Kaplan 92], a tool for the construction of groupware applications. One application based on ConversationBuilder is Scrutiny [Gintell 93], a tool that supports inspection and review of software engineering products.

Table 3.2. Groupware ratings

data management	process management	tool integration	human communications
low to medium	low	low	high

Process-Centered Environments: Process-centered environments provide a strong process framework in which product development can be guided. Some PCEs may have facilities to explicitly address data management, but many do not, preferring to let supporting tools provide that function. Process management is clearly the strongest component with PCEs. However, tool integration is an essential component for the execution of real-world processes within a PCE. In addition, a PCE must have some modest capabilities for communications between humans.

Table 3.3. PCE ratings

data management	process management	tool integration	human communications
zero to medium	high	high	medium

Software Engineering Environments: The goal of software engineering environments is to provide strong support for software development. Thus features that allow for the integration of software development tools and communication between these tools is often found. Some SEEs, such as PCTE have a major data management orientation [Thomas 93], while others, such as Softbench [Cagan 90] may provide little data management capability, preferring to integrate an existing configuration management or object management tool. In general SEEs do not have features for the high-level description of process, although with complex integrations, process issues may become apparent. In such cases, explicit process representation may have to be developed using low level programming constructs. However, the boundary between what is called a SEE and what is called a PCE can be fuzzy and depends on the degree of process support that the environment provides. While tool integration is critical to the operation of a SEE, human communications is of less significance.

Table 3.4. SEE ratings

data management	process management	tool integration	human communications
zero to high	low to medium	high	low

Workflow Products: There is little distinction between process-centered environments and workflow products, except that workflow products are more likely to provide direct support for data management. Both have a strong emphasis on process management. While the origins of PCEs are in the software engineering community, workflow products are motivated by the needs of the general business community.

Table 3.5. Workflow ratings

data management	process management	tool integration	human communications
medium to high	high	high	medium

Workgroup products: Workgroup products provide mechanisms for allowing documents and information to be routed in office environments. Thus they focus on data management and human communications. They generally allow for the ad hoc movement of documents with little or no process guidance. Workgroup products can be broken into three categories: communications (e.g., e-mail), structured information management (e.g., for editable and image-based documents) and transaction-based data management (e.g., for frequently updated and interrogated data) [Ayre 94]. There is overlap between this category and the groupware category.

Table 3.6. WorkGroup ratings

data management	process management	tool integration	human communications
high	low	low	high

The characteristics that distinguish PCEs (and workflow products) from other software engineering environments are:

- their explicit focus on process mechanisms, and the resulting need for process definition and enactment languages; and
- their emphasis on communication between, and integration of, people and their actions, rather than on the communication between, and integration of, tools.

Agreed-to or de-facto tool integration standards are important for PCEs, if PCEs are to connect to the wider field of CASE. Within the CASE integration community, there are several developments that are helping in this direction. For example, the conventions introduced by BMS [Brown 93a], CORBA [Soley 92], or PCTE [Brown 93a] are providing an impetus to third-party developers to be "compliant". Indeed, the two PCEs that we will be investigating have mechanisms to address tool-integration issues.

Much research and commercial work has also been done on the integration of CASE tools. On the commercial side, integration has been traditionally tool-to-tool, with limited process implications. An example of such a tool-to-tool integration is the linking of a word processor with a configuration management (CM) tool in order to manage document versions [CaseWare 93]. More ambitious efforts to develop integrated tool sets have been attempted, but usually in research-oriented settings. For example in [Brown 94] a software development scenario was constructed with Soft-Bench as the framework and using a variety of tools for C-code development, testing, metrics collection, and configuration management. With this level of complexity, it was found that a process model, written in C, was required to manage the sequencing of events.

Many configuration management systems have also addressed practical process issues. While earlier CM products had built-in hard-wired process models [Dart 91], more recent systems have started to provide the capability for end-user process customization (e.g., CaseWare). However, the emphasis in CM systems is more (but not exclusively) on the management of product than on the management of process. PCEs and CM products are likely to have different notions of process management, and integration of PCE and CM services will be painful unless some standards are agreed to. Otherwise a PCE will only be able to call on a limited subset of the services supported by a CM tool.

In the longer term, merging of the concepts in process automation and configuration management may occur in which there is a fusing of data management and process management features. Indeed, CASE integration may benefit from such a union, since tools will then be supported by a compatible and consistent set of product and process services.

3.2   The Experimental Approach

In order to understand the technology behind process-centered environments, the experience of building and executing models within PCEs is invaluable. This section reviews such an investigation. The document update process defined in Chapter 2 forms the basis of implementations built in both ProcessWeaver and SynerVision. In order to evaluate end-user reactions to these executable models, several roles plays were performed with two groups; a technology-oriented group and a process-oriented group.

3.2.1   The Eight Phases of the Experiment

To investigate ProcessWeaver and SynerVision, a modified version of an evaluation methodology, developed for software engineering environments, is used [Weiderman 86]. This methodology is based on several criteria that, in the context of this investigation, involve the following:

- Since detailed functionality may vary from PCE to PCE, the evaluation attempts to focus on the activities of the users of a PCE rather than the low-level features implemented in that PCE.
- The evaluation postpones the inspection of specific features of a PCE as long as possible. This approach forces one to keep a broad perspective and thus helps with comparisons of PCE functionalities (as opposed to detailed implementation).
- The evaluation is based on a PCE-independent example of a process. This ensures that the PCEs are being assessed against the same criteria. It also reduces the effort since the same process model is used on each PCE.
- Objectivity and repeatability are assured through performing the same well defined tests on each PCE. Different experimenters, using the same process example, should come to the same or similar conclusions when evaluating the same PCE.
- Prior to examining the PCE, it may not be possible to determine all appropriate aspects of the evaluation. Thus the experimental approach should allow for iteration and refinement of the approach during the evaluation.
- The methodology should be extensible in the sense that the experiments can be easily modified, expanded and improved upon.

The original approach suggested by Weiderman focuses on end users. Such an application to project management tools is discussed in [Feiler 88]. However, in evaluating PCEs, there are two classes of user: the developer of the executable process and the subsequent end-user of this process. Thus, the approach is modified somewhat to account for this difference. In addition, some of the original methodology has been simplified. These simplifications result in less formality and detail in the area of evaluation questions as compared to Weiderman's original approach.

While Weiderman's approach involved six phases, the approach used here involves eight shorter phases. The details of these phases and the relationships between them are illustrated in Figure 3.1. The vertical line down the center of Figure

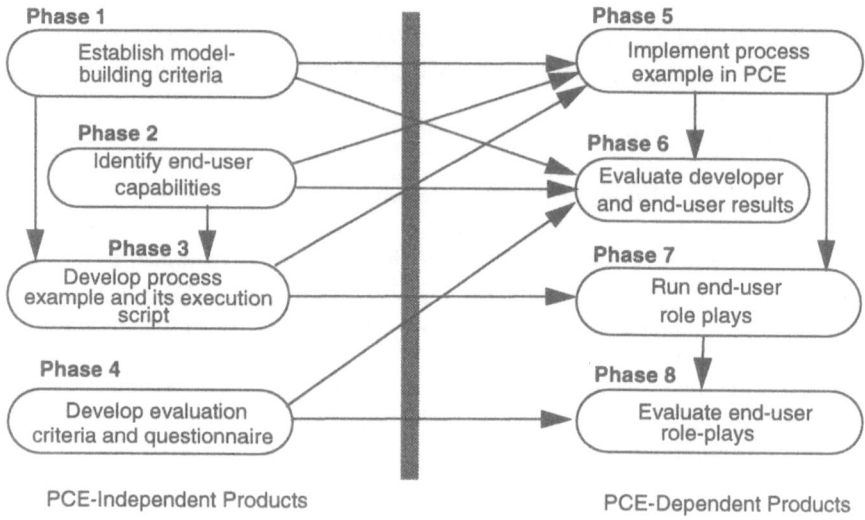

Fig. 3.1. Simplified evaluation process

3.1 separates the development of the PCE-independent experimental set-up (Phases 1 through 4) from evaluations of each PCE (Phases 5 through 8), while the arrows represent dependencies. For example, Phase 1 provides Phase 3 with criteria on what is needed in the process model. A textual description of each phase is given below.

1. *Establish model-building criteria.* Establish the functional capabilities against which the PCEs are evaluated. This includes both the capabilities for developing and debugging process programs based on the process example. For example, we may wish to investigate the ability of the PCE to model the communication between agents (human or otherwise) or the ability of the PCE to perform syntax checking of the process program.

2. *Identify end-user capabilities.* Identify end-user capabilities that the PCEs might provide. Examples are: personal task management, project planning, or metrics collection. In reviewing these capabilities, one has to be careful not to conclude that product A is better than product B because it includes tool X. One

design philosophy may result in a suite of tools being integrated into the product, while another design philosophy may focus on providing process

3. *Develop process example and its execution script.* Given the information of Phases 1 and 2, develop the process example against which the PCEs are to be tested. The process example used in the evaluation is the document-modification process described in Chapter 2. This example is defined independently of the PCE on which it will later be implemented. An execution script is also developed to guide the end users through the end-user role plays (see Phase 7).

4. *Develop evaluation criteria and questionnaire.* Develop a set evaluation criteria, that is independent of both the PCEs and the process example, and against which both the developer and end-user evaluations will be performed. The criteria used are very similar to those identified in [Weiderman 86] and consist of such items as "ease of learning", "performance", "portability", etc. Also develop a questionnaire to be filled in by the end-users in the role plays.

5. *Implement the process example in the PCE.* In each PCE, implement the process example defined in Phase 3, using the Phase 1 criteria for guidance in the building process.

6. *Evaluate developer and end-user results.* With the experience gained from the PCE-specific model-building exercise (Phase 5), assess the capabilities of the PCE using the evaluation criteria developed in Phase 4, supported by the model-building criteria of Phase 1.

7. *Run end-user role-plays.* Perform a set of end-user evaluations, in which several persons act out the process enactment scenario. These simulations will be guided by the execution script. A copy of the materials provided to the end-users (including the execution script) is provided in Appendix F.

8. *Evaluate end-user role plays.* Analyze the end user role-plays using the Phase 4 evaluation criteria. Also use the Phase 4 evaluation criteria to address end-user issues that are not part on the end-user process enactment scenario.

The next four subsections describe respectively the first four phases (i.e., the PCE-independent phases) of the of the experiment.

3.2.2 Model-Building Capabilities (Phase 1)

In order to define the process example, a set of features that a PCE may be expected to support is identified. These features provide requirements for the design of the process example and are placed in the following categories given in Table 3.7: *development, enactment, resource, communications* and *debugging*. The categories are similar to those identified in [NIST 93] (see Appendix E). In addition, [Kellner 90] was reviewed in helping to identify some of the elements listed in Table 3.7.

Table 3.7. Model-building capabilities

1	Development issues	Discussion
a	Scoping of variables	If a process is composed of subprocesses, then there should be mechanisms for passing variable values from process to sub-process and back.
b	Modeling hierarchies	Models of any realistic complexity cannot be defined as one monolithic entity. Thus the PCE must allow activities to have internal structure (i.e., contain sub-activities) that can be broken out and defined separately.
c	Supporting model development	In order to construct process models, the PCE must provide support for model building. This support may be through a textual language with an editor, a graphical language, or a mixture of text and graphics.
d	Creating a process library	In order to enact a process multiple times, it must be possible to store the process program (i.e., the template) with its variables (e.g., roles) uninstantiated. See also item 2.a.
e	Supporting work-ahead	Humans perform tasks in an opportunistic manner that cannot always be predicted by a process model. For example it may be legitimate to prepare for a task before all the formal preconditions for the task have been met (as defined in the process model). Thus the ability to specify differing degrees of control over task initiation is desirable.
f	Modeling standard programming constructs	The process modeling language in a PCE must have a means of expressing the usual programming constructs such as iteration, conditional testing, and variable instantiation.
g	Performing parallel, aggregated processes	Consider the situation where twenty identical processes feed a downstream process. The PCE should have the ability to invoke the same template for all twenty upstream processes. Further, because the number of upstream tasks may not be known until run-time, it would be helpful if specification of this number could be delayed until run time.
h	Selecting sub-processes at run time	Selection of a particular sub-process alternative (out of a set of similar subprocesses) may depend on parameters that are known only at run-time. In this way sub-processes may be treated as variables to be instantiated when execution takes place.

Table 3.7. Model-building capabilities (Continued)

2	Enactment issues	Discussion
a	Assigning agents to roles	A PCE must be able to distinguish between roles (usually defined in the process model prior to run-time) and the agents who actually perform the actions (defined at the start and possibly throughout process enaction). The concept of roles and agents applies equally to humans and machines. The ability to instantiate roles with specific agents must be supported.
b	Supporting on-the-fly process modification	The ability to modify process models on the fly during execution may be important. Things go wrong during process execution, and changes may have to be made promptly. It may not be possible to wait until an automated process has terminated before modifying action can be taken.
c	Logging process data	Logging of process can be important in order to: 1) debug the process (see also item 5.g), 1) roll back an ongoing process to correct an error, 2) provide post-project verification that the defined process was followed, and 3) provide metrics for the support of process improvement.
d	simulating the process	There are many reasons why process simulation can be an important tool. Qualitative simulation supports debugging and process buy-in. Quantitative simulation supports project planning, bottleneck analysis, and process improvement.
3	Resource issues	Discussion
a	Invoking tools	A PCE must provide the mechanisms through which tools can be invoked. Such invocation may involve simply starting the tool or it may involve accessing a specific aspect of its functionality.
b	Managing artifacts	There is a close relationship between the tasks in a process and the artifacts produced by the tasks. These artifacts may be versions of a product. Thus, having some means to manage versions of products is a useful capability.
4	Communication issues	Discussion
a	Modeling communication between agents	Central to process enaction is the notion of communication, either from human-to-human, human-to-computer-agent, computer-agent-to-human and computer-agent-to-computer-agent. The PCE must provide mechanisms for such communication.

Table 3.7. Model-building capabilities (Continued)

b	Modeling automatic actions	As a result of an event occurring, automatically triggered actions may be necessary. These actions may send messages to humans or may trigger other automatic events. Means to model automatic actions must therefore be provided.
5	**Debugging issues**	**Discussion**
a	Checking syntax	This is the ability to identify and clearly define the source of programming errors.
b	Performing reachability analysis	This is the ability to evaluate an enactable process model to assure that all of its parts are accessible during process enaction.
c	Performing deadlock analysis	This is the ability to evaluate if there are process states from which it is impossible to exit.
d	Tracing process dynamics	The ability to trace the dynamics of the process as it is being enacted can provide significant insights for process model validation.
e	Querying	This is the ability to check on the values of variables during process enactment (simulation or actual use).
g	Spying	This is the ability to insert breakpoints in the simulation of a process in order to examine the status of variables, etc.
g	Logging process data	See 2.c above.

3.2.3   End-User Capabilities (Phase 2)

End-user applications may be built in to the PCE or invoked using external tools. In either case, application tools will be needed to support the large majority of processes. Some of the capabilities that are particularly well suited to integration are reviewed in Table 3.8.

3.2.4   Process Example and Its Execution Script (Phase 3)

Most of the items in Table 3.7 (with the exception of debugging issues) influenced the design of the process example in some significant way. This example was described in Section 2.5.2 and portrays a simple document update process that is defined using ProNet notation.

Table 3.8. End-user capabilities

	Application	Discussion
a	Scheduling periodic work	A simple but important application of process support is the ability to initiate tasks (e.g., time card generation) or present personal reminders (e.g., weekly meetings) on a periodic basis.
b	Collecting metric data	A PCE provides many mechanisms that can facilitate the automatic collection of process and product metrics.
c	Supporting project management tasks	Both process enactment and project management require information on tasks, resources, and agents and the relationships and dependencies between them. Thus there is significant overlap in the data needs of process enactment and project management and each can leverage off the other.
d	Supporting the individual user	There are many modest personal tasks with which process automation can help. Examples include: managing "to do" lists, planning work estimates, tracking work effort, and capturing personal metrics.
e	Supporting group communications	A variety of group activities do not require a full process model to drive them. Examples include: delegating, negotiating, reassigning and coordinating tasks.

Note that items 1a, 1b, 1c,1d, 1f, 2a, 3a, 3b, 4a, and 4b of Table 3.7 are explicitly tested by the process example. It should also be noted that there are aspects of the two PCEs being addressed that are not being tested. For example, both PCEs have additional capability in the area of external communication and tool encapsulation. However, as will be seen, some of the capabilities in Table 3.7 are supported by neither tool.

The execution script for the process example is now reviewed. Appendix F provides the evaluation materials that were given to the participants of the end-user evaluations. This script, which is part of the end-user evaluation materials, is shown in Table F.1 and follows one of many possible process scenarios. In this particular scenario, the manager receives an incoming change request to modify a document (item 1 in Table F.1) and identifies his initial choice of editor (item 2). Both technical writers (A and B) initially refuse to accept the role of editor (items 3 and 5), and this forces the manager to impose the editor role on Technical Writer A (items 7). After Technical Writer A has performed the requested modification (item 10), the documents are sent for review to Technical Writer B who in turn adds a comment in the supporting document *Review Comments* (item 11). The next task is then automatically sent to Technical Writer A who again edits the document (item 12), after which it is sent back to Technical Writer B for a second review. At this point, Technical Writer B accepts the modification (item 13), the document is automatically saved in the repository, and the manager is notified that the modification has been successfully completed (item 14).

3.2.5   Evaluation Criteria and Questionnaire (Phase 4)

In order to assess the adequacy of the two PCEs, a set of evaluation criteria is established. These criteria are defined independently of the model-building capabilities (Phase 1) and the process example (Phase 2). They are, in fact, a modification of the set suggested in [Weiderman 86], and are shown in Table 3.9. These form the basis for the evaluation that the author performed. Also, an end-user questionnaire is developed. This questionnaire, shown in Table F.2, lists the questions that the role players answered after performing in the simulated document update process. An analysis of the responses to these questions is provided in Section 3.5.

In summary the sequence of tasks that will be performed in evaluating SynerVision and ProcessWeaver is as shown in Figure 3.2

Table 3.9. PCE evaluation areas

#	Evaluation Area	Comments
1	Model-building capabilities	Completeness of major functional areas for development, as identified in Table 3.7.
2	End-user capabilities	Completeness of end-user functional areas as defined in Table 3.8.
3	Developer issues	a) Ease of learning. b) Ease of use. c) Effectiveness of support for development. d) Quality of on-line help. e) Error handling.
4	End-user issues	a) Ease of learning. b) Ease of use. c) Clarity of presentation.
5	Performance	a) Execution time efficiency. b) Space efficiency.
6	System interface	a) Ease of tool integration. b) Portability. c) Interface to operating system.
7	Off-line user support	a) Support from customer representatives. b) Clarity of documentation. c) Availability of hands-on training. d) Availability of encoded process examples.

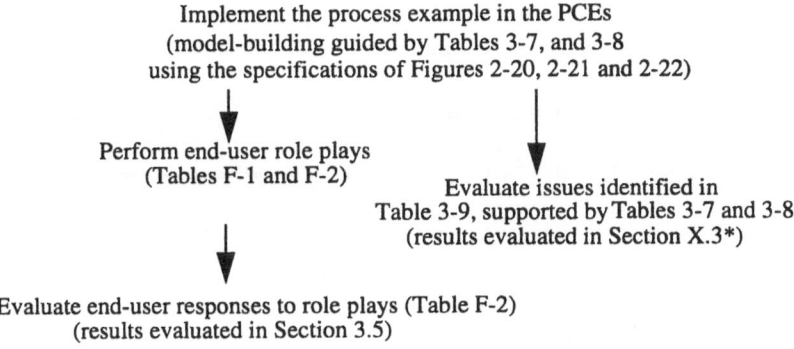

Fig. 3.2. Sequence of evaluation tasks

3.3 The ProcessWeaver Experiment

This section starts out with a review of ProcessWeaver's approach to process automation. The latter subsections then deal with ProcessWeaver in the context of the
evaluation experiment.

3.3.1 Review of ProcessWeaver

ProcessWeaver provides a suite of tools for the management of individual tasks and
for process automation (i.e., sequences of tasks). The end user of ProcessWeaver is
provided with a main window called the *Agenda,* and it is through this window that
tasks, called *Work Contexts*, are sent, received, or worked on. Work Contexts appear
as icons in the Agenda and can be opened to provide detailed tasking information.
In addition, there are several windows to support the development of processes.
These are the *Method Editor*, the *Activity Editor*, the *Cooperative Procedure Editor*,
and the *Work Context Editor*. The Method Editor provides the capability for defining activity hierarchies, while the Activity Editor allows task inputs, outputs, and
roles for these activities to be specified. Through the Cooperative Procedure editor,
one can model the detailed task-level processes for each activity. Finally, the windows through which the end user performs tasks, are designed using the Work Context Editor[1]. These elements of ProcessWeaver are reviewed in more detail in the

---

1. In this section, we equate a task with the activity performed in a Work Context.

following subsections. The final subsection (Pulling the Elements Together) provides an "integration" view, since there are many components to ProcessWeaver and the relationship between these components is not at first obvious.

Agenda Window: The Agenda window acts as a central location for managing an individual's tasks. The current tasks are displayed as icons in the Agenda window as shown in Figure 3.3. In this instance, the task *UpdateDocument* is the Work Con-

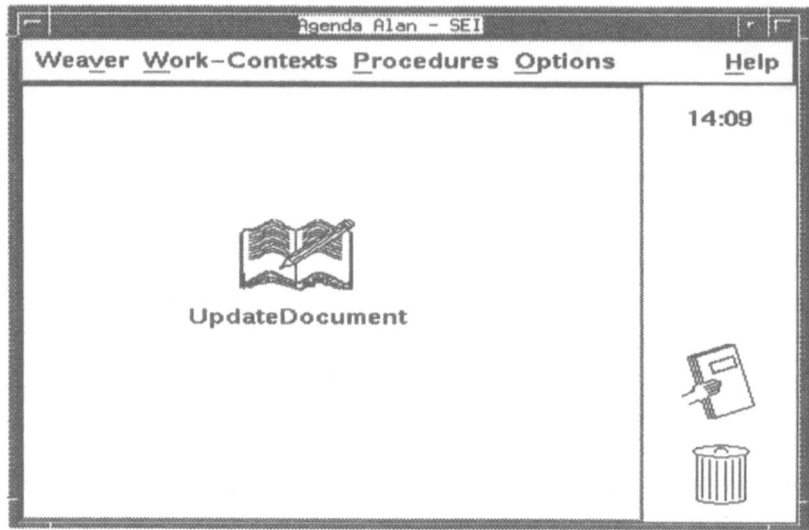

Fig. 3.3. An *Agenda* window

text icon. Such tasks may either be isolated "to do's" or may be elements of a more complex process. If they are isolated "to do's", they may be delegated from someone else or they may originate locally from the person who "owns" that Agenda. In the latter case, the Work Context could reflect a personal task that has to be performed on a periodic basis (e.g., defining monthly objectives) and automatically appears on the first day of the month. Delegation of a task is performed simply by dragging the Work Context icon over to the Delegation icon (the report) on the right of the window. This generates a predefined list of candidates, from which one or more are selected. A completed task can be eliminated by dragging its icon over the garbage can icon.

The menu bar along the top of the window provides a variety of options. The *Weaver* option allows one to access the editors for Work Contexts, Cooperative Procedures (i.e., processes), and Methods (i.e., activity hierarchies). The *Work Context* option primarily allows one to select individual Work Contexts to be instantiated for a specific task and perhaps delegated. The *Procedures* option allows one to generate a new instance of a process, while the *Preferences* option allows one to customize some setup parameters, such as setting an alarm when a Work Context is received.

Work Context Window: On double clicking a Work Context icon in the Agenda window, its associated window appears. A typical Work Context window is shown in Figure 3.4. Notice that there are three different types of objects. These are: mes-

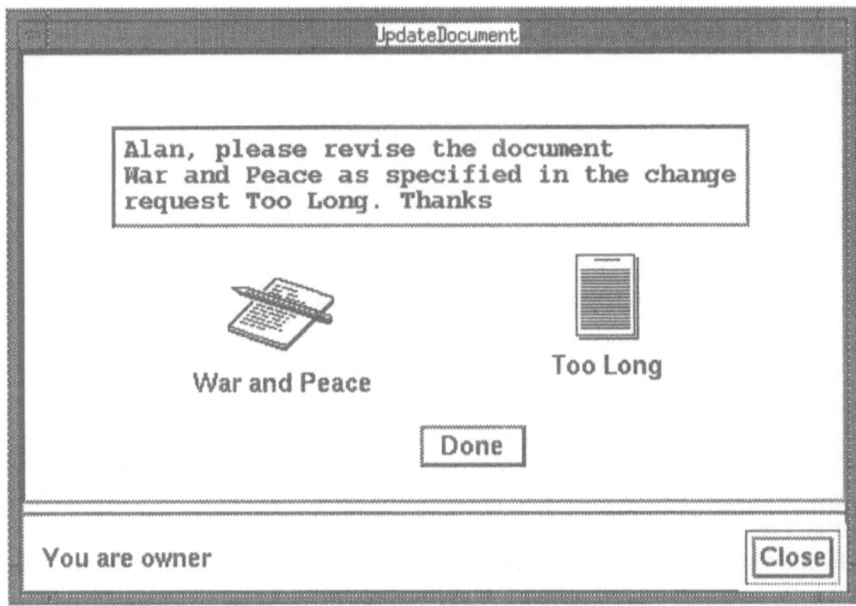

Fig. 3.4. A *Work Context* window

sage boxes, icons representing elements of the task to be worked on, and control buttons. These three items are all the object types that need to be supported by Work Contexts. In the message box, variables can be embedded in the text. Thus in the example above, a role variable (e.g., *$person*) can be instantiated at run-time with a name (e.g., *Alan*). These boxes can also be used to input information into the process. By clicking on an icon, the user can activate the corresponding object. This could be a text editor, compiler, or CASE tool.

Individual Work Contexts can be developed or modified using the Work Context editor. This function allows the developer to customize Work Contexts with any combination of text boxes, icons and buttons that is appropriate to support the end user. A wide variety of icon designs is provided, and one can associate an icon with an appropriate tool or document. A default tool set is provided and this set can be extended by the developer if necessary. Buttons are given identifiers so that they can be associated with a particular decision path of a process model.

Method Editor: As mentioned above, the two previous views (the Agenda and the Work Context) support the end user of the process while the next three views (the Method, Activity, and Procedure Editors) support the process developer.

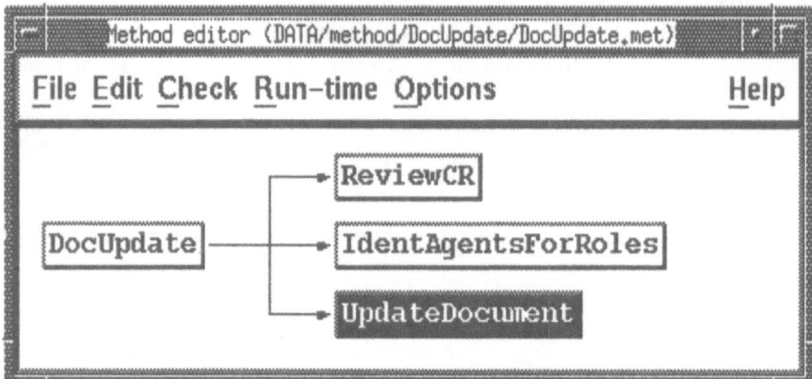

Fig. 3.5. Activity hierarchy for the example process

ProcessWeaver models projects by structuring them into a hierarchy of activities An example of a simple hierarchy is shown in Figure 3.5. The window in Figure 3.5 supports a variety of functions. First through the *Edit* option one can add, delete, and append both activities and decomposition levels to the hierarchy. Through the *Check* option one can examine measures related to, for example, the consistency of input and output products between activities, and this can be very useful for the verification of large models. The *Run-time* option allows one to generate simple default cooperative procedures (processes) automatically that are attached to the activities; these are discussed in the *Cooperative Procedure Editor* section below. Each of the activities has associated with it an *Activity Editor* that defines the inputs required by that activity, the roles required to support the activity, and the outputs generated by that activity.

Activity Editor: Each Activity Editor window displays information related to one activity; a typical Activity Editor window can be seen in Figure 3.6. This window can be accessed for a particular activity by double clicking on that activity in the Method Editor window. The main items displayed in the Activity Editor window are the inputs, outputs, and roles associated with the activity. It is these items against which the Methods Editor can perform consistency checking, over the whole process model, as discussed in the *Method Editor* section above. By clicking on the Edit button, one activates the Cooperative Procedure Editor window.

Cooperative Procedure Editor: The Cooperative Procedure window defines the detailed processes using the Petri Net [Reisig 82] notation. This notation was briefly described in Section 3.1.1.

Down the left hand side of the Cooperative Procedure window shown in Figure 3.7 is a set of transition icons. The graphical part of the process model can be rapidly constructed simply by dragging icons from the left-hand edge of the window and placing them in the model definition area. These can then be connected by dragging

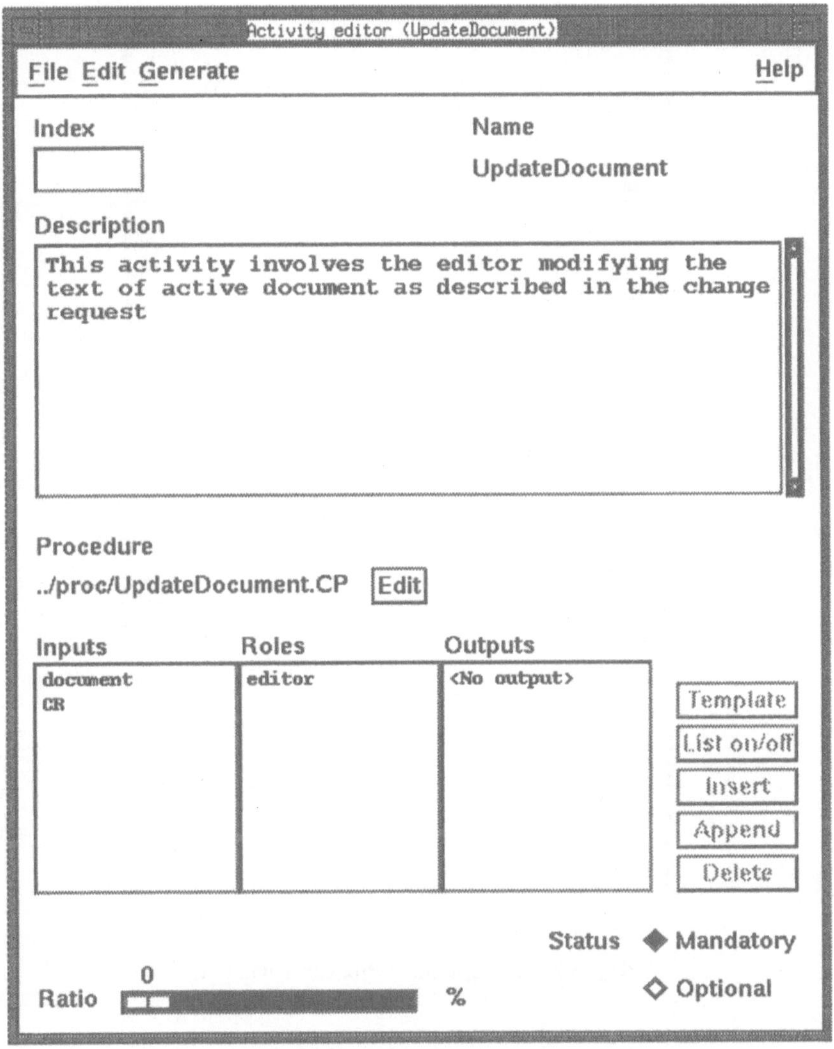

Fig. 3.6. An *Activity Editor* window

a line between (legally-connected) icons. In the graphical model, each transition is composed of two parts – a condition part and an action part. Upon double clicking one of these icons, an information box, customized for that type of icon, appears and lets the model developer enter appropriate information. During execution, the condition part must be satisfied before the action part can be initiated. In addition to the null (always true) condition, there are four other types of condition (Event, Wctxt, Collect and Proc). These are described briefly below:

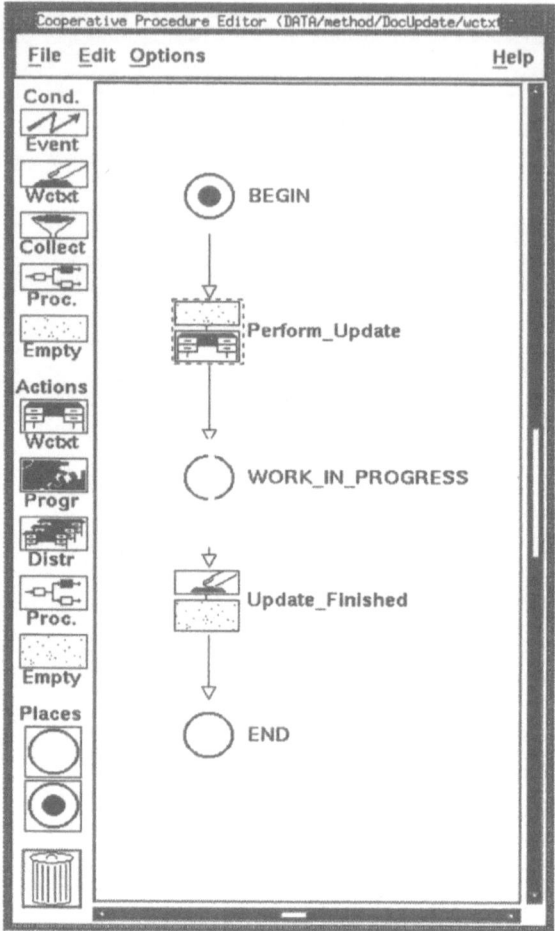

Fig. 3.7. A *Cooperative Procedure* window

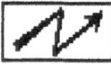 *Event*: This icon implies "waiting for an external event". For example, it could mean that some set of external logical conditions has occurred, such as a word processor updating a file, in conjunction with "Joe" being the editor on that file. External events can also include events on the ProcessWeaver communication bus.

 *Wctxt* (work context). This icon implies that a cooperative procedure is waiting for an answer from a work context currently being performed. For example, when a button named *Done* is pressed inside a work context, the Wctxt condition is set to TRUE.

 *Collect.* This icon evaluates a set of conditions – either work contexts or events. It can be made to fire when all the incoming conditions are TRUE or when only one of the incoming conditions is TRUE.

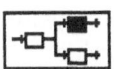 *Proc* (procedure). This icon waits for a given state (e.g., completion) of a sub-process previously launched.

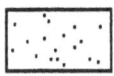 Empty. This icon implies that the condition is always TRUE.

In addition, there are five types of action, each action having an associated icon. The action associated with one of these icons is taken when the corresponding condition is TRUE. These actions are named: Wctxt, Progr, Distr, Proc, and Empty. These are briefly described below:

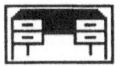 *Wctxt* (work context). When this icon is activated, a work context is sent to the person designated in an information box attached to this icon.

 *Progr* (programming). Allows one to describe required actions, using ProcessWeaver's Co-shell programming language. This language provides many functional features such as:

- manipulation of variables and lists,
- ability to perform arithmetic and logical operations, and provision for constructs in tests, and control, etc.,
- communication with users through work contexts,
- manipulation of events on ProcessWeaver's communication bus through constructs that are similar to Hewlett Packard's Broadcast Message Server, and
- support for development of user-defined Co-shell functions.

 *Distr* (distribution). This icon allows for the sending of a work context to multiple recipients. Its behavior is similar to the Wctxt action.

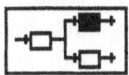 *Proc*(edure). This icon initiates a sub-process of the current process at run-time.

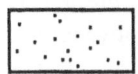 Empty. This icon implies that there is no action.

A very simple default process model is illustrated in Figure 3.7. In this figure, the process begins at the place with the inserted token. An event at the next higher level in the activity hierarchy may initiate this sub-task. The *Perform_Update* transition has no entrance condition as indicated by the *empty* box. The window associated with the action (not shown) provides three elements. First, actions can be taken by executing some code written in ProcessWeaver's Co-shell scripting language. Second, the agent who will perform the action is identified. Finally, the Work Context, that will be sent to the agent, is identified. When the agent has finished the work, a *Done* button (defined in the Work Context) is pressed, the transition *Update_Finished* is completed, and the token moves to the place marked *END*.

Pulling the Elements Together: Given the number of elements that contribute to a ProcessWeaver model it can be a challenge for the novice to understand how all these elements tie together. Figure 3.8 provides a simplified description of such an integrated picture. For the process developer, the *Method Editor* provides a hierarchical view of the major activities. Each of the activities defined in the *Method Editor* window has two associated windows: an *Activity Editor* that specifies the inputs, outputs, and roles required for the activity, and a *Cooperative Procedure Editor* that defines the lower level elements of the process using the Petri Net notation. Each transition in the Petri Net is composed of a condition part and an action part, the action taking place when the condition is met.

In the end-user view (at run-time), a process template is instantiated by a user (e.g., project manager) who invokes an existing *Cooperative Procedure* under the *Procedures* menu in the *Agenda*. This user does not see the Petri Net process model, but is presented with a window (not shown) in which the roles, documents and other artifacts to be used in this specific process are instantiated. For example, the role *$editor* may be instantiated with the specific agent (e.g., *Mary*) who carries out the operation, while the file to be modified, $doc, may be instantiated by the document *War and Peace*. Upon receiving this information, ProcessWeaver can start to enact the process (initiating Work Contexts, performing automatic tasks, etc.).

Through its activities, a cooperative procedure may perform a variety of types of functions. These were reviewed in the *Cooperative Procedure Editor* section. One of the important types of function is to be able to send Work Context messages to human agents who are responsible for tasks. These messages appear on the receiver's *Agenda* window as Work Context icons. (In Figure 3.8, the task is *UpdateDocument*.) On opening the icon to view the full Work Context window, the agent should find sufficient information to perform the task. In the example shown in Figure 3.8, a document icon (*War and Peace*) is seen on the Work Context window, and when this is opened, the actual document to be worked on appears. Note that you can also open the change request *Too Long* as well. When the task has been completed, the *Done* button on the Work Context window is pressed. This state change, resulting from pressing the button, is detected by the *UpdateFinished* condition in the Cooperative Procedure which then allows the process to move forward.

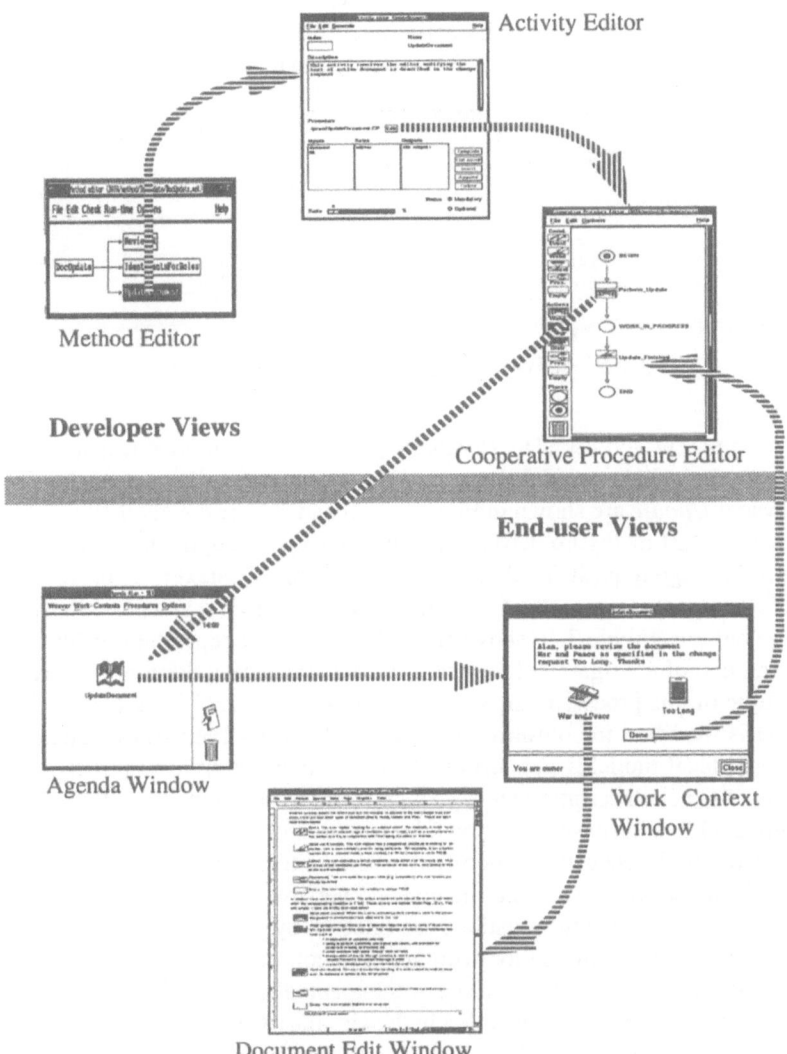

Fig. 3.8. Overview of ProcessWeaver elements

3.3.2   Developing the ProcessWeaver Process Model

To develop the ProcessWeaver model, it was originally intended that the activity hierarchy shown in Figure 3.5 be used. However, this had to be modified because of a variable scoping problem that was encountered. It was intended that the persons taking on the roles of editor and reviewer be identified in the sub-activity *Ident-*

AgentsForRoles. However, as ProcessWeaver was structured (in Version 1.2), a variable that was instantiated in a certain activity could only have the instantiated value used in that activity or in child activities. Hence the activity structure had to be simplified as shown in Figure 3.9. The activity *ReviewIdentify* in Figure 3.9 thus

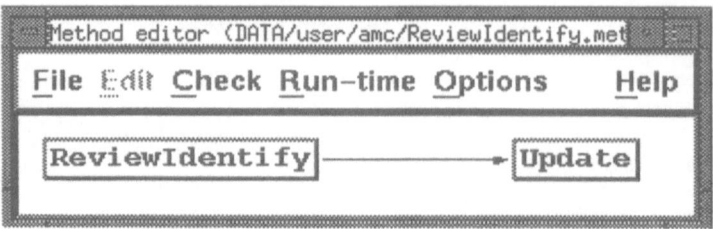

Fig. 3.9. Activity hierarchy for the example process

includes the parent activity (*DocUpdate*) and the child activities (*ReviewCR* and *IdenAgenForRoles*) shown in Figure 3.5. The Cooperative Procedures for *ReviewIdentify* and *Update* are shown in Figures 3.10 and 3.11 respectively.

The upper part of Figure 3.10 defines the process through which the manager reviews the change request. To do this review, a Work Context is displayed on the manager's terminal allowing the CR to be accessed for review and providing *accept* and *reject* buttons. Figure 3.10 shows the two paths taken depending on his choice. The second part of the figure defines the process for selecting the editor and reviewer. The logic of this process is the same as that of Figure 2.21, although the implementation is modified to conform with ProcessWeaver's Petri Net notation. Note that this graphical model is not sufficient to completely define the process model; fragments of Co-shell scripting are associated with many of the transition icons.

Figure 3.11 is a fairly straightforward adaptation of Figure 2.22. The document is checked out of the repository, modified by the editor, and sent to the reviewer. If the reviewer passes the document, the updated version is checked back into the repository. Otherwise, the modifications are rejected by the reviewer, and the document is passed back to the editor with suitable comments in a *review comments* notebook. Check-out and check-in are implemented using the Unix SCCS commands *get* and *delta* that are embedded in the auxiliary Co-shell functions shown in Figure 3.12. Libraries of such functions can be developed for general process use and are attached to a Cooperative Procedure for use within that Cooperative Procedure.

Notice at the end of Figure 3.10 that the subprocess *Update* (Figure 3.9) is initiated through a procedure call to the action *StartDocMod*. The procedure *EndDocMod* watches for the termination of this subprocess.

Clearly, the graphical model cannot be expected to define the detailed logic required for execution. For example, as noted above, calls to SCCS functions have to be made. In other cases, conditions require explicit tests to be performed, and actions may require that assignments of roles to agents be made. These statements are

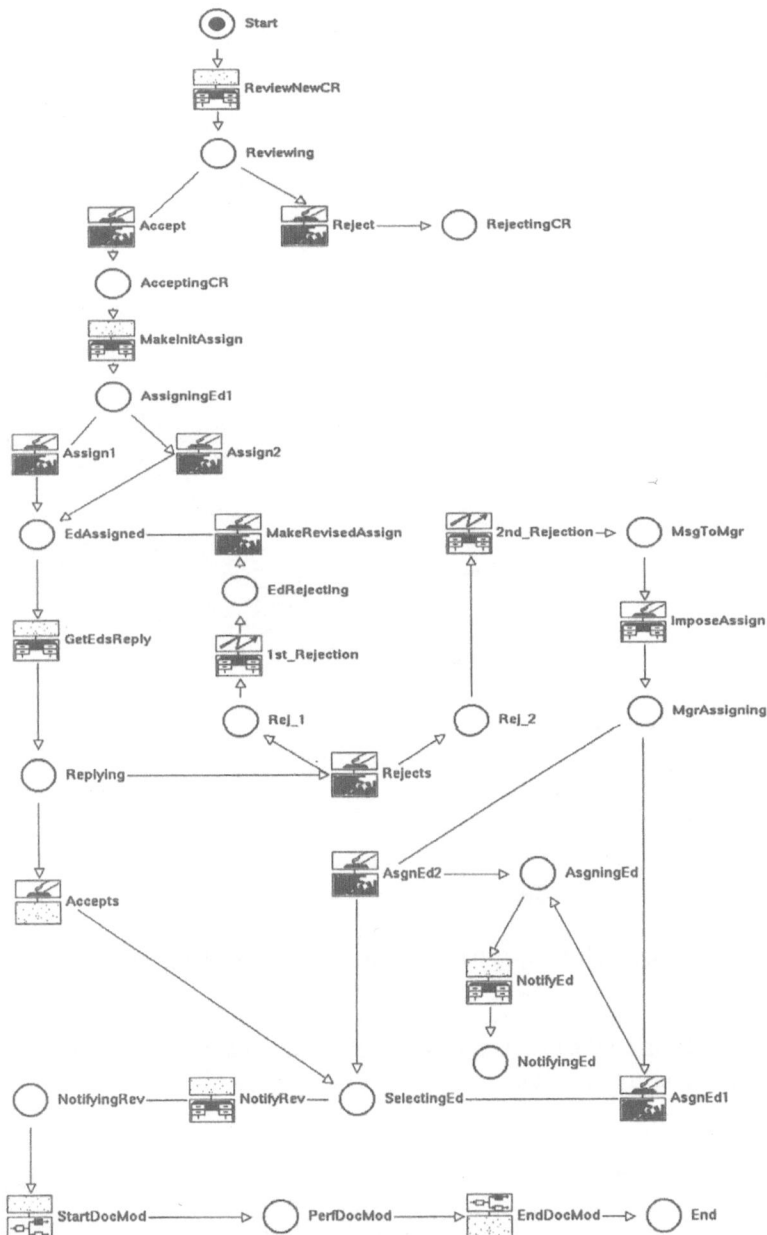

Fig. 3.10. Cooperative Procedure for the activity *ReviewIdentify*

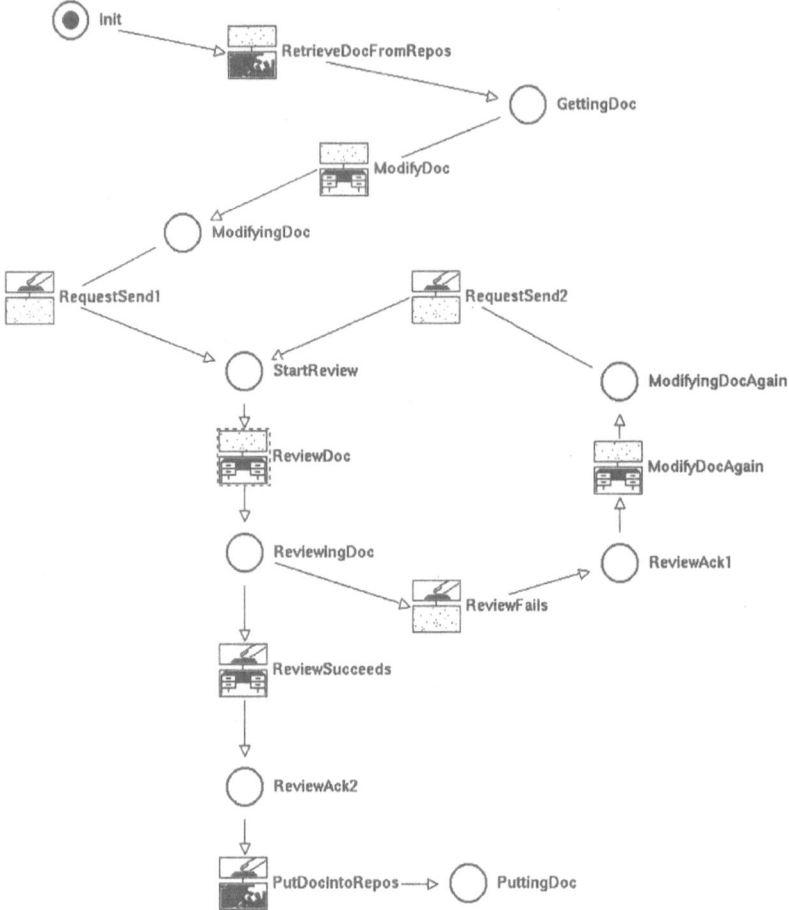

Fig. 3.11. Cooperative Procedure for the activity *Update*

generally made using the Co-shell language windows that can be accessed through the condition and action icons.

3.3.3   The Evaluation

In reviewing the issues to be evaluated, Table 3.9 is the primary focus. Each of the items in categories 1 through 7 of Table 3.9 will be discussed below.

```
define sccs_get($path, $file)
        $command=format("cd ", $path, ";", "/usr/ucb/sccs get -e s.", $file,
        "sccs.out 2>&1");
        system($command);
end;

define sccs_del($path, $file)
        $command=format("cd ", $path, ";", "/usr/ucb/sccs delta s.", $file,
        "sccs.out 2>&1");
        system($command);
end;
```

Fig. 3.12. Co-shell library functions to retrieve and save document files

Model-building Capabilities: Category 1 of Table 3.9 is the largest of the six categories, since it is expanded to include an assessment of the capabilities defined in
Table 3.7.

Development – Scoping of variables. ProcessWeaver allows the value of a variable,
instantiated in one activity, to be used in activities of children (and their children,
etc.). However, variables instantiated at the child level do not have their values prop-
agated up to the parent or higher levels. Consequently, the most natural work-breakdown structure, as seen in Figure 3.5, had to be simplified, making its structure less
intuitive (see Figure 3.9).

Development – Modeling hierarchies. ProcessWeaver models activity hierarchies
using the Method Editor. While this breakdown describes parent-child relationships between activities as a tree, it does not specify the sequencing of child activities within the parent. This sequencing is specified by the process flow for the
parent activity as defined in the Cooperative Procedure. The Cooperative Procedure uses the *Procedure* action (see Section 3.3.1) to initiate sub-activities under it.
Because of the scoping problem discussed in the paragraph above, there were significant restrictions imposed on the way the activity hierarchy for the experiment
could be constructed. (See also the first paragraph of Section 3.3.2).

Development – Supporting model development. Process models are developed with
graphical notations to support high level decomposition of activities (through the
Method Editor) and to define the lower level process (through the Cooperative Procedure Editor). Both of these graphical views are supported by textual information
that is input through forms linked to the graphical editors. This graphical approach
helps productivity by allowing a rapid development of the overall process model.
In addition, fewer syntactic and semantic errors are introduced in comparison to a
purely textual approach. The graphical form of the model also allows for better
communication with persons unfamiliar with process modeling.

Development – Creating a process library. ProcessWeaver stores processes in templates and these templates can be reused. Each process is stored in multiple files each of which uses ProcessWeaver's Universal Storage Mechanism. This mechanism uses an ASCII format that aids in porting process from one platform type to another. Different file types are created for Methods, Cooperative Procedures, and Work Contexts. These files are humanly readable and can be manipulated using certain Co-shell functions. However, they are created primarily as means to capture, in textual form, the graphically-defined process models.

Development – Supporting workahead. Humans can be very creative at starting tasks in an opportunistic manner. Thus they may wish to start tasks before all the preconditions for these task have been satisfied (as defined in the process model). For example, a certain task may require the integration of ten software components, and cannot formally begin until all the components are available. However, preliminary integration work can reasonably start when only five of the components have been completed. In this case, one would like to relax the constraint that all components must be available before the task can begin. Allowing for different degrees of constraint on task initiation is thus an important feature that should be incorporated into the process programming language.

Currently, ProcessWeaver does not allow such flexibility in task initiation. When one defines the Petri Net associated with a Cooperative Procedure, all tokens must be in the places preceding a transition before that transition can be acted upon. A more flexible approach would be to provide for two types of places: the first type (as now exist) are mandatory, i.e., the transition cannot start without a token being in the place preceding the transition. The second type of place is non-mandatory, i.e., a transition can start without there being a token in the preceding place. While the transition could be initiated without a full compliment of tokens, the transition could not terminate until all tokens are in place.

Development – Modeling standard programming constructs. Because of the graphical nature of the process modeling approach, there is a reduced need for conventional programming. This reduction is enhanced by the fact that much information is supplied through fields in standard forms. However, ProcessWeaver does have an expressive textual language called Co-shell with which to describe lower level constructs to support list manipulation, variable assignment and testing, and flow of control. Co-shell programming scripts are most commonly found in the *Prog* actions described in Section 3.3.1.

Besides supporting these standard programming constructs, Co-shell also provides functions to support the manipulation of data and events. ProcessWeaver files conform to an ASCII-based humanly readable format (called the Universal Storage Mechanism) and are used to store the elements of a process. For example, Work Contexts and Cooperative Procedures are stored in USM files. A suite of functions is supplied that allows for the manipulation of these files at a low level. A suite of functions is also supplied to manage events and communication. These allow Co-shell to send and receive messages, allowing components (Unix processes) to communicate through the network. Co-shell can thus, for example, listen for the saving of a specific file and take action when this occurs. Finally, a useful feature of the Co-shell facility is that the shell language can be invoked from a Unix window and can be used to interactively debug Co-shell scripts.

A second method of invoking tools is through direct calls to the Unix operating system using the Co-shell language. This was the approach used in the experiment to invoke the SCCS tools *get* and *delta*, in order to automatically extract and return the document to the configuration management repository (see Figure 3.12).

Development – Performing parallel aggregated processes. There are many situations where multiple, identical subprocesses converge into a single downstream process. An example of this is where several software components are integrated to produce a complete system. To facilitate the development task in such cases, ProcessWeaver allows one to create a default Cooperative Procedure and then load this into multiple parallel activities. Thus, for example, one could load the Cooperative Procedure shown in Figure 3.11 into each of the three parallel activities shown in Figure 3.5. However, there are no mechanisms for allowing the process initiator to specify the number of parallel processes at the start of, or during process execution.

Development – Selecting sub-processes at run time. The ability to select one of multiple possible sub-processes during process execution is desirable. While it is always possible to explicitly incorporate every sub-process in the parent model, doing so could be unwieldy and does assume that all sub-processes are known when the parent process is defined. ProcessWeaver does not support the run-time capability to select one sub-process from a number of possible sub-processes.

Enactment – Assigning agents to roles. ProcessWeaver has a very explicit approach to role assignment (or variable assignment in general). In a process template, any process entity (e.g., role, product) can be defined as a variable, to be instantiated when the process starts. Associated with each Cooperative Procedure is a list that specifies the variables needed to run the process. These variables can be instantiated by hand through the procedure parameters list, or, in the case of a child process, the parent process may instantiate them.

Enactment – Supporting on-the-fly process modification. The ability to modify an on-going process may be important, either to adapt to unforeseen circumstances or to improve some procedure (e.g., replacing someone who has left the project, or adding an improved testing tool). Currently there are no mechanisms to allow this.

Enactment – Logging process data. Process data logging is a useful feature for multiple reasons. First, a historical log of process data generated during a debugging run can provide insights into a process model's logical correctness. Second, if a product or process error is made and requires correction, a historic log of the performed process can, in principle, allow this process to be rolled back to an earlier state and restarted. Third, a historic log of a performed process can support process verification, i.e., a post-project analysis can be performed to assure that the process was adequately followed. Finally, process improvement can be supported by process data logs as they allow analysis of the effectiveness of the process. Process-Weaver does not explicitly provide the capability to gather historic data. However, it does provide the underlying functionality for such a capability to be built. It does not, however, provide the capability to perform process roll-back.

Enactment – Simulating the process. ProcessWeaver provides a capability to qualitatively simulate processes (see Debugging – Tracing process dynamics). However, it does not provide explicit capability to perform quantitative process simulation. With such capability, values of process parameters (e.g., decision values, task durations) are specified on a statistical basis, and the consequent quantitative behavior is analyzed.

Resource – Invoking tools. Tools can be invoked in two ways. First, when a tool is invoked through a Work Context icon, it must first be defined in a *weaver.tls* file. A *weaver.tls* file provides a mapping between a tool function and the corresponding specific tool for a specific platform. Thus, when a Work Context calls for a word processor, the *weaver.tls* file can be set up to call FrameMaker for the Sun4. In the experiment, Emacs was invoked to display and edit the text files.

Resource – Managing Artifacts. During software product construction, multiple versions of intermediate and final products will be produced. There is therefore a close tie between process management and product management. (This can be seen in Figure 2.7) Having the capability to retrieve, store, and test for product versions as an integral capability within the Co-shell language could be useful. As it currently stands, one has to use external version control functions. (SCCS functions were used to support the *Document Update* process).

Communication – Modeling communication between agents. Communication between human agents is modeled principally using the Work Context concept. Work Contexts can be used in two ways. First, individual Work Context templates can be instantiated for simple tasks. After selecting the appropriate Work Context from the Agenda, the initiator of the task fills out a Work Context parameters form, in which the task roles are instantiated with the specific entities (e.g., names of people and documents). The appropriate Work Context icon then appears on the initiator's Agenda window and can be dispatched to the appropriate person by dragging the icon over the Delegation icon. Thus ProcessWeaver supports simple task management and communication between team members.

Second, Work Contexts can, of course, be embedded within processes. This has been described at some length above. As with simple task initiation, process initiation requires that roles be instantiated with specific entities prior to process execution. However, unlike simple task delegation, the initiator of a process does not have to explicitly dispatch Work Contexts to assignees; this is done automatically since the process knows which roles are associated with which tasks, and agents have been associated to roles.

ProcessWeaver can respond to messages broadcast by tools using a protocol that conforms to Hewlett Packard's Broadcast Message Server. This can be implemented through the *Event* condition (see Section 3.3.1). ProcessWeaver can also access tools that are already available within IBM's WorkBench/6000 (or equivalently Hewlett-Packard's Softbench) using the Co-shell language. This communication is performed by creating a Unix script supported by the ProcessWeaver command *wb_send*, that allows WorkBench messages to be sent. This form of communication was not investigated in the experiment.

Communication – Modeling automatic actions. Automatic actions (i.e., elements of the process that are performed without human intervention) can be easily implemented as was demonstrated in the experiment. The experiment applied this in two areas: requests to end users for decisions and invocation of SCCS tools.

Debugging – Syntax checking. Syntax checking is supported both in the Method Editor and in the Cooperative Procedure Editor. With the Method Editor, one can check that all the inputs, outputs and roles between activities are consistent. Another type of check is the *Run-Time* check. This check evaluates whether there are inconsistencies between an activity and its related Cooperative Procedure (e.g., it can identify inconsistent parameters).

Supporting the Cooperative Procedure Editor is a syntax checking feature. This graphically highlights any conditions or actions that have faulty syntax statements in attached Co-shell scripts. If one has a condition or action box open, this option will also highlight the offending line of Co-shell script.

Co-shell scripts can be interactively debugged off-line by typing *coshell* in any Unix window. This provides a vehicle for debugging routines such as shown in Figure 3.12.

Debugging – Tracing process dynamics. One can graphically view an executing process by selecting the *View* button located in the Cooperative Procedures main menu. In this mode, the Petri Net tokens can be observed to move from place to place as the process evolves, thus providing good insight into behavior characteristics. of the process. Ongoing processes can likewise be viewed with the *View* feature, and this provides a window into the real-time status of project tasks.

Debugging – Querying. At any point in the process, the *interact* option allows the user to implement Co-shell commands thus, for example, allowing values of variables to be examined.

Debugging – Spying. While one cannot spy on the variables of the process, ProcessWeaver is supported by a simple spy function that provides information on the messages that are broadcast on the communication channel (e.g., for event notification and reply).

Debugging – Reachability, deadlock, logging of process data. These are not explicitly supported in the reviewed version of ProcessWeaver.

End-User Capabilities: Category 2 of Table 3.9 is expanded to include an assessment of the capabilities defined in Table 3.8 as described below.

Scheduling periodic work. ProcessWeaver has the ability to initiate periodic Work Contexts. The period can be set, for example, so that the Work Context for a task appears on a particular day of the week or on a particular date in the month.

Collecting metric data. ProcessWeaver has no explicit mechanisms for collecting metric data. Events can, however, be recorded using the event handler functions of the Co-shell language. These mechanisms could be used to construct a metric gathering capability.

Supporting project management tasks. ProcessWeaver provides the capability to communicate with project management tools through a supplied Cooperative Procedure that starts up a project. This can invoke either MicroSoft Project for Windows or Project Management Workbench 3.1 under PC/DOS.

Supporting the individual user. ProcessWeaver (V1.2) is primarily designed to support processes management, and, other than scheduling periodic Work Contexts, does not support, for example, "to do" lists or the tracking personal tasks.

Supporting group communications. ProcessWeaver provides effective communication through the Work Context feature. This feature can be used to initiate and delegate individual tasks (or just send messages) and is also the communication mechanism used when tasks are embedded within processes.

Developer Issues:

Ease of learning. The graphical nature of ProcessWeaver is a considerable help to developing processes. ProcessWeaver allows the major activities to be defined through a work-breakdown type of diagram, with each activity having its own process defined though a Cooperative Procedure (Petri Net diagram). This is intuitively appealing and helps with learning. The novice user may however find the connection between all the diagrams and associated text boxes somewhat confusing at first, although this decreases as the user gains experience with the system. The graphical component of ProcessWeaver is supported by the textual Co-shell language. This provides lower-level constructs that are difficult to describe graphically. Use of simple Co-shell scripts was made in the experiment and little difficulty was experienced.

Ease of use. Once ProcessWeaver's organization is understood, one can develop process models quite rapidly. The graphical approach to model development is fun, easy to use, and less likely to promote errors than a textual approach. A generic Cooperative Procedure (that may be user-defined) can be generated for each activity specified through the Method Editor, and this is useful for developing and debugging prototypes of the model. However, experience gained during this investigation indicates that Cooperative Procedures will most likely need customizing.

The window that displays Cooperative Procedures works well for small process models, like those discussed in this book. However, ProcessWeaver does not currently have the ability to zoom in and out of a diagram and scrolling across and down the window is quite slow. These implementation details are likely to cause some frustrations when larger models are constructed.

Effectiveness of support for development. ProcessWeaver's graphical approach to process definition significantly simplifies and speeds up model-building. The Method Editor provides a range of options with which to construct and edit activity hierarchies; the Cooperative Procedure editor allows process elements to be rapidly accessed, linked, and rearranged, while the Work Context editor provides a very straightforward means of creating the end-user interface. Navigating between the editor windows and other supporting windows was found to be very easy, once the relationships between the elements was understood. In addition, support for model debugging (to be described later) was found to be quite comprehensive.

Because each Method, Cooperative Procedure, and Work Context is stored in a separate text file, the number of files associated with a complete process model can become quite large. (There were 15 files for the simple example model.) Thus file management and version control could become an issue. Transmitting all the files for the example model was found to be somewhat tedious.

Quality of on-line help. On-line help is not implemented in the version (1.2) of Process Weaver that was used.

Error handling. ProcessWeaver provides a variety of high-level process-oriented error messages. For example, if one attempts to generate a default Cooperative Procedure for an activity before any inputs, outputs, or roles have been defined, the message *Activity "XXX" has not been edited yet => no inputs/outputs/roles* appears. In some cases, errors cannot occur as syntax checking prevents illegal states.

For example, in constructing a Cooperative Procedure, the system prevents the linking of two contiguous transitions or places.

End-User Issues:

Ease of learning. There is a spectrum of end users from those who simply respond to Work Contexts sent (from an ongoing automated process), to those who develop Work Contexts in order to communicate requests, and to those who develop simple Cooperative Procedures to automate short processes. Each of these end-user categories requires different levels of expertise. Technical learning for the first group is likely to be minimal, although significant behavioral adjustments will be needed for such people. In the second category, development of Work Contexts can help an individual in scheduling periodic tasks such as writing end-of-the-month reports, as well as for interaction between individuals. Such development requires knowledge of a limited subset of ProcessWeaver's functionality (making and instantiating a Work Context template), so learning should be straightforward. The third category of end user will require a lengthier period of training, as knowledge of a significant fraction of ProcessWeaver's capabilities will be required.

The current ProcessWeaver manual does not address end-user categories, or how ProcessWeaver should be implemented by an end user. Having some guidance in this area (perhaps through an end-user manual) would thus be of considerable help. End-user learning in the broader sense must also address technology adoption issues, since a PCE such as ProcessWeaver can potentially have a dramatic impact on the way people work. Teaching personnel to work within a process that is driven by automation will be a greater challenge than simply training these personnel on these technical issues.

Ease of use. ProcessWeaver provides a standard Work Context format for presenting information related to one task to the end user. This format allows for:

- the display of textual information that explains what the task involves,
- document icons that allow access to the documents themselves, and
- control buttons, that allow for decision making such as indicating that the task has been completed (see Figure 3.4 as an example).

This format was found to be intuitive and easy to use. For some more complex applications it might be useful to have the functionality provided by pull-down menus, but this is not currently provided.

Clarity of presentation. As indicated in *ease of use*, the format of basic Work Context windows through which information is presented is well designed. ProcessWeaver cannot of course be responsible for process models that have poor explanatory text, inappropriate icons, or badly chosen controls.

Performance:

Execution time efficiency. With respect to response times, there were no long delays experienced. The following times are for the experimental model that was implemented on a Sun 4 SPARC station running under Sun OS 4.1.2. For the end user, loading a new cooperative procedure took about one second, while after the roles had been instantiated with agents, it took about eight seconds for the first Work Context icon to appear in the Agenda window. Transmitting a Work Context from one user to another took about four seconds. Delay times associated with developing process models were also modest. Opening the method window took about a second, opening a Cooperative Procedure window took about five seconds, while opening a Work Context window took about three seconds. These times are approximate, as a regular watch was used, and there was some minor variability in the times resulting from different machine loadings. Note that the process model used was small, and the results do not indicate how response times will vary with model size, nor is it known how response times will vary with larger numbers of users.

Space efficiency. The ProcessWeaver files take about 13.5Mb of disk space (in the *bin* directory). User files for the process example took up about 15.8 Kb, half of this being for the Work Contexts. Additional memory is taken up by each instantiated (run-time) process model. For the experiment, each instance took up about 8Kb. Since these can accumulate, they can take up an increasing amount of space if they are not managed. They are deleted if the process successfully terminates.

System Interface:

Ease of tool integration. As discussed above, tool integration was implemented:

- using the *weaver.tls* file that associates a tool class with specific tools on specific platforms, and
- making Unix calls through Co-shell scripts.

Both approaches were found to work with few problems. These interfaces are relatively simple and essentially allow one to start and stop tools.

Portability. ProcessWeaver runs on Unix platforms from Hewlett Packard, DEC, and Sun that support X-windows, X11R4, Motif, NSF 4.0. The Agenda can also be run on PCs running Microsoft Windows 3.1.

The process model files are all defined using ProcessWeaver's Universal Storage Mechanism that is based ASCII-based. They are therefore portable between machines.

Interface to the operating system. Bourne shell commands can be embedded in Co-shell scripts through the Co-shell *system* function. Using this mechanism, file read-write access and the SCCS calls were implemented. Within ProcessWeaver, only files owned by ProcessWeaver can have their access permissions changed. This constraint is more a consequence of the Unix system design than of ProcessWeaver design. In a large project, such files would all have to be owned by the "process" rather than appropriate individuals, and this might have restrictive consequences.

Off-line User Support:

Support from Customer Representatives. ProcessWeaver does not yet have a large support staff in the US, although Cap Gemini is planning to expand this function. However the support that was provided for the work associated with this book was both responsive and technically knowledgable.

Clarity of Documentation. The current manuals (User and Reference) [Process-Weaver 92] are good for reference but not as tutorials. The User's Manual does an effective job of explaining many of the low level details. However, it is weak on providing the broad picture, i.e., explaining how all the functional elements of a process model are linked together. The User's Manual could also be improved if it provided examples of use, such as leading a model developer through the process of model construction, including the use of the Co-shell. In the Reference Manual, code fragments illustrating the use of Co-shell functions are provided with the function definitions and these are necessary but not sufficient. A set of functions is provided to manipulate the ProcessWeaver data files, but little explanation is provided on why these functions are needed or how they are used. Finally, if the user wishes to use the event-driven features of ProcessWeaver, he/she must have a working knowledge of this subject – again little more than a listing of the functions is provided. Thus, a separate tutorial manual covering model construction, use of the Co-shell language and its event-driven features, etc., would be of great value and would make ProcessWeaver more accessible to potential users. As mentioned earlier, a separate manual covering both end-user applications and automated process adoption issues would also strengthen the product.

The ProcessWeaver manuals are logically organized and in general information can be found rapidly. The indexes for both manuals are good, but could be more complete. For example, none of the terms associated with "viewing" a running co-operative procedure (see *Debugging: Tracing of process dynamics*) such as *view, kill, stop,* and *sleep* are in the User's Manual index.

Availability of Hands-On Training. Currently training sessions are limited by the small number of support personnel in the US. However, Cap Gemini intends to expand this area as it does with customer support.

Availability of Encoded Process Examples. To date there are few available encoded examples. The version supplied (1.2) came with one working demonstration. A variety of enactable examples of varying size and application would be of great benefit, not only for learning the system, but also as a foundation for customized applications.

3.3.4   Improvements in Functionality

ProcessWeaver Version 1.2 was reviewed in this book. However, this version has now been superceded by Version 2. Some of the significant updates, that relate to the preceding discussions, are summarized below. Note that, at the time of writing, the author has no hands-on experience with this new version. Version 2 is believed to include, but not be limited to, the following:

- Links will allow integration with Hewlett Packard's Broadcast Message Server (or equivalently IBM's WorkBench 3.0).
- A change will be made in the scoping rules to remove the restrictive scoping problem discussed in Section 4.2.
- A tutorial manual with large example and "how-to" section will be included with the documentation. Also, user documentation will be available as on-line context-sensitive help.
- Folders will be provided for organizing Work Contexts.
- Through selection lists, an event can be generated without terminating a Work Context, as is required in Version 1.2.
- A set of application tools covering configuration management, software testing and test tracking, and general office automation will be available.
- An Activity Instance Manager (AIM) will be added. This will provide project management with functions for planning, process tracking, and graphical browsing of the process model. It is anticipated that the feature will remove the need for use of external project management tools.

By adding the end-user application capabilities described in the last two items, ProcessWeaver is no longer a framework but takes on some of the characteristics of an environment. Thus, like SynerVision, ProcessWeaver, Version 2, may be called a process-centered environment (PCE).

3.4 The Synervision Experiment

As in Section 3.3 on ProcessWeaver, this section starts out with a review of SynerVision's approach to process automation. The subsequent sub-sections then deal with SynerVision in the context of the evaluation experiment.

3.4.1   Review of SynerVision

SynerVision provides four "use-models" that address increasingly broad measures of process support. These use-models cover:

- management of personal tasks,
- management of group tasks,
- process enactment through the use of process template,
- process-centered environments.[2]

In the management of personal tasks[3], personal task hierarchies can be created, and attributes associated with these tasks can be attached. Such attributes may be associated, for example, with management of time or with dependencies between tasks. In this way the owner of these tasks can track and monitor their status. In addition to these personal functions, the use-model for group tasks contains functionality to support group interactions. Thus tasks can be delegated, and broader use is made of attributes to support project management such as task status and time spent on tasks. More formal support is provided through the process-enactment use-model. At this level, processes (i.e., task hierarchies and their behavior) are captured in templates that can be reused. These templates support facilities for communication, tool invocation, metrics collection, etc., and provide the "glue" that embeds these facilities in user-defined processes. Process-centered environments (the final use-model) apply the concepts of the three previous use-models to implement major process enactment applications, and Hewlett Packard foresees that commercial vendors will be mainly responsible for their development. Once developed, process-centered environments will be customized to meet the needs of individual organizations. To date, the only significant process-centered environment built on the SynerVision framework is HP's ChangeVision, a product for managing change request tracking and software updating.

Given the discussion of Section 4.2, a possible relationship between SynerVision's use-models and the levels of the Capability Maturity Model (see Chapter 4) can be seen to exist. At CMM Level 1 SynerVision's first two use-models can be effectively adopted, since neither use-model needs to have strong notions of defined process. At these levels, individuals can be helped in the informal management of personal tasks, and modest group communications are supported. It should be noted, however, that use of these models is an effective precursor to having processes defined, in that identification of tasks and gathering of simple task metrics are encouraged. In the third use-model, enactable processes are defined, and this encourages CMM Level 2 behaviors. Having the processes automated prevents groups from sliding back into informal, ad-hoc practices. The final use-model (process-centered environments) envisages ambitious use of process automation, with defined processes being adopted throughout an organization. To the extent that such process

---

2. By an unfortunate coincidence, SynerVision's name for their last use-model (process-centered environments) is the same one as used in a more general context within this book. (See Appendix E for the book's definition). However, the term *process-centered environment* is only used with SynerVision's meaning in Section 3.3, and it is made clear when referred to in this sense.

3. In SynerVision's terminology, all activities in a hierarchy are called tasks, so we will use this convention in Section 3.3

models are accepted consistently by multiple groups within an organization, this use-model may support CMM Level 3 behaviors.

Managing Personal Tasks: The variety of functions that SynerVision provides for the management of personal projects, are briefly reviewed below. Central to task management is the notion of the task and task hierarchies. Figure 3.13 shows the

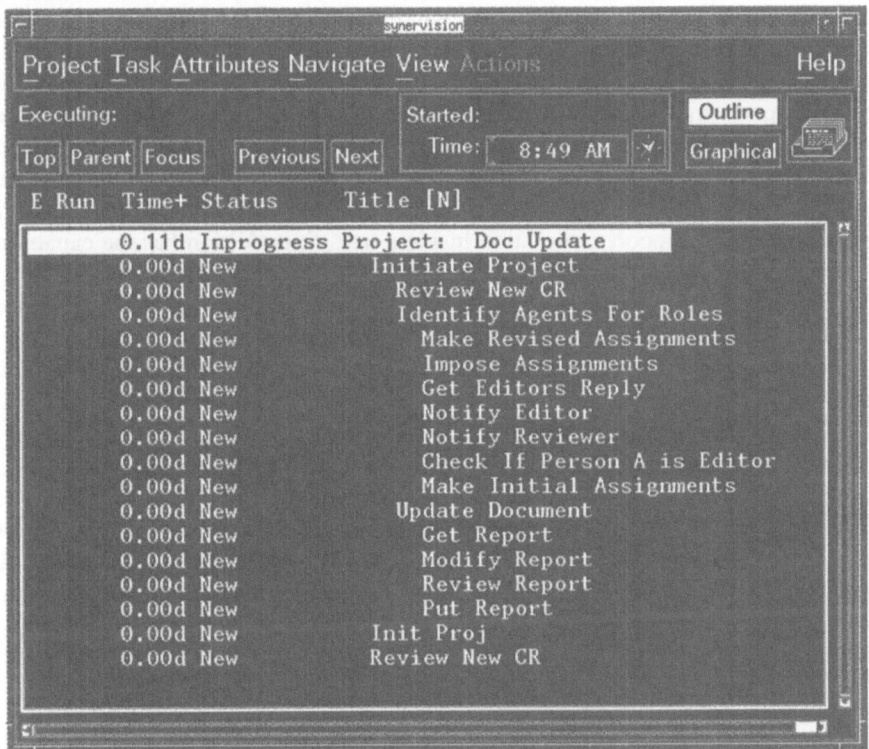

Fig. 3.13. SynerVision main window illustrating a task hierarchy

main SynerVision window in which a simple task breakdown structure is illustrated. Note the task information columns to the left of the tasks themselves. This information can be customized, and a variety of display options such as *earliest start date* can be included in these columns.

Lists of current tasks, such as shown in Figure 3.13, can be developed for individual use. When a task is executing (i.e., it is highlighted and has an "E" in the cell of the column marked with an "E"), time is allocated against it. The times spent on higher-level tasks reflect the durations spent on child tasks. This time-recording mechanism provides support for such activities as managing monthly objectives and distributing time between projects. One can also filter tasks according to the task's attributes using such attributes as task status or priority. For example, one can suppress all the tasks that have the status *Inprogress* from the task structure shown in Figure 3.13. In a similar way, one can also sort tasks according to task attributes such as status or priority.

SynerVision provides a set of windows through which one can customize the attributes of tasks to be performed. The first of these windows is the *Basic* window. This window allows the user to input information such as task priority, earliest start time, and estimated task duration. The window also displays how much time has been spent to date on a task. The second window (*Notes*) allows one to attach one or multiple textual notes to a task. This can be useful for recording either what should be performed in this task or information on how the task was performed. The *Dependency* window then allows one to set constraints on the sequence through which the tasks are performed. Thus one can state that task B should be started before task A is completed and whether this constraint is only advisory or whether it is mandatory. To support automation inside a task, SynerVision has the capability to attach action scripts through the *Actions* window. These scripts are written in the language of the Unix Bourne shell with Synervision extensions and can thus support a wide range of functionality. As a minimum, one can call on utilities such as for e-mail or word processing, but more complex requests can be made through this feature.

A major advantage of automating the software process is that metrics can be collected relatively accurately and painlessly (as compared to manual approaches). Because SynerVision contains or generates information related to tracking project progress, it can provide the user with a variety of standard and customized reports that are useful to track both individual and project efforts. These data are useful, not only to control an ongoing project, but for subsequent process improvement. Standard process reports include:

- Estimation accuracy (planned vs. actual times)
- Hierarchical results (copy of the task information shown in Figure 3.13)
- Planned vs. unplanned tasks
- Process adherence by user
- To do list
- Total tasks by project
- Total tasks by user

Standard project reports include:

- Blocked tasks
- Completed tasks
- Project completion
- Project time
- Quality status
- Task time

Managing Group Tasks: The major extension that the group feature provides is the ability of group members to communicate about tasks. The project leader can set up a task (with a sub-task structure) and can define which members of the group have access privileges to each task. Tasks in a task hierarchy can only have one assigned owner, and sub-tasks in the hierarchy can be created and delegated by individuals. During project execution, individuals can accept, or reject, delegated tasks. This team-oriented task structure and related task status information can be viewed by members of the project. However, read permissions are attached to all tasks to control visibility of task information, and write permissions are attached to control execution/modification privileges.

In order to set access permissions on a task, the original owner of the task uses the *Access* window shown in Figure 3.14. This window allows control of who has

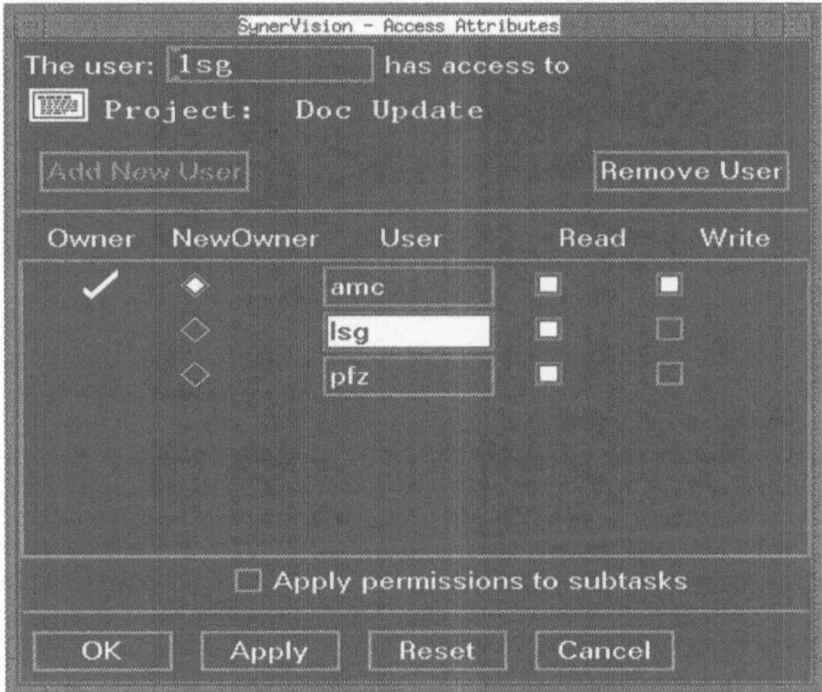

Fig. 3.14. SynerVision access attributes window

read and write permissions for that task. It also allows for the forwarding of the task to the person identified under the *NewOwner* column. Upon receiving notice of the task (the in-box shown in the upper right of Figure 3.13 becomes full), the new owner can open the *task in-box* shown in Figure 3.15 and has the option of accepting, reassigning, or rejecting the task.

Process Enactment Through the Use of Templates: Within SynerVision, there is an incremental growth of concepts from personal processes to group processes and then to process enactment through the use of process templates. Processes that have been developed for personal or group support can be automatically captured in tem-

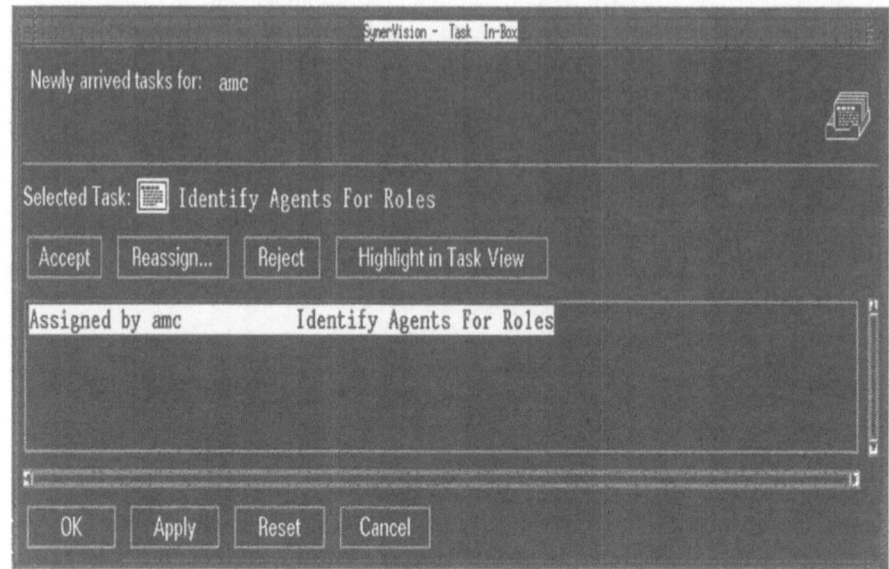

Fig. 3.15. Synervision task in-box window

plates and reused. Thus personal and group processes can be modified and improved upon and, when they are considered effective, can be transformed into templates for adoption by similar groups. In this way, there is less likely to be a major cultural impact, since they have not been imposed from outside, but were evolved within the organization's culture [Kellner 93a].

When a template is automatically generated from a personal or group process, a text-based script is generated and stored in a file. This file is humanly readable since the process description is compiled into a script that is based on the Unix Bourne shell language [Sobell 89] with extensions to account for process needs. Alternately, partial scripts can be automatically generated from a task hierarchy and then completed by hand, or they can be fully written by hand.

The template language (as an extension of the Borne shell language) provides features that are not available in automatically generated scripts. In this context, one of the more important additions to the process-template use-model is the AUTO-MATIC_ACTION function. The section *Managing Personal Tasks* discussed the *Actions* window, a window in which commands can be placed to invoke actions. If such actions are compiled into a template, they are embedded in what are called MANUAL_ACTIONs and, to be initiated during process enactment, require human intervention. On the other hand, AUTOMATIC_ACTIONs can be initiated by the machine, with no human intervention. However, they cannot currently be generated from the *Actions* window and must be written into the script. An overview of this scripting language will be given in Section 3.4.2.

One does not need to follow a process script from beginning to end. For example, one can start at a task in the middle of a process script, provided that the preconditions are consistent with that task and its children. However, doing so may be contrary to the project's policies. Thus SynerVision provides a function *Process Adherence*, that analyzes that tasks have actually been performed. This information is also useful from a metrics analysis point of view.

Figure 3.15 shows the standard communication dialog window. However, this does not always provide sufficient functionality. For example, it does not allow text to be entered into the system. Thus SynerVision provides a Bourne shell-based function *svprompt* with which allows custom dialog windows can be designed. These dialog windows allow for buttons, text display, and input. One such window is shown in Figure 3.16. This type of dialog window is used extensively in the process example, and is the equivalent of ProcessWeaver's Work Context window.

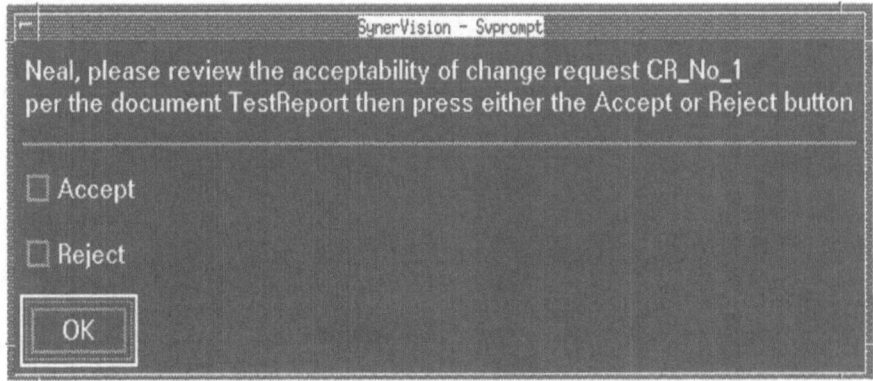

Fig. 3.16. Dialog window generated through the *svprompt* command

Process-Centered Environments: The final use-model is called the *process-centered environment* (SynerVision's term). This use-model provides little in the way of technical extensions to the previous use-models, but focuses mainly on tailoring existing large-scale process templates for specific applications. Hewlett-Packard envisions that these large models are likely to be developed commercially and cite their ChangeVision as an example of such a case. Customizing existing process models is seen as requiring much less investment of effort than having to develop the processes from scratch. Precedents for this exist, for example with building one's own CM system or word processor. Often these systems come with features that make them user-tailorable.

3.4.2 Developing the Synervision Process Model

In this section we will discuss the development of the enactable SynerVision process scripts from the process graphs shown in Figures 2.20, 2.21, and 2.22. For a complete understanding of these scripts, a knowledge of the Bourne shell scripting language is useful but not essential for the following discussion. Appendix D provides a full listing of the complete enactable script that was developed for the experiments, and for illustrative purposes, Figure 3.17 shows a short, simplified, but executable, version of the Appendix D script. This script implements the top-level task (Figure 2.20) breakdown, but does not expand the lower-level tasks *Review New CR* and *Identify Agents for Roles*.

The top-level task has three sub-tasks or children, and associated with each of these is an action defined by the associated AUTOMATIC_ACTION statement. The task breakdown structure can be created manually by simply typing in the text, or it can be generated automatically using the facilities provided by the main SynerVision window. In either case, the associated AUTOMATIC_ACTIONs have to be generated manually.[4] Some comments on this script are appropriate.

A task can be automatically activated when the value of either the *executing* or *status* attribute of that task is changed. For example, at the end of the first AUTOMATIC_ACTION in Figure 3.17, the ATTRIB function sets the *Executing* condition of the task *RevNewCR* to *Running_Foreground* (see line A). The second AUTOMATIC_ACTION is fired when the status of its associated task (*RevNewCR*) changes from *New* to *InProgress* (see line B). Since *RevNewCR*'s initial state is *New* and *Running_Foreground* implies a status of *InProgress*, the activity *RevNewCR* is activated automatically at the end of the *InitProj* activity. Similar state transitions can be followed for the other tasks. Thus each task may activate and deactivate other tasks through the *ATTRIB -i -v -t $task...* command. This does not, however, prevent one from starting a task in the middle of a process sequence; one is free to start anywhere, although errors may occur if, for example, the preconditions for that task are incorrect. In order to force a task to complete before another one begins, the DEPENDENCY function (not used in the example) may be applied.

3.4.3   The Evaluation

As with ProcessWeaver, the six categories of Table 3.9 and the items within these categories provide the basis for the review of SynerVision.

Model-building Capabilities: Category 1 of Table 3.9 is the largest category, since it is expanded to include assessments of the capabilities defined in Table 3.7.

Development – Scoping of variables. SynerVision allows variable values, defined anywhere in the process hierarchy to be used anywhere else. However, visibility of the variable's value in the hierarchy is controlled using the ATTRIB function.

---

4. Some automation of this is currently possible, and it is anticipated that future versions of SynerVision will be able to accommodate both MANUAL_ACTIONs and AUTOMATIC_ACTIONs.

```
#######################################################
# identify task structure (main task and child tasks) #
#######################################################

TASK "Initiate Project"
InitProj=$last_TASKID

CHILDREN_BEGIN

  TASK "Review New CR"
  RevNewCR=$last_TASKID

  TASK "Identify Agents For Roles"
  IdenAgForRI=$last_TASKID

  TASK "Update Document"
  UpdateDoc=$last_TASKID

CHILDREN_END

################################################
# Define AUTOMATIC_ACTIONs associated with tasks #
################################################

# Initialize variables
AUTOMATIC_ACTION  -t $InitProj Status New Inprogress perform <<EOF
    ATTRIB -i -v manager "Paul"
    ATTRIB -i -v report "War and Peace"
    ATTRIB -i -v CR "Change Title"
    ATTRIB -i -v -t $RevNewCR "Executing=Running_Foreground" ### line A ###
EOF

#send message to manager identifying document to be reviewed
AUTOMATIC_ACTION -t $RevNewCR Status New Inprogress perform <<EOF ### line B ###
    CR=\'GET_ATTRIB CR\'
    report=\'GET_ATTRIB report\'
    manager=\'GET_ATTRIB manager\'
    result=\'svprompt -p "\$manager, please review change request \$CR
for document \$report and identify whether to accept or reject." -L -d "accept
reject"\'
# mark this task completed
    ATTRIB -i -v -t $RevNewCR "Status=Completed"
    if [ \$result = "accept" ]; then
# start the next task
                ATTRIB -i -v -t $IdenAgForRI "Executing=Running_Foreground"
    else
# mark parent task as abandonded
                ATTRIB -i -v -t $InitProj "Status=Abandoned"
    fi
EOF

AUTOMATIC_ACTION  -t $IdenAgForRI Status New Inprogress perform <<EOF
    svprompt -p "Now performing Identify Agents For Roles"
    ATTRIB -i -v -t $UpdateDoc "Executing=Running_Foreground"
    ATTRIB -i -v -t $IdenAgForRI "Status=Completed"
EOF

AUTOMATIC_ACTION  -t $UpdateDoc Status New Inprogress perform <<EOF
    svprompt -p "Now performing Update Document"
    ATTRIB -i -v -t $UpdateDoc "Status=Completed"
EOF
```

Fig. 3.17. Example of a short SynerVision script

Development – Modeling hierarchies. SynerVision models task hierarchies through a textual task breakdown structure. An example of such a structure is shown is Figure 3.13. Also provided in this view are columns of user-customizable information on the tasks, such as time spent on the task. One can also illustrate this task structure graphically. However, the textual form provides a more compact and useful view of the task information than the graphical form.

Development – Supporting model development. As discussed in Section 3.4.1, SynerVision processes can be developed incrementally, from personal processes to group processes to formal process templates. All of this can be performed with little or no programming. In this lies a real strength. However, if one has to develop processes with any complexity, templates are likely to require significant hand-coding. This requires a knowledge of the Bourne shell language, and in this there are two drawbacks. First, development time can be lengthy and error prone. As discussed in the following subsection, SynerVision currently has few debugging aids to support development. Second, it is likely to be difficult to communicate the resulting process descriptions, using the templates, to the people who either have to use the processes, or have to sign off on their acceptability. In this regard, a front-end graphical interface for process definition would be very helpful

Development – Creating a process library. One can build SynerVision process templates for library creation in two ways. In the first approach, the menu items in the window interface (see Figure 3.13) provide the functionality necessary to define logically simple processes. The *Generate Template* feature can then be used to automatically generate a permanent template script for that process. In the second approach, the template script is written by hand. Of course, an automatically generated script can subsequently be modified or expanded by hand.

Development – Supporting workahead. SynerVision allows the end user of a process to start intermediate tasks at any time. For example, one may wish to start writing code, even although the formal code design has not yet officially been signed off. In this case, it is the user's responsibility to make sure that the inputs to the task are correct. However, SynerVision also provides the means to control task initiation, if necessary, through the DEPENDENCY function. In addition, a task attribute *dependency-enforcement* can be used to specify whether this dependency is mandatory or can be overridden. Dependencies can also be used to implement AND and XOR relationships between tasks. This flexibility of task control in SynerVision reflects a practical understanding of real-world user issues.

Development – Modeling standard programming constructs. Since the SynerVision template language is based on the Bourne shell scripting language, it has all the standard programming constructs that the shell contains, i.e., looping, conditionals, variable binding, etc.

Development – Performing parallel aggregated processes. For a discussion of this topic, see *Performing parallel aggregated tasks* in Section 3.2.3. SynerVision does not include any explicit capability in this area. If one wishes to have identical processes performed in parallel, one would have to program this into the script by hand, either by placing the common process in a shell function that is called multiple times, or by duplicating the appropriate segment of script for the common process.

Development – Selecting process at run time. As with ProcessWeaver, SynerVision has no explicit mechanism for the run-time specification of sub-processes. All tasks (i.e., sub-processes) must be specified in the process model at model definition time.

Enactment – Assigning agents to roles. There is no explicit concept of "role" within SynerVision (other than the system administrator function) and thus there is no end-user window support for such assignments. This lack of support is true for variable assignment in general. One must therefore write a low-level function to support this capability. For simplicity in the experiment, roles and other variables were instantiated within the script itself (see the first AUTOMATIC_ACTION in Figure 3.17).

Enactment – Supporting on-the-fly process modification. From practical considerations, there may be times when modification of a process that is currently being enacted is required. For example, a task performed late in a process may have to use a product different from that specified at the start of the process.[5] In SynerVision, a process is guided by executing its pre-defined process script. The script cannot be changed during this execution and thus adapting processes on-the-fly is not allowed. In the above example, this means that once the product has been specified, it cannot be replaced by another, unless the possibility for this change has been accounted for in the process script.

Enactment – Logging process data. For a discussion of this topic, see *Logging of process data* in Section 3.2.3. SynerVision provides a feature called Process Adherence through which reports of tasks actually performed can be generated. Additional data logging capability could be incorporated into a SynerVision script by saving information about tasks performed to a file. In theory, process roll-back could be implemented if appropriate process and product data were logged. However, considerable thought would have to be given to its implementation, particularly with respect tracking back through product versions – and SynerVision does not provide any explicit capability to manage product versions. (See *Managing Artifacts* below.)

---

5. However, if such modifications are allowed, they must be very carefully planned, or there could be serious side effects on the execution of the rest of the process.

Enactment – Simulating the process. No explicit support is provided for performing simulation.

Resource – Invoking tools. Tools can be invoked in the template language through Bourne shell calls. This approach provides the simple ability to start and stop a tool, and was used in the experiment (see Appendix D). HP's Broadcast Message Server can be used to provide greater encapsulation functionality, but is not used here.

Resource – Managing Artifacts. For a discussion of this topic, see *Managing Artifacts* in Section 3.3. SynerVision process scripts are based on the Bourne Shell language and as such have full access to all the Shell's commands, including the SCCS version management functions. There is, however, no explicit support for version control at the process management level.

Communication – Modeling communication between agents. Communications can be performed in several ways:
- Tasks can be assigned from one person to another using the Access Attributes window (Figure 3.14). Such assigned tasks appear in the receivers Task In-Box (Figure 3.15). Tasks assigned automatically (using the ATTRIB function in a process template) can also appear in the Task In-Box window.
- Communications between human agents or from the machine to a human agent is supported inside scripts using the *svprompt* function. *svprompt* generates a customized dialog box that provides optionally for textual messages, a text input field, and buttons (Figure 3.16).
- Communications can also be established through a connection to Hewlett Packard's Broadcast Message Server. Since this is not an explicit part of SynerVision's functionality, it is not used here.

Communication – Modeling automatic actions. If a task needs to initiate an automatic action, or a sequence of actions,(i.e., actions without human intervention), the function AUTOMATIC_ACTION is used. This was discussed in Section 3.4.2.

Debugging – Syntax checking. SynerVision provides error information when a model is instantiated and also at run-time. Since the template language is an extension of the Bourne shell, one can interactively debug expressions or redirect values of variables.

Debugging – Tracing process dynamics. Tracing of the real-time status of tasks can be performed by viewing the *status* column of the SynerVision Main window (see Figure 3.13). As a process evolves the status of tasks change and provide a limited indication of what is happening. During the execution of a process, this feature also allows participants in the process to view task status. However, this trace feature is fairly limited as an aid for debugging.

Debugging – Logging process data. Selected process data can be logged to a file during process execution through manually inserted statements in the process script.

Debugging – Reachability, deadlock, querying, spying. SynerVision does not support these functions.

End-User Capabilities: Category 2 of Table 3.9 is expanded to include an assessment of the capabilities defined in Table 3.8 as described below.

Scheduling periodic work. The ability to automatically schedule periodic tasks such as weekly meetings can be very useful. However, SynerVision does not explicitly provide this capability (at least not without writing some Bourne shell script). This is an example of where some built-in higher-level functionality could improve end-user effectiveness.

Collecting metric data. One of the advantages of adopting a PCE is its potential for gathering accurate and complete metric data automatically, thus relieving the end-user of a distasteful chore. SynerVision provides very effective support for the collection and review of time- and task-related metric data. For example, it will track actual-to-estimated task times, and percentage of tasks complete.

Supporting project management tasks. Project management is supported through the metric data described above. Thus a project manager can maintain current knowledge of task status and can generate customized reports providing information about the status of a project.

Supporting the individual user. The individual user is supported in a variety of features for:

- generating personal task metrics,
- associating notes with tasks for guidance on the task, or for journaling,
- specifying task dependencies, and
- automating tasks (e.g., for tool invocation).

Supporting group communications. Users are supported with a variety of features for:

- setting up and operating a shared project,
- communicating between project members, and
- providing metric information on project status.

Developer Issues:

Ease of learning. SynerVision is in a conceptually new class of software product, is quite complex, and has many features. The novice to SynerVision must understand such concepts as tasks (their ownership, status, behavior, etc.), processes (task hier-

archies and dependencies, construction of personal and group processes), communication (accessing information, communication between project member and event
management), metrics specification and capture, and process template construction
(using the Bourne shell and its SynerVision extensions).

Of these items the most challenging (in this author's estimation) is the manual
development of process templates. As previously mentioned, this requires, as a basis, a good working knowledge of the Bourne shell language. Significant use is
made of the *here* feature of the language and this, combined with the need to distinguish between variable binding at process instantiation time and process run-time,
can be a considerable challenge for new users.

However, the development of simple processes (i.e., those not requiring manual
construction of templates) for either personal use or group use is well supported and
much easier to do. It is likely that an organization investing in SynerVision would
start with these processes, work up to template customization, and then go on to the
development of hand-written process templates. This incremental approach provides a safe way in which to gain the necessary experience.

Ease of use. SynerVision can be used in several ways. First, individuals can develop
process templates for personal task management. Second, limited-size process templates can be developed to support group activities. Both of these functions can be
handled without a detailed knowledge of the SynerVision template language. These
templates can be generated automatically and can thus be quickly and informally
prepared, tested, used, improved, or discarded without too much investment of time
or resources. Greater thought has to be given when standard templates are developed for complex processes in which the greater power and expressiveness of the
template language has to be used. This is likely to require significant developer
training, investment in requirements definition, coding, testing, etc., and a broader
consideration of the process adoption issues.

Effectiveness of support for development. The developer's view is accessed through
the SynerVision main window (Figure 3.13) and is supported by the SoftEdit editor.
The SynerVision main window contains all of the capability to develop processes
and automatically define their templates. Pull-down menus are used to select supporting functionalities, such as who has access to tasks (Figure 3.14). Through the
Task item in the menu-bar (Figure 3.13), one can select options to create sub-tasks
in the task hierarchy, to instantiate a process from a template file, or to generate a
new template from a defined task hierarchy. This approach is effective for developing process templates but could be enhanced in two ways. First, a more effective
means for testing and debugging process models is needed, and second, a process-
oriented graphical front end would help define the model and communicate its nature to affected individuals.

Quality of on-line help. SynerVision has an extensive and excellent on-line help capability with hypertext support. The path taken through the current hypertext sequence of selections is provided above the current help page. This prevents the user from becoming lost. The major elements of the SynerVision help feature are the Step-by-Step Instructions and the Guided Tour. Also provided is an on-line Information OverView of ChangeVision. As an example of the Help features, Step-by-Step Instructions include the topics:

- Basics of Using SynerVision
- Creating and Manipulating tasks
- Setting Task Attributes
- Annotating a Task with Process Guidance Notes
- Viewing Tasks the Way you Prefer
- Project Metrics and Reports
- Creating and Manipulating Manual Task Actions
- Using Shared Projects and Tasks
- Creating and Manipulating Process Templates

However, this on-line help does not cover programming in the SynerVision template language, a feature that could be very useful.

Error handling. SynerVision provides both instantiation and run-time error messages. Instantiation error messages provide some insights to problems, but do not, for example, identify template line numbers where errors have occurred. The run-time error messages usually provide insightful information. In developing and running the process models, no system crashes occurred.

End-User Issues:

Ease of Learning. There are two main classes of end-user and each has different learning issues. The first class of end user will develop personal or group processes for its own immediate use through the automated generation of process templates. While some learning is required, a major investment in time is not, since a high percentage of a process script is generated by the machine with appropriate end-user guidance. With this class of end-user, process adoption is not a primary issue since, by developing their own processes, such users are internally motivated to apply them. The second class of end user will only be expected to use pre-defined templates, and thus need not be closely involved with their technical development. Learning to use the templates should not be difficult, since the process guides the user through the sequence of tasks. However, these end users are more likely to have the automated process imposed upon them and thus may show resistance to change. Learning for them is thus less technically focused and more culturally focused.

Ease of use. Using the automated process is not, by itself, difficult since the user is guided through the needed process steps. In fact, if not designed effectively from a behavioral perspective, this ease of use may well make the user feel like a cog in a machine, with the potential for reducing creativity to button pushing and form filling.

Clarity of presentation. The standard end-user windows provided by SynerVision are shown in Figures 3.15 and 3.16. These allow for the sending and receiving of task delegation information and are straightforward to understand. However, the task information that can be displayed in the Task In-Box (Figure 3.15) is limited basically to the task name and who assigned it.

During execution of a complex process scenario, a large number of currently active tasks may be displayed at any one terminal. The Task In-Box can be used to list these tasks so long as only brief information on the tasks is required. However, if more complex instructions or decision making is required, then the Task In-Box is insufficient. For such tasks, customizing the presentation must be done and this is performed using the *svprompt* function. A typical display generated by this function is shown in Figure 3.16. The clarity of information presented by these displays has more to do with the developer's use of the interface and the process context in which the windows are displayed than it does with SynerVision's underlying features.

However, the currently implemented *svprompt* function provides a less than adequate means for managing its windows. Many task windows, such as shown in Figure 3.16 may reside on the terminal simultaneously, taking up space or hiding each other. In addition, the designer of the process interface is not provided with any control over the placement of documents or tools that may be associated with tasks. Management of these windows is an issue with which SynerVision has yet to deal.

Performance:

Execution time efficiency. SynerVision was run on a HP Apollo 9000 Series 700 workstation running under HP-UX. The slowest common procedure with a noticeable delay is the instantiation of a process from its template. A one-task template (with eight lines of code) took 5 seconds for instantiation from the template, while the experimental model defined in Appendix B (184 lines of code) took about 33 seconds. This primarily affects developers who are debugging models and thus are required to instantiate models often, but it can also affect end users, since a process has to be instantiated from its template before it is used. Run-times for executing the process model are usually of less importance, since instant responses are not required. (For example, when one end user sends a message to another end user, the communication time is generally not critical.) As with ProcessWeaver, these times are approximate, as a regular watch was used. Variability in times, resulting from different loadings on the machine, was not a problem with SynerVision since the machine was isolated from other users.

Space efficiency. With respect to space efficiency, files in the SynerVision 'bin' directory takes about 7.2Mb of disk space. The experimental model (Appendix B) takes about 8Kb of disk space.

System Interface:

Ease of tool integration. Invoking Unix tools in process templates was simple to do using Bourne shell constructs (see Appendix D). However, directing SynerVision output to the appropriate end-user terminals created some frustration. This is in part because higher-level constructs for directing output were not available in SynerVision; this functionality had to be built up from the Bourne shell. This is one area where some simple extensions to the scripting language could be a real benefit to the process developer.

More complex integrations using Hewlett Packard's Broadcast Message Server were not attempted.

Portability. SynerVision is available both on Hewlett Packard Apollo computers and on Sun SPARC stations.

Interface to the operating system. SynerVision process models are based on the Bourne shell language that is part of the Unix operating system. In addition, SynerVision uses the Unix file system to store the process models.

Off-Line User Support:

Support from customer representatives. Customers purchase an annual support contract for phone-in question answering and document update. Customers can also purchase specific services such as for the development of specialized process templates.

Clarity of documentation. The current documents that support SynerVision are:

1. Installing SynerVision and ChangeVision
2. Introduction to SynerVision: Models of Use [SynerVision 93a]
3. Developing SynerVision Processes [SynerVision 93b]

The first document was not used since it had little relevance to the technology behind SynerVision and in addition SynerVision was already installed on the HP platform. The second document provides a good explanation of the different use-models described in this chapter. It was very helpful in understanding the philosophy that guided the development of SynerVision and as a practical hands-on guide for exploring models that did not require template programming. The third document, which is required for template programming, is considerably less helpful and needs revision to be effective. Its principal weakness is the assumption that its readership knows the Bourne shell language. A review of this language, emphasizing the features that are commonly required in SynerVision templates, would be valuable.

The document's other main weaknesses are its poor organization and lack of good illustrative examples (not just code fragments) to clarify the technical points it is making. It might have made more sense for the latter two documents to be organized as a user manual and a reference manual. A tutorial manual would also be of significant help.

Availability of hands-on training. Customer on-site training is currently offered. In addition, a one-day management overview course will be given that focuses on the development and use of SynerVision-supported processes.

Availability of encoded process examples. Since it is an example of a conceptually new class of product, SynerVision should provide some simple application examples. This would help support the successful transfer of the technology to early adopters. As a minimum, examples of simple templates for personal processes and group processes could be very useful. In addition, template programs, manually developed using the Bourne shell constructs, would help more advanced users.

3.5   End-User Role Plays

This section deals with feedback obtained from persons who performed the end-user role plays. Two groups of three persons performed these role plays; one technology oriented group of three persons and one process-oriented group of three persons. Each group performed the document review scenario with both the SynerVision implementation and the ProcessWeaver implementation. It should be noted that the number of persons participating in the role plays was small and further studies, that involve larger numbers of people, would be worthwhile. However, the results of this investigation showed some interesting and consistent trends. The script shown in Table F.1 was used to guide the role-plays and, on completion of each role play, the participants filled in the questionnaire shown in Table F.2. Figures 3.18 through 3.20 below summarize the results of the end-user responses to this questionnaire.

ProcessWeaver was run from a Sun 4 host, while SynerVision was run from an HP-9000 host. In both cases, the client machines were either Sun 4 platforms or Macintoshes (using MacX). Thus the hardware environment was quite heterogeneous.

Before discussing the results, some aspects of Figures 3.18 through 3.20 are first explained. Each statement in the questionnaire is associated with five boxes that allow for a range of responses from full disagreement to full agreement. The number of responses for each box was tallied and totals are shown in the figures. These totals range from zero to four. (There were never more than four out of the six responses in any one box.) The 'Bias' column at the right hand side reflects the

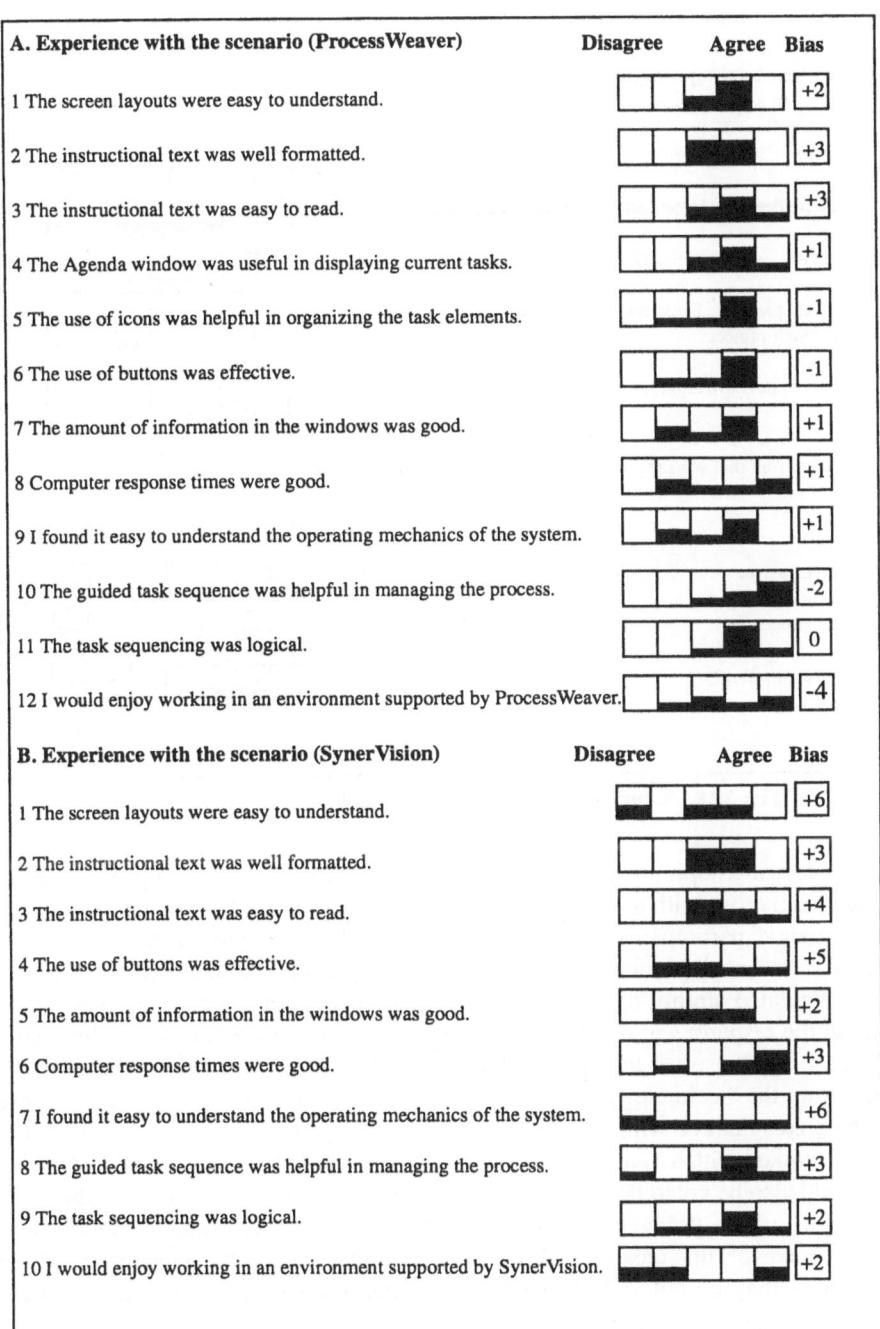

Fig. 3.18. Summary of end-user experiences

Given your brief experience with the process automation scenario, would you feel comfortable working in a process-centered environment if:

	Uncom-fortable	Comfort-able	Bias
1) it were designed by you and only supported your personal tasks,			-4
2) you had input to its design, and it were used within your project,			-3
3) it were predefined, but modified (with your input) for use within your project,			-2
4) you did not have input to its design?			-1

Do you think that working within a process-centered environment is *necessarily*:

	No	Yes	Bias
5) too invasive,			+6
6) too impersonal,			+6
7) too controlling?			+3

Fig. 3.19. Summary of end-user views on adoption of automated process

degree to which opinion differed between those participants with a process background and those with a technology background. A positive bias indicated that the "technology" participants were more favorably inclined to agree with the statement than the "process" participants, while a negative bias reflects the reverse. The bias was calculated simply by assigning the box number (items 1 through 5 in Table F.2) to the responses in that box, summing these assignments for the "technology" responses and also for the "process" responses and then subtracting the "process" total from the "technology" total. For example if the "technology" responses were in the boxes marked with a 2, a 4, and 5 while the "process" responses were in the boxes marked with a 1, a 3, and a 3, then the bias would be (2+4+5)-(1+3+3) = +4. It should also be noted here that the statements were designed to focus on the characteristics of the products' features and not on the process example implementations. However, this clean separation was not always possible. Hence some of the responses may be colored by the way in which the end-user interfaces of these products were constructed.

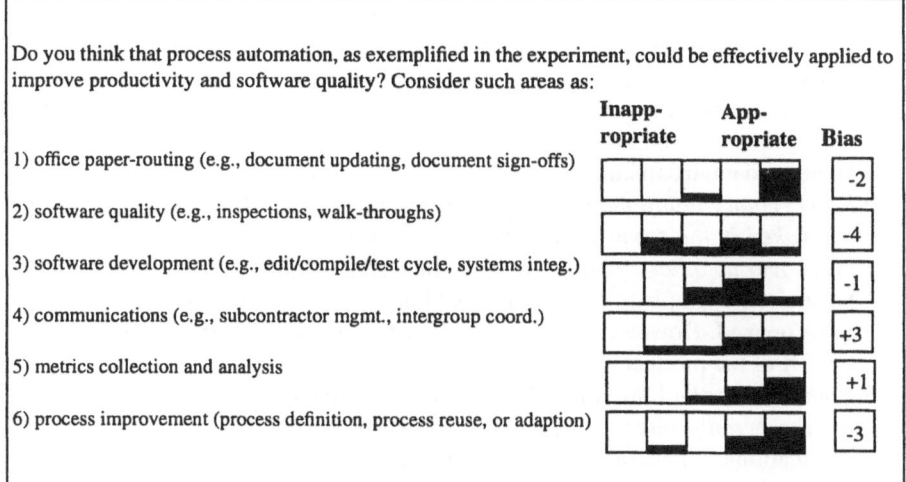

Do you think that process automation, as exemplified in the experiment, could be effectively applied to improve productivity and software quality? Consider such areas as:

	Inapp-ropriate	App-ropriate	Bias
1) office paper-routing (e.g., document updating, document sign-offs)			-2
2) software quality (e.g., inspections, walk-throughs)			-4
3) software development (e.g., edit/compile/test cycle, systems integ.)			-1
4) communications (e.g., subcontractor mgmt., intergroup coord.)			+3
5) metrics collection and analysis			+1
6) process improvement (process definition, process reuse, or adaption)			-3

Fig. 3.20. Summary of end-user views on appropriate applications

3.5.1 User Interface

Examining the data in Figure 3.18, it appears that there is a slight tendency to agree with the statements rather than disagree. If one considers the response range being from 1 (total disagreement with the statement) through 5 (total agreement), a neutral response is reflected by a 3. Averaging across all ProcessWeaver's responses (across all statements and all participants) the mean response is 3.64. The corresponding mean response for SynerVision is 3.21. The three categories in which ProcessWeaver's had a noticeably higher rating than SynerVision were:

- The screen layouts were easy to understand.
- The guided task sequence was helpful in managing the process.
- I would enjoy working is an environment supported by ProcessWeaver.

This result may, in part, be because ProcessWeaver manages all tasks (i.e., the Work Contexts) as icons inside its Agenda window and thus provides mechanisms for organizing and controlling ones tasks at a symbolic level. The SynerVision interface lacked this level of abstraction (see *Clarity of presentation* in Section 3.4.3).

It is interesting to note the technology/process bias in Figure 3.18. The bias column clearly indicates that the technology participants were more positively inclined to the interfaces (particularly SynerVision's) than the process participants. The one significant counterpoint to this general conclusion is the response to statement A12. Here, the process participants appeared to be more favorably inclined to working within the ProcessWeaver environment than the technology people. The following is an itemized list of (paraphrased) comments from the participants. The comments are italicized, followed by the author's remarks (non-italicized).

- *Little context is provided when tasks arrived − I may know what I have to do, but I am not be provided with adequate context. For example, when the technical writers rejected the role of editor, there is no opportunity for them to provide the reason(s) why.* This is a design problem with the process model, not a problem with either product. However, the example does point out the importance of providing human communication channels when developing an automated environment.
- *SynerVision window management was lacking functionality. When a document is invoked in the scenario, the document is simply thrown on the screen, and may cover up other ongoing work.* An inelegant solution to this problem could be devised by implementing additional buttons to allow documents (and tools) to be opened. However, a built-in feature to support this functionality should be part of the product.
- *Both products lack the capability to undo an erroneous action (such as clicking on the wrong button).* This is a necessary capability for a real-world applications. A generalization of this is process roll-back (discussed in Section 2.7.2), also missing in both products.
- *I really liked the idea of the Agenda window in ProcessWeaver, where one could keep track of outstanding work in one place.*
- Training: Comments clearly indicated a need for training in understanding the process. With the role play, little training was supplied. In a real-world setting, setting end-user expectations through training will be critical.
    - a. *End-user training in the use of the process automation is essential.*
    - b. *In practice, users need some form of tutorial on PCEs, either classroom style or through access to self-help materials.*
    - c. *In some cases in the scenario, it would be nice to have a bit better description of what exactly to expect and when to expect it. In this way I would know that the scenario was proceeding according to plan or not.*
- *The foundations of process automation, as exhibited by both products is impressive, but the technology has some way to go before it can be considered mature.*
- *When I shut off my terminal, do I lose all the tasks currently on the screen?* This question was answered for the Macintoshes by exiting MacX (the Macintosh software that allows Macintoshes to act as terminals for X window applications). This action disconnected the running SynerVision model from the Macintosh and the connection could not be reestablished. For ProcessWeaver, tasks (i.e., Work Contexts) did persist when the same procedure was performed. On shutting down, and restarting SynerVision on the HP-9000, the Synervision task structure and the task status was recovered, but the process seemed to lack information about the process status prior to the shutdown. Thus the process could still not be continued. On the other hand, ProcessWeaver appears to store this status information since shutting down and restarting ProcessWeaver did not appear to affect the Work Contexts in the Agenda window.

3.5.2 Adoption Issues

Adoption issues are addressed here independently of either SynerVision or Process-Weaver. Figure 3.19 provides the adoption-issue data generated by the end users. The responses to items 1 through 4 clearly indicate a greater willingness to accept automation if one has control over the process. Greatest acceptance is found when the processes are developed for personal use, although there appears to be significant support for these processes in which the users have input to the design. There was a consistently negative reaction to having an imposed external process.

The bias factors in Figure 3.19 indicate that process-oriented individuals were less concerned with adoption issues than were the technology individuals. This trend is particularly noticeable with statements 5 through 7 where the issues of invasiveness, impersonality, and control are examined. However, the *trends* shown by both groups were similar. (Note that the sign reversal between items 1 through 4 and 5 through 7 reflects the manner in which the statements were made and not a reversal of opinion.) Typical of the comments in this area are:

- *I would like to see the wider scope of what is happening.* This might be helped by providing workers visibility into the status of activities in the project, and by providing the ability to send explanatory or confirmational messages.
- *Whether I felt comfortable in an automated environment would depend on how process-driven I was.* Acceptance might also be easier if one were new to a project or if the project itself were new (i.e., there are no built-in expectations) rather than if a unfamiliar process were imposed upon an existing project.
- On working in a process in which the user does not have input:
  a. I would be uncomfortable working in someone else's process.
  b. If I do not have any input to the design of the process, there's a chance I could live with it, but if it does not match my reality, I would be dissatisfied.
- Comments of the 'too invasive' issue:
  a. It could be too invasive if it tells me how to accomplish work instead of telling me what needs to be accomplished.
  b. Unlike e-mail I cannot elect when to receive information.
  c. It's too invasive only to the extent that windows get popped in front of you while you are concentrating on something else. The second issue is one of metrics gathering coupled with personnel evaluations. If this is not handled well (i.e., the ground rules are well established, well known and accepted), it could be a really big issue. Otherwise I don't feel a process-centered environment is too invasive.
- Comments on the 'too impersonal' issue:
  a. It's no more impersonal than with e-mail. As with anything else, process automation is not a substitute for communication between staff.
  b. Automated environments would likely reduce personal interaction with other human beings.

- Comments on the 'too controlling' issue:
    - *a. I find the elimination of process navigation concerns to be a relief. I can have the files and tools I need when I need them. It allows me to concentrate on the work, not the setup.*
    - *b. Where do I get a chance for input other than "yes-no"? The machine controls my destiny with no human on the other end (or so it seems).*
    - *c. The only way it would be too controlling is if the process-centered environment restricted all of my efforts to exactly what the process is scripted for. As long as this is not the case, and the environment is providing timely guidance, this is OK with me.*

3.5.3   Application Issues

Contrary to the results in Section 3.5.2 where concerns were raised about adoption of process automation technology, Figure 3.20 indicates that there was a fairly positive response to applying the technology to particular areas. In this section, the Bias indicator did not show any consistent trends between the technology and process individuals. The three applications where process automation was thought to be most suited were: office paper routing, metrics collection and analysis, and process definition and improvement. The following are typical comments:

- Office paper routing:
    - *a. Somewhat helpful, particularly in getting sign-offs.*
    - *b. Excellent application, particularly if the tool supports tracking.*
- Software quality:
    - *a. Too people-intensive, a PCE doesn't add much.*
    - *b. I think the quality of inspections would decrease without face-to-face meetings.*
    - *c. For coordinating inspections, walk-throughs and for follow-up action items, this would be good.*
- Software development:
    - *a. Good for the individual.*
    - *b. Good for automating a tasks that are (almost) always followed in the same sequence.*
    - *c. If it is supported by automated metrics collection, such as time spent in each phase.*
- Communications:
    - *a. Yes – if it makes sure everybody gets appropriate mail and info.*
    - *b. Only appropriate if everyone has PCE support.*
    - *c. PCEs should make communication as easy as with e-mail.*
    - *d. A great way to ensure some form of recorded communications.*
- Metrics collection and analysis:
    - *a. Definitely could make these activities easier.*
    - *b. Must watch out for gathering too much, or irrelevant information.*

- Process improvement:
    a. I think it would be a BIG mistake to encode process this way for a development group.
    b. Looks like a winner for assisting activities in process improvement.
    c. Good for process definition. However, need for a process asset library.

As can be seen from the results above, there were clear differences of opinion, ranging from enthusiasm to concern, as to the effectiveness of applying automation to software development process. There was a slight but noticeable and fairly consistent divergence of opinion between those with a technology background and those with a process background. As might be expected, the technology-oriented participants viewed process automation with greater degree of scepticism. Since involving technical personnel will be central to successful implementing process automation, it is important to identify and deal with the issues technology-oriented individuals raise.

3.6 A Comparison of ProcessWeaver and Synervision

The objective of the experiments conducted with SynerVision and ProcessWeaver is to explore an emerging technology using these products as examples. Both of these process-centered environments have powerful mechanisms for enacting process and both, as members of a new class of software, have their weaknesses. In any case, the successful application of either PCE (or other PCE as listed in Appendix C) is likely to depend as much on organizational and human factors as on the product selected. Such issues as having an effectively defined process, good developer and end-user training, and sensitivity to technology adoption issues will be at least as important for success as the chosen PCE.

ProcessWeaver and SynerVision have many similar capabilities, but implement these capabilities in different ways. Currently, both SynerVision and ProcessWeaver do not differentiate between the process developer and end user – each PCE provides the same functionality to both groups. This allows end-users to implement their own personal processes or define processes for local project support, as well as allowing for the development of more ambitious processes. However, there may be a need, particularly with large processes, to distinguish between process-developer and end-user capabilities. Both PCEs implement reuse templates so that a process can be instantiated and enacted from a library of previously defined processes. Both PCEs allow the end-user to enact subprocesses, independent of the parent process to which they are associated. While tasks form the "building blocks" of processes in both PCEs, tasks can also be initiated, communicated, and worked on by end users in isolation from any process.

It should be noted that neither of these PCEs is repository-based, and in that sense they emphasize the control aspects of process rather than the data management aspects. Thus neither has mechanisms for handling versions of products, or for controlling potential conflicts that can arise from multiple agents modifying the same product. Data-centered products that have emerged primarily from the configuration management community are also entering the market place. Such products (e.g., CaseWare) do provide a repository and also allow one to define and enact the processes that focus on a product's evolution. However, these CM products have narrower process modeling capabilities. Integration of PCEs with configuration management products is probably needed, but since CM and PCE products may have different notions of "process," care is probably required in this effort. It should also be pointed out that neither ProcessWeaver nor SynerVision support some of the groupware concepts such as simultaneous, remote collaboration on work, for example, in editing a document.

There are also some noticeable differences between the two products. Process-Weaver emphasizes a graphical approach to process definition. This approach defines a process by graphically specifying an activity hierarchy, each activity being supported by a lower-level Petri Net model. In SynerVision, processes are defined in a text-oriented manner using an activity hierarchy, supported by scripting that specifies task behaviors and dependencies. SynerVision integrates some end-user applications,[6] while a design decision was made with ProcessWeaver to focus strictly on process support,[7] allowing for application extensions to be added as required. The following topics highlight some of the similarities and differences in more detail.

Developing process models: With both ProcessWeaver and SynerVision, simple process models can be developed without any knowledge of their textual scripting languages. Because of its built-in project management and metrics tools, SynerVision allows one to develop reasonably sophisticated models without knowledge of its textual language. Also, as discussed in Section 3.4.1, SynerVision's design provides a smooth incremental learning curve from supporting simple personal tasks to managing of group tasks. However, when one needs to describe processes that require the explicit writing of SynerVision scripts, the learning curve becomes much steeper.

As stated above, ProcessWeaver (Version 1.2)does not provide built-in metrics and project functionalities that SynerVision provides. Thus, to include such capability in ProcessWeaver, one may have to start using ProcessWeaver's scripting language at an earlier point than with SynerVision. However, because of the graphical nature of much of the ProcessWeaver model, the degree to which the scripting language has to be used may not be significant. Through ProcessWeaver's graphical approach, both the activity hierarchy and the process models associated with each activity are defined. This approach provides two advantages:

---

6. That is, it has characteristics of a process-centered environment (PCE) since it supports end-user capabilities for metrics collection and project management.

7. Version 1.2 of ProcessWeaver is, strictly speaking, a process-centered framework (PCF).

- model development is faster, and
- fewer syntactic and semantic errors are introduced.

SynerVision's approach to model definition is textually oriented (see Figure 3.17). The activity hierarchy can be displayed graphically, but this is somewhat superfluous as the textual view is quite adequate (see Figure 3.13). However, because of the textual approach, building SynerVision process models by hand requires a greater investment in learning the language and is more time consuming than with ProcessWeaver's graphical approach. Productivity in constructing SynerVision models could also be improved if SynerVision had a richer set of higher-level functions. During the construction of the experiment, it was found that time was spent developing supporting functions from Bourne shell elements and it would have helped if these had been built in.

While the graphical process support provided by ProcessWeaver is very helpful in developing models, neither SynerVision nor ProcessWeaver supported by a true graphical process enactment language. A graphical process enactment language is desirable in order to communicate all the essential process elements to others who will either have to sign off on a process or who will have to live within it. In addition to defining the relationships between all the major process elements, such a graphical language should be able to display tasks, artifacts used by tasks, and the agents (or roles) who perform the tasks.

The software underlying both SynerVision and ProcessWeaver was found to be robust in the sense that no system crashes and no significant system bugs were encountered during development.

Templates, roles, and process instantiation: Both SynerVision and Process-Weaver have explicit mechanisms to allow for the initiation of isolated tasks and for sending these tasks off to the persons responsible for their execution.

With respect to processes (that embed tasks) SynerVision and ProcessWeaver provide for the development of process templates that allow for the repeated use of defined processes. If one develops a process in SynerVision, there is an explicit step that must be taken to generate a template from an existing runable process. However, in ProcessWeaver, one develops models as templates (which, in turn, may embed default Cooperative Procedure templates). In either case, an instance of the template is generated and executed at run-time.

Every Cooperative Procedure in ProcessWeaver provides a *parameters* box to the process developer in which variables required for the execution of that process are placed. Later, at run-time, ProcessWeaver presents the process executor with a *procedure parameters* box in which the variable instances are filled in. In SynerVision, the process developer must explicitly build such mechanisms into the model using the scripting language. This is an example of where the process developer's task could be simplified if higher level functionality were built into SynerVision.

A SynerVision process model is basically contained within one file. This was found to be very useful for electronically transmitting the model to a remote location when debugging support was needed. Because a ProcessWeaver model consists multiple files, such a procedure becomes less convenient.

Process rollback: Process definition in ProcessWeaver is based on a Petri Net formulation, and this has resulted in one overly restrictive characteristic. Before a task in a Cooperative Procedure can begin, all the upstream tasks must have been completed. In real situations, it may be possible for someone to start a task before all the formal conditions for task initiation have been met, and indeed this opportunistic behavior may result in greater productivity. Section 3.3.3 discussed a possible resolution of this problem.

SynerVision does not exhibit this modeling constraint. Unless explicitly specified to the contrary, an agent responsible for performing a task can begin at any time. Clearly there will be tasks that must not start prior to other tasks ending, but this can be specified in the model.

Accessing external tools and the external environment: SynerVision allows access to external tools using the standard Unix mechanisms and can communicate with its external environment using the functionality provided by Hewlett Packard's Broadcast Message Server. ProcessWeaver supports similar mechanisms for tool invocation and communication. ProcessWeaver and SynerVision both provide a convenient means for associating tools with tool classes. Thus on different platforms or with different users, different tools within the same class may be invoked.

SynerVision provides project management and metrics capabilities that are seamlessly integrated into the product. Processes can be developed incorporating these tools without a knowledge of the SynerVision scripting language. In addition the metrics tools provide the capability to gather metric data such as time spent on a task without any intervention on the part of the task owner.

ProcessWeaver provides project management support through integration to external tools, but this is not as integrated as SynerVision's support. Two tools are supported by ProcessWeaver (Version 1.2) are: MicroSoft Project for Windows and Project Management Workbench 3.1 (under PC/DOS).

Debugging: ProcessWeaver provides a variety of tools to support debugging. These include support for consistency checking (e.g., between inputs and outputs of Cooperative procedures), syntax checking of scripts, interactive debugging for the Co-shell language, and process visualization (that allows one to view tokens as they move around the Petri Net and to spy on variable values during this process). SynerVision does not currently support any debugging aids other than that provided by the interactive *shell* that comes with Unix.

Documentation and examples: Neither SynerVision nor ProcessWeaver currently provide adequate documentary support. SynerVision's manual *Introduction to SynerVision: Models of Use* [SynerVision 93a] provides an excellent grounding in those aspects of SynerVision that do not require one to program. However, the more advanced manual, *Developing SynerVision Processes* [SynerVision 93b], is less well organized, needs improved explanations of the concepts, and should contain a greater number of complete examples rather than just code fragments. This manual tries to be both a reference manual and a tutorial, and these two focuses should probably be separated. SynerVision has extensive on-line help that supports these development of processes not needing manually-encoded scripts.

The ProcessWeaver manuals (User and Reference) have three significant weaknesses. First, the User Manual lacks a good explanation of how the high-level elements of ProcessWeaver (Methods, Cooperative Procedures and Work Contexts and their supporting information boxes) relate to each other. Second, the Reference Manual needs to provide expanded coverage of the concepts in event handling supported by illustrative examples. Third, the Reference Manual should provide more background into the functions that support the manipulation of the files stored under ProcessWeaver's Universal Storage Mechanism format. In this version of Process-Weaver (1.2) on-line help was not implemented.

The end-user view: ProcessWeaver provides a means of easily customizing, within a limited format, the information that is sent, either from one person to another, or that is sent to a person as a result of an automatic action. This window is called a Work Context (see Figure 3.4) and allows for text boxes, document or tool icons, and control buttons to be displayed. Upon clicking on an icon, a window containing the document or tool is opened for use. This end-user window management in ProcessWeaver was found to be quite effective.

SynerVision provides three main types of window for displaying end-user information. First, a Task In-box (see Figure 3.15) is provided that simply lists a person's assigned tasks along with the names of the task assigners. The main purpose of this window is to allow the assignee to accept, reject, or reassign a task. Second, customized windows can be developed that contain both textual information related to the task, and control buttons. However, neither the Task In-box nor the customized windows can display icons representing documents or tools. A supporting document or tool can, however, be opened as needed to support the task, and this is done by writing a line or two of Bourne shell script. However, this approach is not very elegant and SynerVision could incorporate improved functionality for managing end-user windows, particularly with respect to the support of task-related documents and tools. Finally, the *Notes* feature may be used to supply the end-user with guidance on the task at hand or to document how a task was accomplished.

In summary, each PCE has different strengths and weaknesses. There is no "best" product – it truly depends on one's needs. For example, ProcessWeaver provides developer-friendly support for graphically-based model building, while SynerVision has effective built-in support for project management and automatic metrics gathering. SynerVision provides more extensive capability for the project with modest process enaction objectives (when one can build models without having to resort to hand-coded shell scripting), and supports an approach that allows for incremental growth in process sophistication. On the other hand, the higher-level functionality for building and debugging process models may make ProcessWeaver a more attractive choice when large models are being considered. The choice of which product to use (including the others listed in Appendix C) has to be made based on the requirements of the project for which the process enactment model is being built. Both reviewed products show significant insights into what is needed for effective process enactment, but the implementation paths have gone in different directions. The technology has some way to go before reaching maturity, and practical field experience will make it more robust and provide the vendors with greater application knowledge.

4 The Application of Process-Centered Environments

4.1 Why Use a Process-Centered Environment?

Process-centered environments represent a new class of software that integrates the people in the organization with the development process and with the supporting technology. Unlike compilers, editors etc., PCEs primarily affect how work is performed rather than what is produced. PCEs provide the "glue" that actively manages the flow of work between people and their tools. Thus the issues that must be addressed in their adoption are significantly different from those for standard CASE tools. Some of these issues are already known through experiences with the software factory concept [Cusumano 91], but there may be novel issues which, because of the lack of practical application of PCEs in real-world settings, we have yet to discover. In fact much of the information provided in this chapter is based on experiences in areas related to process automation; there is as yet too little actual experience in the use of process-centered environments. The primary motivations for using a PCE are improvement of quality and productivity; each of the items discussed below directly supports these goals. There are some significant advantages to using a PCE and some disadvantages. These are also discussed below.

4.1.1 Advantages of Using a PCE

Use of a PCE inherently forces one to define one's processes in a rigorous enactable sense. This discipline alone is a major benefit. It allows for improved communication and understanding between the human participants and for consistency in how things are done. While use of a PCE cannot guarantee process improvement, used correctly it can certainly support the improvement effort by encouraging process definition and use. Training new employees in the process [Kellner 89] is supported both off-line and on-line. Off-line training is supported by use of the defined model to teach the novice the overall structure of the process. On-line, the novice (like other parties using the process) is guided through the process and thus requires a less detailed knowledge of the process in order to do his/her job effectively. In this way, fewer process-related errors are likely to be made. Whether the user is a novice or not, a PCE can eliminate the need for project personnel to perform many mundane tasks. Automated actions can be initiated on the basis of certain process states being reached, information can be presented to the user when appropriate, and messages can be sent between agents (human or not) when necessary.

As a by-product of having one's processes defined in an enactable sense, one can build up an enactable-process reuse library. This library can be of enormous help to others in the organization who have similar process needs [Basili 91, Kellner 93b]. Thus a project that has developed a particularly effective process (say, for peer review) can save the process in the corporate reuse library for access by others. By so encouraging this consistency and uniformity of process use, the organization is not only saving resources, but it is supporting Maturity Level 3 characteristics as described in Section 4.2.

If a process cannot be measured, then improvement is a matter of opinion. However, collecting metric data manually has several drawbacks. First, developers generally do not want to spend their time manually filling out metric data forms, for either time-dependent data or code-dependent data, if they see no direct benefit to their work. Second, manually-generated data is likely to be error-prone and inconsistent,[1] particularly if the data is collected with resentment and suspicion. Resentment and suspicion are related to the issue of intrusiveness, that is, management "spying" on developers and using the collected data as fodder for job evaluations. However, this problem exists whether a PCE is used or not. (Suggestions for its solution are addressed later in Section 4.4.) Metrics collection and analysis can be major time consumers, and use of automation in this area could thus be a significant contributor to productivity. Of course, the collection of complete and accurate data also enhances product quality. Analyses of this metric data should lead to improved automated processes, and these improvements can then be permanently captured in the corporate reuse library.

In a traditional software development organization, it is often difficult for management to obtain current information on project status, etc., particularly if the project is large. Since the automated control of a process requires a current knowledge of task and product status, decisions taken etc., this information can also be made immediately available to management. Thus management can request reports on such current information as "list of tasks completed" or "status of change requests".

An indirect advantage of PCEs is that they may make CASE technology more effective. CASE tools are too often viewed at a tactical level (see Section 4.2), that is, organizational issues such as process adoption and improvement are not seen as important elements to success. However, PCEs force one to address these very issues. Thus embedding CASE tools into a PCE may provide those CASE tools with a context to make them more effective.

---

1. Of course, automated collection of metrics can be prone to its own types of errors, for example, if the duration of a task is equated with the task effort.

4.1.2 Risks of Using a PCE

Being a young technology, specific commercial PCEs may exhibit a variety of technical limitations that detract from their usability. Some of these limitations were discussed in Chapter 3 and should be addressed as the technology matures. There is, however, one disadvantage that could be pervasive. This is the inflexibility of process programs as they are implemented in today's PCEs. Process programs allow for the rigorous management of a defined process, and may be executed many times with no deviations. However, unanticipated events will undoubtedly occur during the execution of a process, and it is difficult to manage these "on the fly" with an automated system. Quoting [Lehmann 89]:

> [T]he real world is essentially dynamic, forever changing. Even without feedback effects, exogenous changes in the real world will change the facts on which the assumption set is based. However careful and complete the control on the validity of the assumptions at the time they are built into the system some, at least, will, at best, be less than fully valid when the program is executed or better, when the results of the execution are applied.

It is interesting to note that the problems with humans is exactly the opposite those of machines. People have an wonderful ability to improvise in real-time although it is easy to abuse this facility. On the other hand, machines have the ability to assure the application of consistent process, but find "on the fly" adaptation of the process difficult. Perhaps striking a balance, in which the adaptability of humans and the consistency of machines, should be strived for.

Serious impediments to the use of process automation are also likely to originate in organizational, cultural and human factors. First, not all software development organizations have characteristics compatible with high degrees of process automation. This is particularly true for organizations in which conceptually new software is being developed. These organizations may not easily be able to stabilize their processes and may have to operate in a craft manner (i.e., using small teams of highly competent professionals).

Second, the notion of letting a machine control how one works has negative connotations associated with mindless mass production. Designing an automated process to be human-compatible, while challenging, is critical to success. Thus, in addition to understanding the mechanics of building process programs, the designer, or team that designs these processes must have insights into human behaviors, motivations, and expectations, and must be sensitive to the needs of the project for which the processes are being developed. As will be discussed later, it is probably essential for success that those who will use the automated processes should also be involved in their design. Process users will, for example, have insights into appropriate process patterns, and these can be used to advantage when the process is formally defined. While management may see process automation as a means to control the developers (through, for example, greater access to status information), developers will only accept such automation if it is perceived to support their developmental needs (e.g., it liberates from chores rather than enforces unrealistic constraints). An example of a badly designed system might be one in which management can too easily interfere in the minute-to-minute activities of developers.

Not only may developers feel threatened by process automation, but managers may feel a loss of control, since tasks they previously had to perform by hand may now be managed automatically. Likewise, some of the decision-making that was previously performed by managers is now automated. Finally, while developers are likely to feel comfortable with technology in general, this is less true with managers who may not have the technical background or who may not have been involved with technology for many years. While outwardly supporting automation, such managers may be inwardly fearful and consequently may not be truly committed to its implementation [Gray 94].

4.2   Issues Related to CASE and Process Improvement

In attempting to move software development away from the craft approach (that is highly skilled and individualistic) to a more rational means of production, two approaches have been pursued:

- using technology to support, automate, and to some extent reduce the skill level required for software development; and
- improving the process through which the software is developed.

Because these two paths have a direct bearing on the technology of software process automation, they are discussed below in some detail. These paths also cross, and it is at this intersection that process-centered environments exist.

The first approach involves the use of CASE tools to help produce software more efficiently. At the developer level these tools support such activities as design, code generation, test, reverse engineering, and document production. At the management level these tools support such activities as configuration management, planning, scheduling, tracking, and cost estimation. However, to date, CASE tools have not lived up to their early promise in the sense that a very large fraction of those purchased become "shelfware" [Page-Jones 92]. This is, in part, a consequence of the exaggerated claims of CASE tool vendors. It also results from a too narrow focus on CASE technology. As stated in [Boone 91]:

The current attempts at CASE implementation have only been at the tactical level, dealing with such issues as tool evaluation and selection, and choosing pilot projects for applications of these tools. These tactical approaches have met with extremely limited success, and a growing number of experienced users are sharing the opinion that the situation will continue unless CASE is approached strategically.

By strategic thinking, Boone suggests that four elements, closely related to total quality management, are required:

- pursuing continuous improvement,
- putting quality first,
- using process engineering, and
- facilitating change.

This chapter focuses on the last two of these items. Practical guides to addressing some of these CASE issues are provided in [Bouldin 89, Fletcher 93, Humphrey 89b, Oaks 92]. In particular, these guides provide approaches to CASE adoption, addressing some of the "strategic" issues identified in [Boone 91], and have relevance to the adoption issues to be discussed in later in this chapter. Also, many of the issues addressed by Boone's four elements involve human factors and thus may give a degree of discomfort to many who are technically trained and naturally look for technical solutions. However, as Boone points out, the success of CASE will be just as dependent on non-technical, as on technical considerations. These non-technical issues have much in common with the spirit of the Capability Maturity Model [Paulk 93a] that provides a practical incremental approach to process improvement. Because of its relevance, the CMM will be discussed below within the context of tools and process automation.

The above issues are even more acute when dealing with integrated tool sets. To date, tool vendors have developed some direct tool-to-tool integrations (for example, IDE's integration of Software through Pictures, CodeCenter, and FrameMaker). However, successful use of integrated tools, as reflected in actual day-to-day use for product development, is quite limited. As stated in [Rader 93]:

[I]nformal discussions with practicing software engineers from the defense and engineering communities indicate that few of the concepts, standards and products that purport to provide CASE tool integration have found their way into operational use.

Given the problems associated with the adoption of individual CASE tools, it is perhaps not surprising that adoption of integrated CASE tool sets has met with resistance. In addition to the issues associated with the introduction of single CASE tools, integrated CASE tool sets are more expensive, magnify the process and adoption issues, and will incur significant training costs. While the above issues are also relevant to PCEs, PCEs may provide the critical ingredient, process structure, that will help CASE tools and integrated tool sets overcome some of these barriers. Some itemized reasons why this is so are given below:

- Specific elements of tool functionality can be matched to the needs of the process.
- Training in the use of the tools can be seen in the context of the process.
- Tools can be more rationally evaluated and selected.
- The process provides a framework for communication between tools.
- Metrics collection on tool-related data can be given a more rational basis.

Of course, commercial off-the-shelf tools may have their own notions of process that are not necessarily compatible with those of the PCE. Thus process trade-off will have to be made if a particular tool is incorporated into the automated environment.

In summary, CASE tools and integrated tool sets have failed to reach their full potential in part because of issues that are less technical and more organizational or cultural. PCEs may force some of these issues to be addressed more explicitly, and may thus be important in the successful adoption of CASE.

Let us now turn to the second approach to moving software production away from its craft origins – process improvement. Software process improvement has its roots in the work of pioneers in quality improvement such as W. Edwards Demming [Demming 82] and Joseph Juran [Juran 89]. In particular, Demming had a significant influence on the re-industrialization of Japan after the Second World War. Through his efforts, and the earlier influence of Walter Shewart, many Japanese companies adopted statistical process control as a mechanism to improve product quality. However, Demming's philosophy also placed significant importance on human and organizational factors in the drive to improve quality. He identified fourteen points that management should follow if it is to be competitive through emphasizing quality. These points will not all be stated explicitly here, but can be found in Demming's book. However, some of these points, such as emphasizing training and education, driving out fear in workers, breaking down communication barriers and encouraging pride of workmanship are central to the adoption of process automation. These points will surface later in this chapter when specific approaches to adoption are discussed. The fifth of Demming's 14 points focuses on continuous improvement to decrease costs: *Improve constantly and forever the system of production and service, to improve quality and productivity, and hence constantly decrease costs.* This point provides a basis for incremental and continuous software process improvement as prescribed by the Capability Maturity Model briefly described below.

A project that does not have a clear understanding of the processes through which it develops its software is likely to produce an inferior product. This is particularly so for large projects having many people and producing large, complex software systems. It was because of the consistent failure to successfully manage the development of such large software systems that the Capability Maturity Model was developed. The CMM provides a framework for establishing effective processes for software development and does so in a manner that prioritizes the implementation of the practices necessary to build effective processes.

The CMM is based on five levels:

- Level 1: Initial
- Level 2: Repeatable
- Level 3: Defined
- Level 4: Managed
- Level 5: Optimizing

The general characteristics of these are summarized in Figure 4-1 [Paulk 93a]. At Level 2 (Repeatable), there is a strong focus on developing effective management practices within projects. At Level 3 (Defined), standard processes are defined across the whole organization and tailored for use within individual projects. Level 4 (Managed) then sets quantitative quality goals for both processes and products, making extensive use of metrics to achieve this objective. Finally, at Level 5 (Optimizing), the emphasis is on continuous process improvement through technology innovation and quantitative cost-benefit analysis on alternative processes. Before a particular level can be achieved by an organization, all the requirements of the lower maturity levels must be met. Each level is composed of a set of Key Process Areas (KPAs), such as Requirements Management at the Repeatable Level, while each KPA is in turn composed of a set of specific practices.

This view of process maturity is independent of tools or tool support. However, at higher levels of software maturity, there is increasing overhead associated with maintaining this maturity, as a result of the cumulative number of practices that must be supported. To get an idea of the extent of the effort required to achieve a particular maturity level, Table 4-1 shows the number of pages of practices from [Paulk 93b] that are used to characterize each maturity level. Since each page provides specific and detailed information and guidance, these simple data give an idea of the effort necessary to reach and sustain a particular level. Clearly, not all practices can be automated or even supported by software tools. However, a significant number can have at least partial support, and it has been argued [Ett 91] that *[a]utomated process enactment support is necessary to achieve a process maturity beyond SEI Level 3 in a COST EFFECTIVE manner.* Given the large number of practices at and below Level 3, it is possible that automation may also be a critical component for levels 2 and 3, if cost effectiveness is important.

Table 4.1. Pages of practices at the five CMM levels

Maturity Level	1	2	3	4	5
Pages of practices at Level	0	84	100	32	48
Cumulative pages of practices at Level	0	84	184	216	260

In many instances, there is a clear relationship between tool functionality and the needs of a particular Key Process Area. For example, the Level 2 KPA "Software Project Planning" is likely to make use of project management tools. While

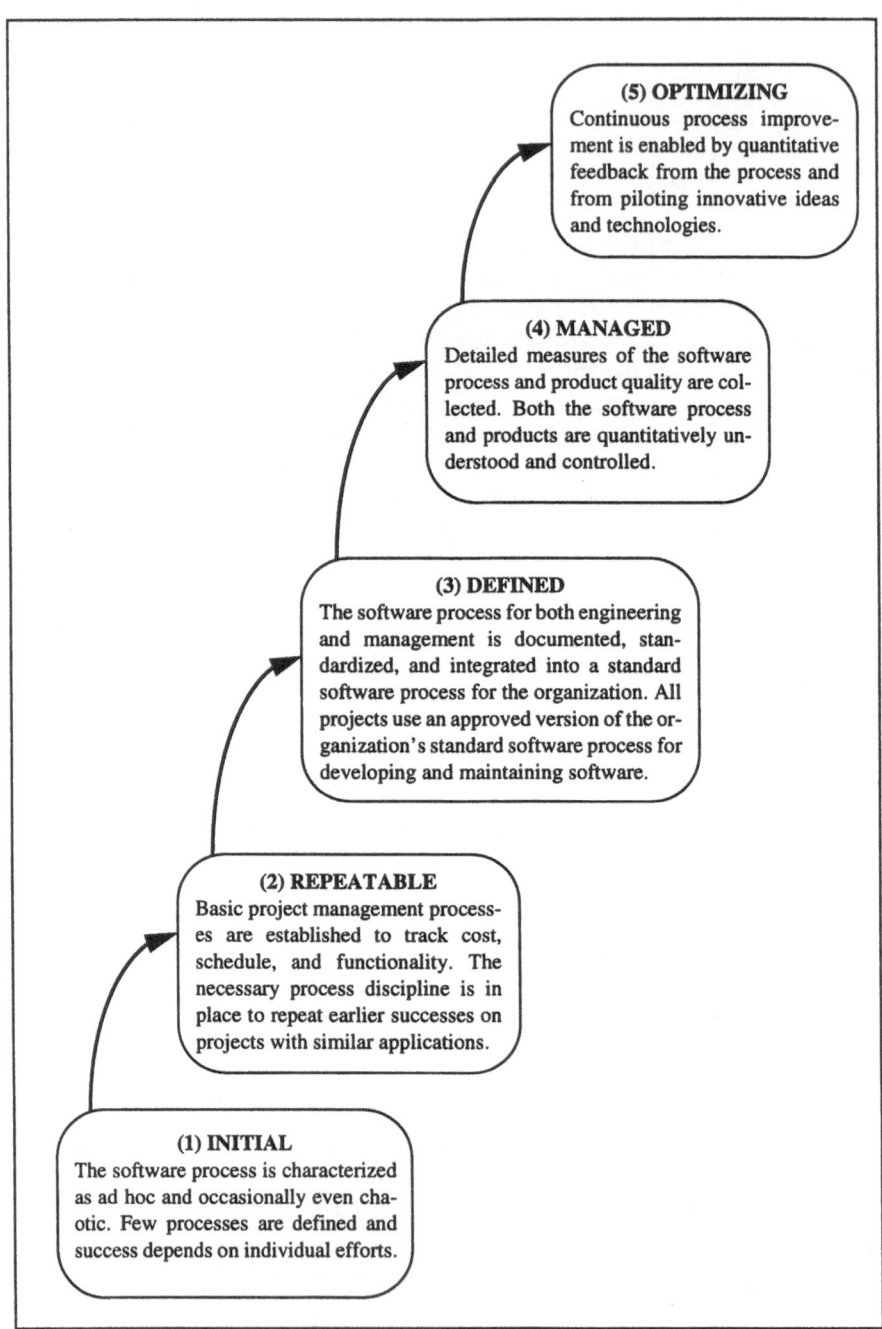

Fig. 4.1. The five levels of the Maturity Model

this relationship is important, it is more useful, in the context of this report, to correlate tool use to the broad goals of each maturity level. Figure 4-2[2] illustrates this other relationship. For example, at Level 2, there will be sets of guidelines on tool selection, tool use, and tool training at the project level. In addition tool use will be integrated into the project-defined processes by which the software is produced. The view of the technology/process relationship shown in Figure 4-2 is useful because it implies that one can start to use a PCE at any maturity level. However, if a PCE is used at Level 1, only limited components of its functionality can be effectively employed (for example, code development at the individual level, personal scheduling, and task routing). At Level 2, a much broader set of functionalities can be invoked, since project processes can be enacted through the PCE.

There is an increasing focus on metrics collection and analysis at Maturity Levels 2 and 3. Process automation provides a vehicle for the consistent and efficient collection of these metrics. In addition, given the precise way in which an automated process must be defined, there is the potential for collecting metrics in a more systematic manner than with a more qualitatively defined manual process. These characteristics can provide a basis for rigorous, quantitative process improvement

Automated processes are more "brittle" than manual processes, i.e., they are less adaptable to unforeseen circumstances and they cannot be modified as easily on the fly. Thus an understanding of one's manually-driven process may provide valuable insights in promoting the success of its automated equivalent. It can be argued that a CMM Level 1 organization should not use a process-centered environment for critical processes if these processes are not already understood, stable, and well-defined. While it is tempting to think that a process-centered environment can help move a organization from Maturity Level 1 to Level 2, stable manual processes (an essential ingredient of a level 2 organization) will significantly reduce the risk of implementing a PCE. There is also a concern that a Level 1 organization will become too preoccupied with the PCE technology rather that focus on the main issue which is process improvement.

This is not to say that a Level 1 organization cannot use some of the functionality provided by PCEs (such as supporting individuals in product development) or experiment with them in small-scale noncritical areas, but experience should be gained before process automation is imposed on critical parts of one's product line. Application to small-scale, noncritical areas will provide a means to learn and gain confidence about both the technology and the adoption issues. Indeed this may be part of the activities that the Level 1 organization performs in order to achieve Level 2. Yourdon [Yourdon 92] makes a point about ineffective use of expensive CASE tools in Level 1 organizations, and this point is equally valid for PCEs:

---

2. This figure was developed by the author to be consistent with the CMM, but is not part of it.

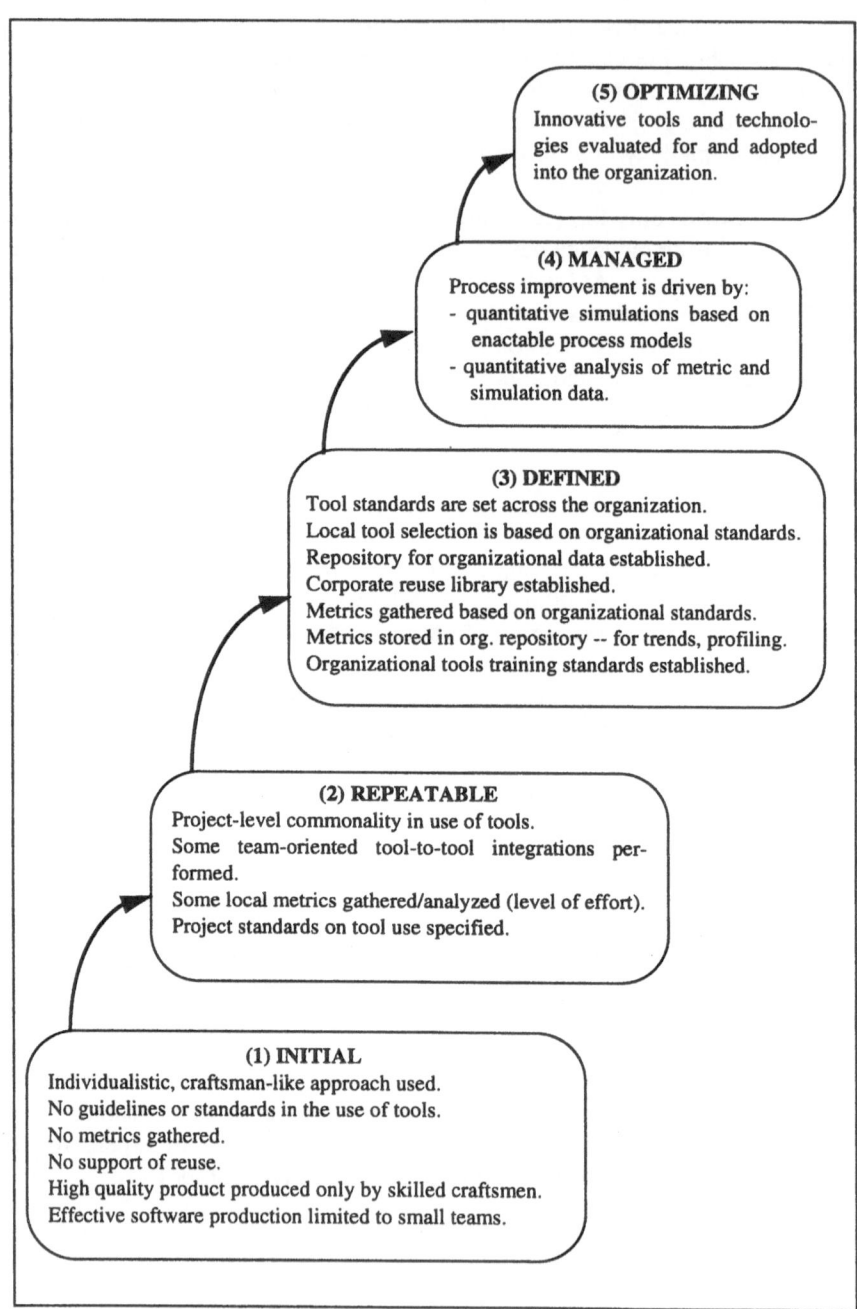

Fig. 4.2. Tool-use characteristics at the five maturity levels

The problem with buying the $100,000 package when the organization is level 1 is that (1) it may not be used at all, (2) it is likely to be overwhelming in its demand for rigor and formality and (3) it may ultimately prove to be the wrong product for the organization, but nobody wants to confess that a $100,000 mistake was made.

At Level 4, process-centered environments can offer significant benefit in process improvement. Quantitative process simulation can be used as a tool for predicting project duration, manpower loadings, and bottlenecks. Simulations, supported by estimated task times and manpower availability, can be run to generate predicted project duration etc. These predicted outcomes can then be compared to the actual project duration etc. Because there is an exact correspondence between the simulation and the automated enactment of the process, the data resulting from the simulation and project implementation can be directly compared. A more sophisticated approach is to run multiple simulations in a Monte Carlo fashion, thus providing insights into the sensitivity of the results to distributions over task times, decisions paths taken, etc. [Kellner 91]. Through this approach, a tight coupling between process simulation and process enactment is achieved and this can provide a rigorous basis for quantitative process improvement.

4.3 Responses to Adopting New Technology

Transitioning to complex technologies is challenging, as is evident from experiences with CASE tools, and transitioning to the successful use of software process automation will be as challenging as most. Installing this technology means a lot more than managers handing over responsibility to technical staff and assuming that they will implement the details. Managers as well as technical staff are likely to be actively involved in the use of the automated system and must be its visible supporters. Education about the impact of process automation and training in its use are essential ingredients at all levels in the organization. Also important is setting the right expectations so that when adoption problems do arise, as they will, they are anticipated.

Figure 4.3 [adapted from Przybylinski 91] illustrates some of the changes that are likely occur as technology is introduced into an organization. This figure illustrates at a high level the human reactions to how the degree of commitment is likely to increase as time progresses (in a successful transition). After the initial exposure through marketing information or presentations (contact), an overview of the technology and its potential benefits diffuses through the organization. Recommendations about its use are then made to the appropriate level of management (awareness). The appropriate people in the organization, probably technical staff, become increasingly conversant with the details of the technology (understanding),

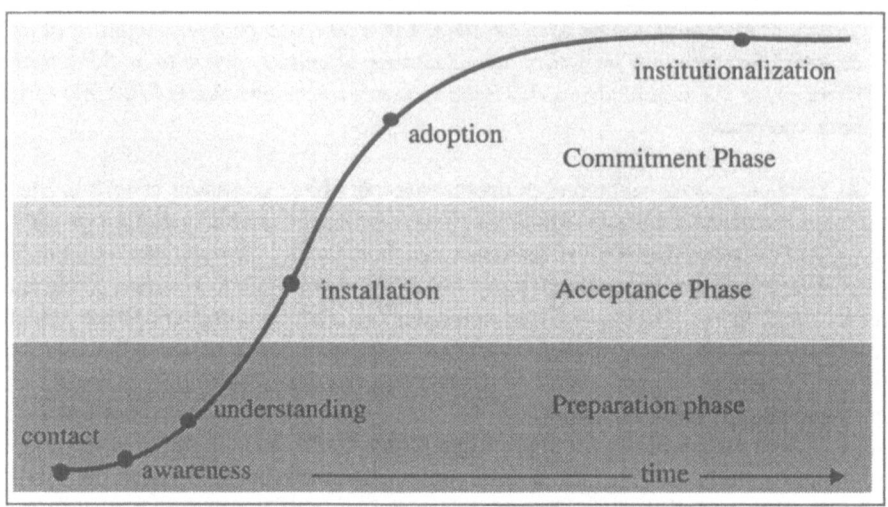

Fig. 4.3. Phases of technology adoption

and a pilot project is implemented (installation). Based on the success of the pilot project, a decision is made to adopt the technology more widely in the organization (adoption). Finally if the adoption phase is successful, the technology becomes an integral part of how business is conducted (institutionalization). At this point the technology becomes so integrated that it is indispensable and members of the organization may wonder how they managed without it. Note in the diagram how later phases tend to be longer than earlier phases.

Figures 4.4 (a), and (b) illustrate how a technology like process automation is likely to affect a project in which it is being installed [adapted from Przybylinski 91]. A stable organization has understood ways of doing business. Any technology that disrupts this comfortable situation is likely to be resisted. Changing the organization's culture is analogous to unfreezing a block of ice in order to refreeze it into another shape. To modify the old culture, the ice must be unfrozen; that is, old assumptions and ground rules are broken, and this can generate discomfort, uncertainty, and suspicion about motives. During this transition phase, experience with the use of the process will be lacking while 'bugs' in the process design or in the process program may be discovered. Thus productivity is likely to suffer (Figure 4.4a) and could be accompanied by increasing costs and decreasing quality. If these transition effects are not anticipated, management may decide prematurely that process automation is a failure and abandon it. While unfreezing is necessary for effective change to be made, it should be done in such a way as to minimize the negative consequences. Suggested strategies are suggested in Sections 4.5 and 4.6.

Figure 4.4b describes changing human reactions to those involved in a technology that directly effects how people work. Although not always, there will generally be an initial interest and curiosity about the technology (although a healthy dose of scepticism may also exist). When the social impact of the technology is more fully

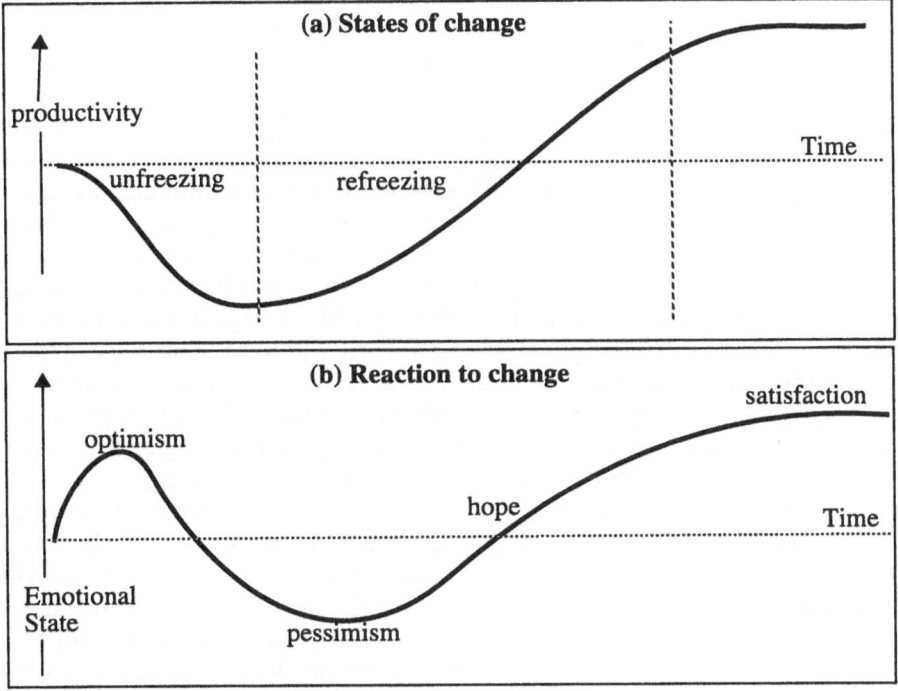

Fig. 4.4. Changes during technology adoption

realized, and particularly when teething troubles arise, the general reaction may swing from positive to negative. Only after the technology is working effectively and there is a general feeling of mastery over it (assuming the transition is successful), does the mood swing back to the positive side. A criterion for gauging the success of the adoption is to assess the reaction to the suggestion that the automated process be removed and replaced by original manual process.

4.4 User-Oriented Issues with PCEs

Previous chapters have dealt primarily with technical issues associated with automating software production. However, implementing a process-centered software environment involves much more than just addressing the technology. Indeed the success of adoption rests at least as heavily on personnel, organizational and cultural elements. This section thus looks briefly at a variety of more user-oriented problems facing organizations wishing to adopt a PCE. Many, but not all, of these issues are also likely to be confronted when CASE technology is introduced.

As mentioned earlier, a significant fraction of software today becomes "shelf-ware", in part because it may not meet users' functional requirements, because of lack of appropriate user training, or because of lack of compatibility with the project's process. Other elements may also contribute. [Boone 91] discusses factors that have been impediments to the successful introduction of CASE technology. Such factors include the difficulty that developers have in adapting to the different philosophy that CASE tools impose upon them, and the discomfort that managers have when coding doesn't begin until much later in the development cycle. These changes in working habits will only be magnified when complex PCEs are introduced. A process-centered environment will be costly to install, in terms of the initial investment in software, in terms of the required training, and in terms of its adaptation to the needs of the projects using it. There will also be financial and technical investments in its long term maintenance. The likelihood of failure in using such a system will be higher than with individual products. Given the high cost of this kind of investment, an organization may shy away from making more than one attempt at installing a PCE if the first attempt is perceived as a failure.

Adopting any new technology is likely to meet with significant resistance. Because of its pervasiveness and potentially impersonal nature, this is particularly true with process automation. As with any new technology, some of this resistance will simply result from the fact that people often do not like to change from their comfortable routine to new and uncertain ways. However, some resistance will also come from reasons unique to process automation technology. Such reasons are related to the controlling nature of the technology and the automated collection of personal productivity metrics. Typical reactions to these changes will include:

- Now I don't talk to people, I only communicate through my terminal.
- I don't want management to know every move I make.
- I don't want to be treated like a cog in a machine.
- I know these metrics are going to be used against me in my annual evaluation.
- I don't have the control over the things that I used to have control over.

Such comments reflect the natural fears of staff members, particularly if management is viewed as authoritarian. Some of the resistance reflects a general reluctance to any change that significantly affects how one does ones job. However, process automation imposes behavioral changes that are unique to that technology. Most computer tools (for software development, project management, etc.) are passive in the sense that they respond to the commands of, and perform actions to support, the human agent. Process automation is different in that it can request actions of the human. While the roles of the computer and human are not entirely reversed, this puts the computer at the same status level as the human (since the human can still request the machine to perform actions too). This question of roles may be difficult for many to take, and is a major reason why adoption issues for process automation technology are so critical.

If management wishes to succeed, then it needs to create an environment of trust that can only be achieved through closely involving the people who will have to live within the system. While Henry Ford may have been able to impose his will on the men in his assembly line by increasing their wages, such a crude approach is unlikely to work in the software field [Womack 90, Yourdon 92]. More sensitive tactics have to be used. The following paragraphs provide some experience-based guidelines that may be useful to address when considering the transition to a process-centered environment.

What should be automated? If not designed properly, automated support may get in the way rather than help. Automating a process because the technology exists can be like building a radar-activated mouse trap - it is too complex, too costly and does not meet the user's simple needs. So what tasks should be automated? These include:

- tasks that are well understood and stable. Thus, for example, automating processes where decision making is based on clearly defined criteria may be attractive,
- tasks that have clear interfaces to and from other tasks,
- tasks that are tedious may be automatable, thus allowing the developer to concentrate on the more creative aspects of the job,
- tasks where manual involvement is error prone,
- tasks that involve significant amounts of routine communications, and
- high integrity tasks, that is, tasks where conformance to the process must be assured.

Two additional points should be noted. First, social factors that are less tangible may also have to be considered. For example if the person is responsible for a process is hostile to the idea of automation, then it may be advisable to look to another process candidate. Second, prior to gaining wide experience with process automation, it is probably appropriate to start with modest-sized processes. Thus islands of automation may be established, with the later possibility of building bridges between these islands.

Areas where automation can be of significant help include configuration management, change tracking and metrics. Others include code reviews, document reviews, requirements management and project management. Today configuration management (CM) is already well automated and certain CM tools [e.g., CaseWare 92] increasingly allow for a customized process to be defined by the end-user. Much work still needs to be done in examining the overlap between CM and process, but systems like ISTAR [Dowson 87] and others [Bernard 89, Mahler 90] have investigated this topic. Process models can provide insight into what artifacts should be placed under CM control and what process metrics should be gathered. The simple process models discussed in Chapter 2 provide some guidance. In a well formed model, those artifacts that connect activities to activities are candidates for CM control. Thus, both product versions and condition versions may be placed under configuration management. In this context, tracking condition versions allows us to roll back in time to any prior part of the process and reconstruct what went on. The required process information also provides guidance on what metrics should be gathered from a process point of view.

Process issues with managers and developers: In general, project management needs include the ability to access information such as quality assurance reports, test reports and status reports on products and tasks. On the basis of this information, the manager can make decisions on future courses of action. These decisions set broad constraints on how developers perform their technical work. The means of imposing management decisions on technical personnel should be through a well defined process, that is, the developers understand the ground rules within which they can perform their work. This may be called the defined management process and is an enabling mechanism for a productive working environment.

While the traditional management view of process tends to be one of control, the developer's view is one of support. Developer's processes involve such activities as design, development and testing of software products [Humphrey 92], and are thus quite different from management processes. The developer wishes to use automated process support to provide guidance when it is requested, and relieve menial chores when possible. Automated process support tools need to provide a sufficiently broad range of functionality to express these different needs. One area where automated support is critical is metrics collection, since developers may be reluctant to invest time in an activity that they may perceive to be of primary benefit to management.

Within these two extremes, there is a third category of process. In larger projects, groups of developers must cooperate [Ellis 91] in product development. In this case, a cooperative process should be defined that involves aspects of both support for and control of products. Clearly, when multiple developers participate closely in a task, issues of control at the developer level must also be addressed. At a minimum, configuration management processes are important here [Dart 91]. In this area, special tools that allow developers to interact, for example in concurrent debugging [Dewan 93], may become more prevalent in the future. Thus the use of groupware technology in process-centered environments needs to be investigated more thoroughly.

If a software technology does not meet the user's needs, it will not be accepted. In a similar way, if a PCE is not well adapted to the way people work and interact, it is likely to be subverted or worse. By enforcing rigid conventions on the software process, an automated environment may not only take away the feeling of personal control but may prevent a developer from showing initiatives that help efficiency. For example, in a rigidly automated process, a developer may be unreasonably prevented from initiating a subsequent task because an earlier task had not been completed. Thus, either the level of granularity of the modeled process was too coarse (i.e. there was insufficient resolution to account for small tasks), or it was too intrusive (it should not even have attempted to control tasks in this way). Section 2.7.1 suggested an alternative solution to this problem.

Automation should primarily liberate the software development team from chores that can be automated (e.g. configuration control, gathering of metrics). Second, it should enforce process in a broad sense i.e. provide a framework into which individual (personal) processes can operate with significant freedom. Other constraints are probably appropriate for specific projects, but in adding them, a trade-off between the perceived benefits (productivity, management control etc.) and the human impact of the constraint should be carefully assessed. As Humphrey [Humphrey 89a] states: *the environment should provide strict enforcement of liberal process*. Humans can be very creative in circumventing systems that do not support their needs.

A PCE needs to consider multiple roles, such as upper management, project management and technical development. Each of these roles has different support and information requirements and in general, lower levels in the hierarchy will support the higher levels. For example, developers will provide their project management with technical and status information related to tasks. In addition, planning and schedule information will flow from project managers to upper management. A PCE must have an understanding of entities such as activities, agents, artifacts and of the relationships connecting those entities. Information about the entities and relationships should be reflected in the data objects underlying the environment.

For different reasons, developers and managers may feel threatened by the introduction of a technology such as process automation. On the developers side, concerns may include:

- reduction of privacy
- loss of control over how one performs ones work,
- fear of redundancy.

Effective strategies must be applied in order to deal with these issues. One means of achieving acceptance of automation is by involving those who work within a process to be, in part, responsible for the design of the process. In this sense, decision making and responsibility are pushed down to those developing the product. Such an approach runs contrary to the top-down decision making philosophy seen with traditional management, but it *is* seen in many quality-oriented US and Japanese companies. However, this strategy may threaten managers with a traditional outlook. In allowing work teams to design their own processes, developers are, in a sense, designing their own supervisor. On the managers side (particularly project and middle-management) concerns may include:

- loss of control due to automated decision making,
- loss of control due to introduction of self-directed work teams,
- loss of control over information
- ignorance (and fear) of the technology, and
- loss of status.

Managers (and others) may also be uncomfortable with loss of ability to control information. For example, if one is able to prevent others from obtaining information, then this situation can be manipulated. With a properly designed automated process, information can be controlled as specified by the process and not at the whim of any individual. However, those who previously abused this power may resent the loss and resist any change.

Finally, management expectations need to recognize how long an effective implementation of process automation will take. Process improvement introduces cultural changes within an organization and these will not occur overnight. This is equally true with process automation which introduces the additional element of technology into the equation.

Lessons from Groupware: Human-computer interaction has been extensively analyzed by people in the field of computer supported cooperative work (CSCW) [Ellis 91]. The products developed (usually called groupware) are aimed at supporting teams of people who use networked computers to facilitate joint efforts. There are generally three functional categories that groupware supports: communication, collaboration, and coordination. A common example of a "communication" package is e-mail, an example of a collaboration package might be an editor that allows simultaneous update from multiple terminals, while an example of a "coordination" package, might be a group scheduler. Most of these tools are of a generic nature to support non-technical or management goals. However, because they have to deal with how humans interact in tightly coupled settings, experience in this field sheds light on the issues relevant to the process constraints on environments.

Within the context of PCEs, there are several areas where groupware technology is likely to be important:

- specification/design
- documentation
- code inspections
- project planning
- reviews (e.g. of change requests)

Some of the above (e.g. code inspections) are truly synchronous activities i.e. the group participates at the same time, either at different terminals at the same location or geographically dispersed. In others (e.g. documentation) the mode of interaction is more likely to be asynchronous. Some lessons learned from groupware evaluations that bear on software PCEs are:

- don't try to get too elaborate with sophisticated functionality. Rather focus on a system that emphasizes basic functionality and ease of access, and does these well from a end-user point of view.
- if non-electronic analogies or metaphors can be used to describe entities and their attributes, use them.
- the system's architecture should be designed from the beginning to reflect seamless data and control integration. The difference between a system where one can move effortlessly between applications and one where such movement is awkward can be crucial to success.
- be careful in adding features that may have advantages for one group while imposing the work on another group. (This is the "what's in it for me?" syndrome).
- don't try to over-automate the process as we cannot predict all possible configurations that the system may encounter.
- design the environment for changing requirements. Human needs are very difficult to predict, and the system must be adaptable to account for user experience.

These points are also discussed in [Bullen 90, Grudin 88, Singh 92]

Resistance to change: Resistance should be expected. Overt resistance is to be encouraged otherwise it can easily become covert and undermining. Issues, such as fear of job loss, being controlled by a machine, or concern about intrusive metrics, should be aired and discussion encouraged. Out of such discussions, ideas and approaches may be found, that, as well as being excellent in their own right, will foster a feeling of "buy-in". Some of the strategies suggested in the paragraphs below relate to resistance and its resolution [Fletcher 93].

The use of metric data should be for process improvement only, not for performance evaluations, otherwise there may be significant reluctance to cooperate in its collection. If used in performance evaluations, this data may not only be perceived as threatening (particularly if it is being collected automatically), but will most likely be manipulated and therefore suspect. Metric data on an individual should only be visible to that individual, while non-attributable group-averaged data is used for process improvement and for higher management review. Individuals can compare their performance with the group average and determine how effective they are relative to their peers.

Process ownership and improvement: The philosophy of pushing down responsibility to as low an organizational level as possible should be adopted. Thus the group responsible for performing a process that is to be automated should help define, and should feel that it has ownership of, that automated process. This may be done by encouraging close collaboration between the user group and a software engineering process group (SEPG) [Fowler 90]. The SEPG should know how to elicit information on the current processes and identify the user-group's requirements on its automated equivalent, by:

- knowing how to define process models,
- knowing how to implement and validate enactable models,
- understanding metrics collection and analysis issues, and
- having the necessary skills to address adoption/transition issues.

In the same way that a group operating a process should feel ownership if it, the group should also have the responsibility for improving it. Thus the group should be responsible for collecting and analyzing its own process metrics, encouraging suggestions for enhancing the process and for implementing changes. These changes should, of course conform to the organizational standards (see *Organizational context* below).

Metrics collected on the process will of course be an important element in making such improvements. The combination of a well defined process coupled with consistent, complete and accurate metrics, makes for a powerful combination in the drive for quantitative process improvement

Training: There are several types of training required for successful implementation. First there is training on the technical aspects of the PCE. Examples of topics covered would be process definition and execution, and tool integration. This training supports the development of the application. Second, there is facilitator training for those who will help transition the environment into use. Facilitators provide a link between the development team and affected end users during the development of the process model, and also support end-users during initial installation. Finally, there is then end-user training on the use of the automated process. This training is not only technical but provides an opportunity for setting expectations with respect to such issues as non-attribution of metric data, and no layoffs as a result of the automation project. Some additional points should be noted. Training should occur close to the time it is used if possible, and practical hands-on workshops will probably provide the most effective means of delivering the information [Brownsword 94]. Training on the technical issues can be effectively provided by persons outside the organization or business unit involved. However, training on transition issues, that have a significant cultural component, needs to be provided by, or at least supported by, some members of the affected organization.

Organizational context: Project processes should be defined within the broader context of the organization. Thus the organization has the responsibility to develop process definition standards (e.g., type of process definition/enactment methodologies), process interface standards (to allow for compatibility between project processes and higher level processes), and data format standards (to allow for information consistency between projects). However, broad organizational standards should only be imposed after sufficient exploratory experience is gained with process automation at the project level.

Broad higher-level process models may be used to guide the organization of the lower-level processes and information flows. However, these higher-level processes should not specify the details of the individual processes. Detailed process definition should be a bottom-up task (using the standards). The top-down model may be periodically revised as a result of bottom-up integration of tasks. In this way the model is organic, being neither completely top-down nor bottom-up.

The manner in which a process is be modeled should depend on the application area. In general, processes closer to technical development should provide increasing degrees of support or guidance and decreasing degrees of imposed control. For example, developers are unlikely to accept a level of overt, external control in which every act in the edit/compile/test cycle is regulated. However, they may wish to support their activities by developing their own personal process scripts. On the other hand, persons managing change requests or document review activities may be very happy to have the support of an externally defined process in order to lift some of the administrative burdens from their shoulders.

4.5 A Transitioning Strategy

In order to install an organization-wide integrated software development environment (not necessarily a PCE), significant planning must be done [Humphrey 89a]. While Humphrey suggests a two-phase strategy, the following approach expands that suggested by him and has three phases. The first phase is exploratory and allows for technical and adoption experience to be gained. This phase should probably be performed by projects having the characteristics of an organization at Maturity Level 2 or higher[3]. The second (strategic) phase involves planning for organizational adoption of process automation. The third phase covers actual implementation of process automation within projects as directed in phase 2.

If the long range goal of process automation is implementation across multiple projects, it is essential that upper management are involved and enthusiastic sponsors. In order to gain that level of buy-in, the champion of the technology must understand the technical issues, the adoption issues, and be able to set the correct management expectations. Expectations to be set include, for example, the fact that adopting the technology will not occur overnight. There is likely to be resistance to working with this technology, both from staff and line managers, and this level of visible commitment from upper management is necessary to sustain the momentum during the adoption process.

It should be noted that the transition strategy described below does not distinguish between the replacement of an existing process with its automated equivalent, and the adoption of an automated process where no process existed before. The latter is likely to be easier in the sense that there is no cultural or technical legacy to contend with. In particular, when no process initially exists, a replacement strategy, as described in below, is not required.

Phase 1 – Exploration: This phase is very important in allowing an organization to assess the appropriateness of process automation for its culture, prior to making significant investments. Thus implementing one or more pilot processes should be the first step. Before starting, it is probably wise to read about technology change management. Little has yet been written explicitly about adopting process automation, but many of the issues are the same as those in the adoption of other technologies. Excellent places to start are [Block 81, Bouldin 89, Fletcher 93, Humphrey 89b, and Oaks 92]. The paper by [Dart 94] illustrates how close the issues of adopting automated configuration management are to that of adopting automated process. The following criteria are suggested in selecting an appropriate process to be automated (see also "What should be automated?" in Section 4.4.).

---

3. The Capability Maturity Model [Paulk-93a] associates maturity levels with organizational character-istics, not project characteristics. However, nearly all of Level 2 practices within the CMM focus on project characteristics. It is in this sense that the term "a project showing Level 2 characteristics" is used.

- the process is modest in size,
- the process is well understood and stable,
- the process is not on the critical production path of external products,
- the project, of which the process is a part, is not constantly putting out "brushfires," and
- the users of the process are positively inclined to automation.

To implement automated processes in an existing project, real-time validation may be required before commitment to the new process is made. One approach to this is to run the old (perhaps manual) process in parallel, side-by-side with the new automated process, making sure that the inputs to both are identical. Outputs are then compared for some time to assure that they are identical. In cases where the old and new processes are not the same, the two processes can still be run side-by-side until sufficient confidence is gained that the new process is providing correct output (called the parallel strategy). Another strategy is to incrementally insert small components of the automated process into the old process in such a way that the change-over to the new process occurs gradually (called the incremental strategy). In either case, off-line simulation of the automated process can help validate its behavioral correctness and generate end-user buy-in prior to installation.

The pilot project will provide valuable experience in the operational behavior of the automated environment. In particular, the pilot will provide information on:

- the timeliness of response of the system from an end-user perspective,
- the design of the process from an end-user perspective,
- the design of the user interface from an end-user perspective,
- the robustness of the environment to "dumb" errors,
- the effectiveness of the adoption strategy,
- the frequency with which the systems crashes or goes off-line.

Gathering data and tracking metrics on these issues is critical, particularly for a first-of-a-kind project. This information will allow for more rapid correction and improvement to be made. It may also be importance to justify to management the expansion of automation to additional projects.

Phase 2 – Strategic planning: Once confidence has been gained through the demonstration process(es), the knowledge and skills gained can be put to use in developing a strategy that will allow wider and consistent implementation throughout the organization. The following activities are suggested:

- Establish an automation focal point (an individual). This person was probably part of the Phase 1 activities, could be part of a software engineering process group, and must have an understanding of issues related to technology, process, and adoption. Communication is also an essential skill for this individual.
- Identify, and obtain buy-in of key individuals who will influence the process automation project (i.e., technical leaders, projects leaders, upper management and corporate staff).
- Develop a high-level standards statement for the automation project. Include standards for:

- process definition,
- process enactment,
- communication,
- user interface
- metric data collection,
- management tools,
- development tools,
- data repositories,
- vendor support, and
- training.
- Establish a strategic plan for PCE for adoption and maintenance.
- Assess the most promising technologies.
- Establish a corporate process reuse repository.
- Develop a practical handbook for the adoption of automated process that covers the technical, adoption, training, and reuse issues. This should be a living document that will be updated with experience.

Phase 3 – Project implementation: With experience in hand from the demonstrations, and the organizational framework provided by Phase 2, implementation throughout the organization's projects can begin. For this phase, the following activities are suggested:

- Establish an implementation group composed of experts in the automation technology and members of the affected project. If necessary train individuals in the PCE and in adoption techniques.
- Identify and evaluate project-based costs, benefits and risks associated with adoption of process automation.
- Develop project and application-specific process automation objectives and implementation plans. Specify what will be accomplished. Try to set quantitative quality, cost and schedules goals for the process.
- Develop a project and application-specific migration strategy based on the handbook for the adoption of automated process.
- Define, develop and implement the process templates based on the handbook for the adoption of automated process.
- Validate the effectiveness of the process by involving future users in simulated process role-plays (see Chapter 3)
- Provide training and hands-on experience for all affected parties.
- Track the progress of the automation project (getting feedback from users), document lessons learned, and improve the process model.

It may be helpful to expand on the activity of defining an organization's migration path by suggesting one possible scenario. This scenario assumes that the first project is involved in Phase 1 and the subsequent projects are part of the Phase 3 activities. As mentioned above, a project showing Level 1 characteristics will not have the process maturity to effectively use a PCE in the broad sense. A project with level 2 characteristics is therefore chosen for the pilot (Phase 1) installation. At this point, the manually-defined process is chosen and adapted for automation using the organization's standards. It is then tested off-line through simulation. Critical project members are closely involved in these activities. The functional elements supported by the PCE may include development tools such as compilers, debuggers, etc., or management tools such as for project planning and cost estimating. At this point a transition strategy must be planned and implemented, and could, for example, use either the parallel or incremental approach discussed earlier. Transitioning the automated process into the project also requires that the project members be trained in how to work and feel comfortable with the automated process.

When sufficient confidence has been reached with the first project, other projects transition to the use of the PCE during Phase 3. These latter projects may concurrently be achieving Maturity Level 2. In adopting the PCE, these projects will have to conform to the data standards set up for the repository. This not only allows projects to communicate, but also sets the stage for the organization to reach maturity Level 3. At Level 3, a major focus is on organizational consistency of process. Thus each project's process will be tailored to reflect the organization's standard process. The process, as defined for each project, will be developed using standard process modeling tools and stored within the organization's repository under CM control. Also, in moving towards Level 3, the organization will support access tools allowing upper management to query the repository. This is possible since data across the organization is now stored in a consistent manner.

The functionality provided by the PCE will need to accommodate changes in the process as process improvement takes place. Increasing demands on process management is to be expected as new requirements, greater process complexity, and product variety are imposed. Significant modification of the process program is also likely since mistakes will be made as experience is gained. If the process model is not resilient and flexible, it is likely that continued modification of the associated software will overstress the original concept. This problem of process evolution and maintenance affects not only the process template design, but also challenges the underlying mechanisms provided by the process programming language.

5 The Past, Present, and Future of Process Automation

The history of software development in electronic form spans barely five decades, a very short time as most histories go. However, this history has many parallels with that of traditional manufacturing. The relationship between the two can provide insights into where the software industry has been, where it is today are where it may be headed tomorrow. So in this chapter we will, in part, explore the relationship between traditional manufacturing over the part two centuries to software development over the past few decades focussing on issues related to process automation. Further insights into evolving nature of engineering and the relationship to software can be found in [Shaw 90, Humphrey 91a].

The industrial revolution generated a great demand for highly skilled craftsmen for the manufacture of guns, bicycles, sewing machines and other mechanical devices. However, the technology of those times produced component parts whose dimensional accuracy was low. Thus parts did not often fit together, and there was a need for craftsmen to do hand finishing work, often filing down metal parts, to accomplish this fitting. Of course, parts from one copy of a product could not replace the same parts in another copy of the same product as each copy was now unique. The need for extensive hand finishing kept production low.

Particularly within the military, there was a strong appeal to develop interchangeable parts, so that "arms could be interchanged as readily as soldiers could be switched" [Hounshell 84]. At least three factors influenced the ability to make parts interchangeable. One was the division of labor: if a workman was dedicated to making multiple copies of the same component, then the reliability went up. The second involved the introduction of technologies such as milling, that replaced the old method of filing to achieve accuracy. Third was the introduction of special-purpose machines, customized for the product in question. These included the use of gauges for accurately measuring part dimensions. Since many of these techniques also required less skill, craftsmen resisted their introduction. This de-skilling of the workforce was also a necessary component for mass production as there were not sufficient skilled craftsmen to fuel the staggering growth of new factories.

Because the craft approach resulted in limited production, manufacturing could not benefit from the economies of scale. Thus craft-based manufacturing shops were small, many products were custom tailored to end-users needs and there was also a strong pride in workmanship. However, the advantage of customization (and its associated high cost) could not, is most cases, compete with the economies of scale introduced with the newer mass-production techniques.

Principally as a result of interchangeability of parts, high volume production was possible. In the automobile industry, Ford experimented extensively with techniques for interchangeability with enormous success, increasing production of the Model T by over six fold between 1909 and 1912. The advent of the assembly line amount 1912 then increased output by over seven fold between 1912 and 1916. Inspection could be reduced as a result of precise tooling, machines were located exactly where they were needed, throughput was scheduled in order to keep the lines running at controlled rate, and metrics were collected in order to assure accurate planning and control of the system. Finally, improved metallurgical control allowed for consistency of components that in turn allowed the machines to be operated faster and throughput to be increased.

To a considerable extent, many software development houses still operate under craft conditions today. There are several parallels with the manufacturing craft industries. First, the use of interchangeable parts has strong similarities to the use of reusable software components. Until recently few software components were reused (although this may be changing). There is resistance among software developers both to design for reusability (it's an extra hassle) or to incorporate reusable components when new systems are developed. In part, there may be a perception that the reuse of parts reduces software developers (the "craftsmen") to systems integrators thus removing the creative element from software development.

Second, the goal of using interchangeable parts is to eliminate costly back-end handwork needed to fit parts together. Lack of accurate dimensions in mechanical components can result in an accumulation of inaccuracies as these components are combined into subsystems and then into systems. The longer it takes to remove the inaccuracies, the greater the downstream problem will be in making corrections. In software, if bugs are not caught early, the ability to correct them at the subsystem and systems levels will likewise become increasingly difficult. Thus software bugs can be viewed as a software analogy to the lack of good tolerance in mechanical systems.

Third, accurate measurement became a critical element in the ability to reproduce standardized parts. This need to measure part accuracy was not threatening to craftsmen as such. However, other forms of measurement were. Fredrick Taylor's ideas of "scientific management" [Taylor 11], in which people could be treated as parts of a large machine, were met with particular hostility. Taylor introduced the concept of time and motion studies and this found practical expression in Ford's mass production lines. Not only was this form of data gathering intrusive, but its use justified increasingly high production rates. In a like manner software developers, as craftsmen, do not like the idea that their productivity or quality is being scrutinized. Nevertheless, the collection, analysis and use of metrics data is still essential for effective software process improvement However, appropriate privacy controls can be placed on who can access which elements of the metric data without significantly reducing its effectiveness. Some strategies on the use of metric data were discussed in the Chapter 4.

The worst aspects of mass production, that is, the mindless assembly line and the dehumanizing treatment that the workers experienced, do not have equivalents in the software area. The aim of mass production was to design the factory so that unskilled immigrants could perform the tasks on the assembly line. Clearly, it is difficult to impose this environment on educated software engineers who identify with the spirit of the craftsman rather than of the unskilled factory worker. As stated in [Humphrey 91a]

Professionals need some control over their working environment. They do not like to be given orders or detailed direction. They like some choice over their working assignments, and they want their concerns recognized by management."

It is from this vantage point that process automation must be viewed.

Craft production gave way to mass production that in turn has, in more recent decades, given way to lean production. After the Second World War, the Japanese and in particular the Toyota Company, were driven to use this philosophy as a means of minimizing costs. An early driving force was the manufacture of sheet metal stampings. Because die changing was a major undertaking, the US automobile manufacturers set up their presses to make long runs of such stampings. However, in its early years, Toyota produced far fewer cars and was forced to devise approaches to allow for quick die changes. Not only did this reduce inventories and their associated costs but, if defects in the stampings occurred, they could be identified much sooner. It also allowed for more rapid response to customer needs as there was less of the old product still left to sell. In this way, lean production was born.

Lean production means eliminating fat wherever it can be found. "Fat" can be identified with excess inventories, overuse of floor space, poor quality components, inefficient use of machines, and not exploiting everyone's intelligence to the maximum extent. Quoting [Womack 90]:

Lean production combines the advantages of craft and mass production, while avoiding the high cost of the former and the rigidity of the latter. Toward this end, lean producers employ teams of multiskilled workers at all levels of the organization and use highly flexible, increasingly automated machines to produce volume products in enormous variety.

Unlike in mass production, workers in this environment were not unskilled laborers performing mindless repetitive tasks. For example, the workers who were responsible for operating the stamping presses were also responsible for changing the dies. They were encouraged to make and implement suggestions for improving the performance of the machines they operated. Thus lean production encourages those who are intimately familiar with their working processes to improve these processes. In the mass production factory, only professional engineers were permitted to make such recommendations. As quoted above, automation can play an important part in the lean revolution. However, it must be viewed with caution. If automation is installed without understanding the limitations of the technology, disaster may result. One of the most expensive lessons to be learned by General Motors was the inappropriateness of attempting to over-automate their Hamtramck plant. Rather that being a shining example of our technological future, it turned into a nightmare: robots spray-painted each other, body parts were installed on the wrong cars, robots smashed into cars and other robots, and assembly lines went down because of software problems. This does not imply that automating processes is inappropriate; only that it must be seen within the broader context of improving quality.

The active cooperation in, and full support of personnel at all levels of an organization is essential for the successful introduction of automation. Thus if the principle motivation of management is to control a work force or to eliminate staff, then the effort will most likely fail. As [Davidow 93] states:

> The Japanese have believed the best way to achieve results is to perfect the processes on which they are based. They have also approached the process of improvement in a conservative way, becoming great believers in taking small incremental steps and pursuing the goal relentlessly over extended periods of time. The Japanese have a word for this approach: kaizen.

Thus the Japanese have approached automation in an evolutionary fashion rather than a revolutionary fashion. This is consistent with the recommendations of Chapter 4, where it is suggested that a) experience should be gained through pilot projects before more ambitious efforts are tackled, b) islands of automation should then be established to gain experience, before c) large-scale integration of these islands of automation takes place. Throughout all these developments, the experience and insights of the personnel who have to work within the processes should be given considerable weight in designing the processes. Again quoting [Womack 90]:

> [L]ean producers change how people work but not always in the way we think. Most people – including so-called blue-collar workers – will find their jobs more challenging as lean production spreads. At the same time they may find their jobs more stressful because a key objective of lean production is to push responsibility far down the organizational ladder. Responsibility means freedom to control one's work – a big plus – but also raises anxiety about making costly mistakes.

Pushing down responsibility to the lowest level and encouraging everyone to take initiative to improve has major implications for the organization. Empowerment of workers leads to a reduced role for project and middle management, and this may be resisted. However, many companies such as Hewlett Packard have improved their competitiveness by making such organizational changes. Computers in general play a significant role in supporting such business re-engineering by providing an information infrastructure. Process automation is beginning to support these changes. Development of large software systems involves many complex and interdependent processes, and may ultimately benefit as much as any field by the introduction of process automation. However, if due consideration is not given to the personnel who have to work within the automated environment, and appropriate adoption strategies have not been worked out, failures such as occurred at the Hamtramck plant could occur.

In at least one sense, manufacture of mechanical devices and software differ significantly. With the manufacture of mechanical devices, a major focus is on making components and assembling them into the final product. However, with software, identical copies of the final product can be reproduced electronically in an almost trivial way. The manufacturing lifecycle of mechanical devices can be considered to consist of four phases: product design and development, tooling for manufacture, product manufacture, and product maintenance. In software, two phases are dominant: product design and development, and product maintenance. Some of the elements of the tooling phase for mechanical devices can, however, be seen in the software design and development phase. For example one may have to implement an appropriate CASE environment to support the software design and development phase. Earlier we discussed how mechanical interchangeability and software reuse were conceptually related. This is a case in which an element of mechanical manufacture corresponds to an element on software design. There are however, significant differences in the notions of mechanical maintenance and software maintenance. In the former, failures in some instances of a product can occur while not in others. However, in software a bug either exists in all copies or it does not. In addition a significant fraction of software maintenance provides enhancements, while this is rare with mechanical devices. Finally a mechanical device will most probably end its life as a result of the mechanical degradation of its components. Software does not suffer from this problem. However, given the rapid change in software technology it may become obsolete, or it may become too expensive to support because of a history of poorly implemented maintenance.

Cusumano [Cusumano 91] identifies three software manufacturing strategies. First is the commercial-off-the-shelf (COTS) strategy. In this category, the objective is to mass-produce a product that dominates its competition, and sells in very large numbers. The second category is to produce specialized one-of-a-kind software product as is often required by the defense industry. This situation uses techniques most closely akin to craft manufacturing, and may be less amenable to process automation. The third strategy involves developing semi-customized products when the product area is well understood, but some adaption is required. Such products re-use generic components to a great extent and these components are adapted using standardized techniques to meet customer requirements. It is in this category where that so-called software factory concepts are most easily applied. It is in this area that process automation may hold its greatest promise. A major category, not addressed by Cusumano, is software maintenance – both corrective and perfective. This category is of significant size and taking an increasing share of software engineering resources. Because maintenance processes are usually well understood, they can often be standardized, and are potentially good candidates for process automation.

In the 1960s, IBM saw the need for a more systematic means to produce software, elevating its importance above that a hardware support function. Thus they built a software factory called the Santa Teresa Laboratory, employing 2000 personnel. (It was not called a factory!) In earlier experience with developing the OS/360 operating system, IBM encountered large numbers of defects, and long delays in delivery. This motivated much change. A significant contributor to this problem was the fact that the operating system was being developed at multiple remote sites each of which had significant autonomy and used varying methods. Coordination and integration proved to be very challenging in this environment. As a result, in part due to the OS/360 experience, IBM decided to build the centralized Santa Teresa facility. IBM "created a highly centralized functionally organized facility with standardized process and physical layout designed to facilitate programmer performance, comfort and communication" [Cusumano 91].

Japanese factories, as exemplified by Hitachi, Toshiba and NEC, were motivated by a similar desire as that of IBM, that is, to develop an effective environment in which people, processes, tools, and standards could all brought to bear to rationalize and improve the means with which software was developed. Quoting Cusumano [Cusumano 91]:

> *Japanese software factories were strategic in that they resulted from long-term rather than just project-centered objectives, with managers systematically identifying productivity, quality and performance goals, and introducing comprehensive measures to meet these goals.*

Of course, due to the state of the technology, none of these factories were able to consider the use of process automation as described in this book. However, during the mid 1980s, IBM was beginning to look in that direction. In an article "Automating the Software Development Process" [Hoffnagle 85] states:

> *Process definition and execution should be made explicit, formally definable and machine processable. There should be an evolutionary capability to move the current process, based upon paper guidelines that are manually monitored and administered, to an automated process control mechanism which uses explicit, formal process definition and rule-based control. The architecture should specify a process mechanism that has functions and interfaces for defining a process, storing it in a facility as a set of rules and using these rules to control the execution of the process. Formal definition and mechanization will permit the recording and monitoring of the usage, performance and effectiveness of the specified process.*

Only after a decade are we seeing the introduction of such process automation in the market place. Progress in the application of a new technology is unpredictable, often being related to the growth of seemingly unrelated fields, to business perceptions or military needs. However, the trend to lower-cost hardware, increased conformance to communication and integration standards, and the arrival of effective PCE technology will help set the stage. Also, the increasing emphasis on both software process improvement and business process re-engineering may encourage moves in this direction. However, it will probably take some well publicized success stories to give the technology the needed credibility to be widely successful.

What is the future for the technology? While organizations need to start with small processes to gain experience, it is ultimately to support large projects that process automation will come into its own. To date there is little real experience in using software process automation as described in this book. However, it is likely that the acceptance of PCE technology will depend at least as much on the way it is introduced and used as on the technical capabilities of any specific process-centered environment. Process automation will affect how management operates in an organization, not just how technical staff operate. By codifying the processes through which software is built and managed, organizational restructuring is likely occur, accelerating the current trend to flatter organizations. Because of the need to involve project members in defining and managing the automated processes, this technology may also accelerate the move towards self-directed work teams.

At the applications level, a process-centered environment may, in the future, provide much broader support than is now realized. Central to this is the fact that a PCE has an understanding of the current state of the process being managed. If this knowledge is combined with a knowledge of the application domain of interest, a significant synergy could take place. Thus application domain support, guidance, and metrics collection could be provided within a process context. Domain/task-specific support for the following areas is possible:

- selecting reuse components,
- selecting appropriate tools, or techniques,
- selecting appropriate algorithms,
- selecting test suites,
- providing information on target machines,
- guiding novices through the task,
- comparing planned schedules with actual progress, and making recommendations,
- performing automatic metrics analysis, and
- providing guidance to support process improvement efforts

In these areas, use of rule-based reasoning is a natural fit particularly with systems where rules are already being used to drive the process model. In addition hypermedia may be valuable techniques for providing supplemental guidance or training information. By increasing the degree of technical support in this way, we could be further reducing the skill-level necessary to develop and manage software. Given the limited availability of highly qualified personnel, this may be necessary, although it could introduce additional human factors concerns.

The future of software process automation has yet to be decided. Potentially it can bring dramatic improvements in software productivity and quality, but questions remain to be answered. Is the technology sufficiently responsive and adaptable to human needs? Conversely will implementers be sufficiently aware of the critical human-factors issues? Will early failures at automation prematurely give the field a bad reputation? Will resistance to working in an automated process be a major impediment? Will process automation products be sufficiently flexible to describe most process characteristics and sufficiently scalable to model "industrial-strength" projects? While answers to these questions will only be resolved in time, awareness of the issues and plans to deal with them will immeasurably improve the chances for success.

Appendix A
The Process Enactment Program, ProSim

Appendix A provides information on the Prolog program, ProSim, that demonstrates simple process enactment. This program does not contain process-specific information, but manages the rules that are process-specific. The rules, and other process-dependent information, are contained in the models *codeDevel* and *docUpdate* that are defined in Sections A.2 and A.3 respectively. These subsections also contain sample output that results from running the process models. All program listings in Appendices A were developed using AAIS Prolog [AAIS 91] on the Apple Macintosh.

These programs can be downloaded through Internet's anonymous ftp facility. The ftp address is: *ftp.sei.cmu.edu*. The files are located in the directory: *pub/procauto/execProcs/ProSim.SEI*

The files can also be downloaded through the World Wide Web [Dougherty 94] 94]. Using this approach, the Universal Resource Locator is: *http://www.sei.cmu.edu/SEI/topics/process_auto/ProcAuto.html*

A.1 The Process Controller Listing

Section 2.4.3 and in particular Figure 2.18 should be consulted in reviewing the process controller program below. In order to run one of the two processes enter either name (codeDevel or docUpdate) when the driver program requests it.

```
/******************** process initiator ********************/

init:-
    write('Enter file name of process model: '), read(FileName), nl,
    reconsult(FileName),
    write('~~~~~~~~~~~~~~~~~~~~~~~~~~~~~~~~~~~~~~~~~~~~~~~~~~~~~~~'), nl,
    write('~~~~~~~~~~~~~~~~~~~~~~~~~~~~~~~~~~~~~~~~~~~~~~~~~~~~~~~'), nl,
    initSystemVars,
    initUserVars,
```

```
    doActivities.




/*********************** driver functions ********************/

doActivities:-
    /* find activities that can start process*/
    findActs(ActList),
    /* start all initial activities */
    perform(ActList),
    doNextAct.

doNextAct:-
    /* sets up the recursive loop for each activity in the process */
    bagof(Act,active(Act), ActListOld),
    retractall(active(_)),
    /* find activities that are candidates or are now in progress*/
    findActs(ActList),
    /* remove activities now in progress */
    newActs(ActListOld, ActList,[],ActListNew),
    /* start all new activities */
    perform(ActListNew),
    doNextAct.

findActs(_):-
    /* test all activity perconditions to find currently valid activities */
    test(Test),
    TestX =.. [Test],
    TestX,
    fail.

findActs(ActList):-
    /* group all currently valid activities into a list */
    bagof(Act, active(Act), ActList).

findActs(_):-
    write('All activities have been completed'), nl,
    abort.

newActs(_, [], DifList, DifList).

newActs(OldList,[A|NewList], X, Y):-
    /* remove all elements from NewList that are in OldList */
    member(A,OldList),
    newActs(OldList,NewList, X, Y).

newActs(OldList,[A|NewList],X,Y):-
    newActs(OldList,NewList,[A|X],Y).

perform([Act|ActList]):-
    /* initiate new activities */
```

```
    ActX =.. [Act],
    ActX,
    perform(ActList).

perform([]).
initSystemVars:-
    /* clear program of all garbage left from previous run */
    retractall(ver(_,_)),
    asserta(ver(0,0)),
    retractall(log(_,_,_)),
    asserta(log(nul,nul,nul)),
    retractall(subact(_)),
    retractall(actList).

/********************* utility functions *********************/
set(X,K):-
    /* initialize version number X to value K */
    retractall(ver(X,_)),
    assert(ver(X,K)).

inc(K):-
    /* increment version number K by 1 */
    retract(ver(K,J)),
    J1 is J+1,
    assertz(ver(K,J1)).

dec(K):-
    /* increment version number K by 1 */
    retract(ver(K,J)),
    J1 is J-1,
    assertz(ver(K,J1)).

put_ent(Store, Val, Condition):-
    /* put an entity into a store and assert exit entities */
    retract(store(Store, Val_list)),
    assertz(store(Store, [Val|Val_list])),
    assert(Condition).

get_ent(Store, Val):-
    /* retrieve an entity from a store */
    store(Store, Val_list),
    member(Val, Val_list),
    assertz(Val).

get_ent(Store, Val):-
    /* retrieve an entity from a store - entity not found */
    write(Val),
    write(' is not contained in '),
    write(Store),nl,
    !,
    abort.

stripParen(X,Y):-
```

```
/* changes repository name xxx(1) to file name xxx_1 */
X =.. [Body, Int],
int2string(Int,Str),
stringconcat(Body,".",Body1),
stringconcat(Body1,Str,Y).
instantiate(VarIn, VarOut):-
    instantiate1(VarIn,VarOut),
    !.

instantiate1(VarIn,VarOut):-
    /* instantiates a subscripted variable e.g., doc(1) => report(1) */
    VarIn =.. [Var1, I],
    Var2 =.. [Var1, X],
    Var2,
    string(X),
    VarOut =.. [X,I].

instantiate1(VarIn,_):-
    write('Could not instantiate variable '), write(VarIn),
    abort.
```

A.2 The *codeDevel* Process

codeDevel represents a highly idealized code development process shown in Figure
2.9. Some of the activities call on lower-level functions to support the performance
of that task. For example *act4* calls on the function *buildAndTestCode*. However, in
this simple model these lower-level functions do little; they are only there to illustrate the decoupling of the rules that select the activities from the associated work
performed in the activities.

A.2.1 The Program Listing

```
/*************** activity preconditions ********************/
/*** these are all tested at each cycle against current activities ****/

test1:-
    ?(startCodeMod),
    not(log(getSourceCode, _,[sourcesRetrieved(1)])),
    asserta(active(act1)).

test2:-
    ver(i,I),
    (?(sourcesRetrieved(I)); ?(testPasses(I,false))),
    I1 is I+1,
    instantiate(codeModule1(I1), CodeModule2),
    not(log(modifyCode1,_,[CodeModule2])),
```

```
    asserta(active(act2)).

test3:-
    ver(i,l),
    (?(sourcesRetrieved(l)); ?(testPasses(l,false))),
    l1 is l+1,
    instantiate(codeModule2(l1), CodeModule3),
    not(log(modifyCode2,_,[CodeModule3])),
    asserta(active(act3)).

test4:-
    ver(i,l),
    l1 is l+1,
    instantiate(codeModule1(l1), CodeModule1),
    ?(CodeModule1),
    instantiate(codeModule2(l1), CodeModule2),
    ?(CodeModule2),
    not(log(buildAndTestCode,_,[testPasses(l1,true)])),
    not(log(buildAndTestCode,_,[testPasses(l1,false)])),
    asserta(active(act4)).

test5:-
    ver(i,l),
    ?(testPasses(l,true)),
    not(log(putSourceCode,_,[sourcesUpdated])),
    asserta(active(act5)).

/*********** activities and postconditions **************/
act1:-
    set(i,1),
    instantiate(codeModule1(1), Module1),
    instantiate(codeModule2(1), Module2),
    get_ent(sourceRepos, Module1),
    get_ent(sourceRepos, Module2),
    outPut1,
    assertz(log(getSourceCode, [startCodeMod], [sourcesRetrieved(1)])),
    assert(sourcesRetrieved(1)).

act2:-
    ver(i,l),
    developer1(Developer1),
    changeRequest(CR),
    (?(sourcesRetrieved(l)), X=sourcesRetrieved(l);
         ?(testPasses(l,false)), X=testPasses(l,false)),
    instantiate(codeModule1(l), CodeModule1),
    l1 is l+1,
    instantiate(codeModule1(l1), CodeModule2),
    modifyCode1(Developer1, CR, CodeModule1, CodeModule2),
    assertz(log(modifyCode1, [X], [CodeModule2])),
    assert(CodeModule2).


act3:-
```

```
    ver(i,I),
    developer2(Developer2),
    changeRequest(CR),
    (?(sourcesRetrieved(I)), X=sourcesRetrieved(I);
         ?(testPasses(I,false)), X=testPasses(I,false)),
    instantiate(codeModule2(I), CodeModule2),
    I1 is I+1,
    instantiate(codeModule2(I1), CodeModule3),
    modifyCode2(Developer2, CR, CodeModule2, CodeModule3),
    assertz(log(modifyCode2, [X], [CodeModule3])),
    assert(CodeModule3).

act4:-
    ver(i,I),
    tester(Tester),
    I1 is I+1,
    instantiate(codeModule1(I1), CodeModule1),
    instantiate(codeModule2(I1), CodeModule2),
    buildAndTestCode(Tester,CodeModule1, CodeModule2, TrueFalse),
    assertz(log(buildAndTestCode, [CodeModule1, CodeModule2],
             [testPasses(I1,TrueFalse)])),
    assert(testPasses(I1,TrueFalse)),
    inc(i).

act5:-
    ver(i,I),
    instantiate(codeModule1(I), Module1),
    instantiate(codeModule2(I), Module2),
    put_ent(sourceRepos, Module1, sourcesUpdated),
    put_ent(sourceRepos, Module2, sourcesUpdated),
    outPut2,
    assertz(log(putSourceCode, [testPasses(I,true)], [sourcesUpdated])),
    assert(sourcesUpdated).

/********************** supporting model data *********************/

test(test1).
test(test2).
test(test3).
test(test4).
test(test5).

/********************** entity definitions *********************/

codeModule1(module1).
codeModule2(module2).
changeRequest(cR_No_1).
store(sourceRepos, [module1(1), module2(1)]).
developer1(leonard).
developer2(cliff).
tester(tricia).
startCodeMod.
/********************** initialize variables *********************/
```

```
initUserVars:-
    retractall(sourcesRetrieved(_)),
    retractall(module1(_)),
    retractall(module2(_)),
    retractall(testPasses(_,_)),
    retractall(sourcesUpdated),
    retractall(rolesAssigned(_)).
```

/********************* supporting functions *********************/

```
outPut1:-
    write("""""""""""""""""""""""),nl,
    write('source code retrieved'), nl,
    write("""""""""""""""""""""""), nl.


modifyCode1(Developer, _, _, _):-
    write('module 1 modified by '), write(Developer), nl,
    write("""""""""""""""""""""""), nl.

modifyCode2(Developer, _, _, _):-
    write('module 2 modified by '), write(Developer), nl,
    write("""""""""""""""""""""""), nl.

buildAndTestCode(Tester, _, _, TrueFalse):-
    write(Tester), write(', did the code pass testing? (y/n): '), read(YN),
    (YN='y', TrueFalse='true'; TrueFalse='false'),
    write("""""""""""""""""""""""), nl.

outPut2:-
    write('modified and tested source placed back in repository'), nl,
    write("""""""""""""""""""""""), nl.
```

A.2.2 Typical Program Output

The following listing illustrates an interactive session with ProSim using the process model, *CodeDevel*, defined above and in Chapter 2. The text of user's responses are shown in bold for clarity.

```
?- init.
Enter file name of process model: codeDevel.
~~~~~~~~~~~~~~~~~~~~~~~~~~~~~~~~~~~~~~~~~~~~~~~~~~~~~
~~~~~~~~~~~~~~~~~~~~~~~~~~~~~~~~~~~~~~~~~~~~~~~~~~~~~
''''''''''''''''''''''''''''''''''

source code retrieved
''''''''''''''''''''''''''''''''''

module 1 modified by leonard
''''''''''''''''''''''''''''''''''

module 2 modified by cliff
''''''''''''''''''''''''''''''''''
```

tricia, did the code pass testing? (y/n): **n.**
""""""""""""""""""""""""""

module 1 modified by leonard
""""""""""""""""""""""""""

module 2 modified by cliff
""""""""""""""""""""""""""

tricia, did the code pass testing? (y/n): **y.**
""""""""""""""""""""""""""

modified and tested source placed back in repository
""""""""""""""""""""""""""

All activities have been completed

A.3 The *docUpdate* Process

The *docUpdate* process (see Figures 2.20, 2.21, and 2.22) is somewhat more complex than the *codeDevel* process. In addition, the complexity of the lower level functions is more detailed. Specifically, text windows appear in order that editing work
can be performed as part of the execution of the process. However, there is no networking capability and all output, including the dialog window appears on the one
screen.

A.3.1 The Program Listing

```
/*************** activity preconditions *********************/
/*** these are all tested against at each cycle to current activities ***/

test1:-
    ?(newCR(_)),
    not(log(revNewCR, _,[accepts(true)])),
    not(log(revNewCR, _,[accepts(false)])),
    asserta(active(act1)).

test2:-
    ?(accepts(true)),
    not(log(makeInitAssign,_,[rolesAssigned(1)])),
    asserta(active(act2)).

test3:-
    ver(i,l),
    ?(rolesAssigned(l)),
    not(log(getEdsReply,_,[edAccepts(l,true)])),
    not(log(getEdsReply,_,[edAccepts(l,false)])),
    asserta(active(act3)).

test4:-
    ver(i,l),
```

```
      I =:= 1,
      I1 is I+1,
      ?(edAccepts(I,false)),
      not(log(makeRevAssign,_,[rolesAssigned(I1)])),
      asserta(active(act4)).
test5:-
      ver(i,I),
      I =:= 2,
      ?(edAccepts(I,false)),
      not(log(imposeAssign,_,[assignMade])),
      asserta(active(act5)).

test6:-
      ver(i,I),
      (?(assignMade); ?(edAccepts(I,true))),
      not(log(notifyRev,_,[revNotified])),
      asserta(active(act6)).

test7:-
      ?(revNotified),
      not(log(notifyEd,_,[edNotified])),
      asserta(active(act7)).

test8:-
      ?(edNotified),
      instantiate(document(0), Document0),
      not(log(getDoc,_,[Document0])),
      asserta(active(act8)).

test9:-
      instantiate(document(0), Document0),
      ?(Document0),
      instantiate(document(1), Document1),
      not(log(modDoc,_,[Document1])),
      asserta(active(act9)).

test10:-
      ver(i,I),
      instantiate(document(I), Document),
      ?(Document),
      instantiate(comments(I), Comments),
      not(log(reviewDoc,_,[passReview])),
      not(log(reviewDoc,_,[Comments])),
      asserta(active(act10)).

test11:-
      ver(i,I),
      instantiate(comments(I), Comments),
      ?(Comments),
      I1 is I+1,
      instantiate(document(I1), Document),
      not(log(modDocAgain,_,[Document])),
      asserta(active(act11)).
```

```
test12:-
   ?(passReview),
   not(log(putDoc,_,[docSaved])),
   asserta(active(act12)).
test13:-
   ?(docSaved),
   not(log(sendMsgToMgr,_,[msgSent])),
   asserta(active(act13)).

/***************** activities and postconditions ********************/

act1:-
   manager(Manager),
   newCR(NewCR),
   revNewCR(NewCR, Manager, TrueFalse),
   assertz(log(revNewCR, [NewCR], [accepts(TrueFalse)])),
   assert(accepts(TrueFalse)),
   set(i,1).

act2:-
   set(i,1),
   ver(i,I),
   manager(Manager),
   techWriter1(TechWriter1),
   techWriter2(TechWriter2),
   makeInitAssign(Manager, TechWriter1, TechWriter2),
   assertz(log(makeInitAssign, [accepts(true)], [rolesAssigned(I)])),
   assert(rolesAssigned(I)).

act3:-
   ver(i,I),
   newCR(NewCR),
   editor(Editor),
   getEdsReply(NewCR, Editor, TrueFalse),
   assertz(log(getEdsReply, [rolesAssigned(I)], [edAccepts(I,TrueFalse)])),
   assert(edAccepts(I,TrueFalse)).

act4:-
   ver(i,I),
   techWriter1(TechWriter1),
   techWriter2(TechWriter2),
   makeRevAssign(TechWriter1, TechWriter2),
   I1 is I+1,
   assertz(log(makeRevAssign, [edAccepts(I,false), i(1)], [rolesAssigned(I1)])),
   assert(rolesAssigned(I1)),
   inc(i).



act5:-
   ver(i,I),
   manager(Manager),
   techWriter1(TechWriter1),
```

```
        techWriter2(TechWriter2),
        imposeAssign(Manager, TechWriter1, TechWriter2),
        assertz(log(imposeAssign, [edAccepts(l,false), i(2)], [assignMade])),
        assert(assignMade).

act6:-
        reviewer(Reviewer),
        notifyRev(Reviewer),
        assertz(log(notifyRev, [assignMade], [revNotified])),
        assert(revNotified).

act7:-
        editor(Editor),
        notifyEd(Editor),
        assertz(log(notifyEd, [revNotified], [edNotified])),
        assert(edNotified).

act8:-
        instantiate(document(0), Document),
        get_ent(docRepos, Document),
        assertz(log(getDoc, [edNotified], [Document])).

act9:-
        set(i,1),
        ver(i,l),
        instantiate(document(0), Document),
        instantiate(document(l), Document1),
        newCR(NewCR),
        editor(Editor),
        modDoc(Editor, Document, NewCR, Document1),
        assertz(log(modDoc, [Document], [Document1])),
        assert(Document1).

act10:-
        ver(i,l),
        instantiate(document(l), Document),
        instantiate(comments(l), Comments),
        newCR(NewCR),
        reviewer(Reviewer),
        reviewDoc(Reviewer, Document, NewCR, Comments, PassCom),
        assertz(log(reviewDoc, [Document, Comments, NewCR], [PassCom])),
        assert(PassCom).

act11:-
        ver(i,l),
        instantiate(document(l), Document),
        instantiate(comments(l), Comments),
        inc(i),
        ver(i,l1),
        instantiate(document(l1), Document1),
        editor(Editor),
        newCR(NewCR),
        modDocAgain(Editor, Document, Comments, NewCR, Document1),
```

```
    assertz(log(modDocAgain, [Document, Comments], [Document1])),
    assert(Document1).
    act12:-
    ver(i,l),
    instantiate(document(l), Document),
    put_ent(docRepos, Document, docSaved),
    assertz(log(putDoc, [Document], [docSaved])).

act13:-
    manager(Manager),
    document(Document),
    sendMsgToMgr(Manager, Document),
    assertz(log(sendMsgToMgr, [docSaved], [msgSent])),
    assert(msgSent).

/*********************** supporting model data ********************/

test(test1).
test(test2).
test(test3).
test(test4).
test(test5).
test(test6).
test(test7).
test(test8).
test(test9).
test(test10).
test(test11).
test(test12).
test(test13).

/*********************** entity definitions ********************/

techWriter1(ed).
techWriter2(paul).
manager(alan).
document(testReport).
newCR(cr_No_1).
comments(reviewNotes).
/*********************** initialize variables ********************/

initUserVars:-
    retractall(accepts(_)),
    retractall(rolesAssigned(_)),
    retractall(edAccepts(_,_)),
    retractall(assignMade),
    retractall(revNotified),
    retractall(edNotified),
    retractall(passReview),
    retractall(testReport(_)),
    retractall(reviewNotes(_)),
    retractall(docSaved),
    retractall(msgSent),
```

```
        retractall(editor(_)),
        retractall(reviewer(_)),
        retractall(store(_, _)),
        retractall(editor(_)),
        retractall(reviewer(_)),
        retractall(active(_)),
        assert(store(docRepos, [testReport(0)])).

/*********************** supporting functions ********************/

revNewCR(NewCR, Manager, TrueFalse):-
        create(file_edit_window, FEW, [200,50, 400,550], NewCR, true),
        write(Manager), write(', do you wish to accept the change request '),
        write(NewCR), write('? (y/n):'), read(YN), nl,
        (YN='y', TrueFalse='true'; TrueFalse='false'),
        destroy(FEW),
        write('~~~~~~~~~~~~~~~~~~~~~~~~~~~~~~~~~~~~~~~~~~~~~~~~~~~~~'), nl.

makeInitAssign(Manager, TechWriter1, TechWriter2):-
        write(Manager), write(', who do you wish to selelct as editor: '),
        write(TechWriter1), write(' or '), write( TechWriter2), nl,
        write('Enter name: '), read(Editor), nl,
        (TechWriter1=Editor,
        assert(editor(TechWriter1)), assert(reviewer(TechWriter2));
        TechWriter2=Editor,
        assert(editor(TechWriter2)), assert(reviewer(TechWriter1));
        write('Illegal name, make another choice'), nl,
        makeInitAssign(Manager, TechWriter1, TechWriter2)),
        write('~~~~~~~~~~~~~~~~~~~~~~~~~~~~~~~~~~~~~~~~~~~~~~~~~~~~~'), nl.

getEdsReply(NewCR, Editor, TrueFalse):-
        create(file_edit_window, FEW, [200,50, 400,550], NewCR, true),
        write(Editor), write(' will you accept the role of editor for '),
        write(NewCR), write('? (y/n):'), read(YN), nl,
        (YN='y', TrueFalse is 'true'; TrueFalse is 'false'),
        destroy(FEW),
        write('~~~~~~~~~~~~~~~~~~~~~~~~~~~~~~~~~~~~~~~~~~~~~~~~~~~~~'), nl.


makeRevAssign(TechWriter1, TechWriter2):-
        (editor(TechWriter1),
        retract(editor(TechWriter1)), assert(editor(TechWriter2)),
        retract(reviewer(TechWriter2)), assert(reviewer(TechWriter1));
        retract(editor(TechWriter2)),assert(editor(TechWriter1)),
        retract(reviewer(TechWriter1)), assert(reviewer(TechWriter2))
        ).

imposeAssign(Manager, TechWriter1, TechWriter2):-
        retractall(editor(_)),
        retractall(reviewer(_)),
        write(Manager), write(', who do you wish to select as editor: '),
        write(TechWriter1), write(' or '), write(TechWriter2), nl,
        write('Enter name: '), read(Editor),
```

```
(techWriter1(Editor),
 assert(editor(TechWriter1)), assert(reviewer(TechWriter2));
 techWriter2(Editor),
  assert(editor(TechWriter2)), assert(reviewer(TechWriter2));

 write('Illegal name, make another choice'), imposeAssign), nl,
 write('~~~~~~~~~~~~~~~~~~~~~~~~~~~~~~~~~~~~~~~~~~~~~~~~~~~~'), nl.

notifyRev(Reviewer):-
 write(Reviewer), write(', you have been selected to be reviewer'), nl,nl,
 write('~~~~~~~~~~~~~~~~~~~~~~~~~~~~~~~~~~~~~~~~~~~~~~~~~~~~'), nl.

notifyEd(Editor):-
 write(Editor), write(', you have been selected to be editor'), nl,nl,
 write('~~~~~~~~~~~~~~~~~~~~~~~~~~~~~~~~~~~~~~~~~~~~~~~~~~~~'), nl.

modDoc(Editor, Document, NewCR, Document1):-
 write(Editor), write(', please modify the document per the change request'), nl,
 create(file_edit_window, FEW1, [200,50, 400,550], NewCR, true),
 stripParen(Document,Doc),
 create(file_edit_window, FEW2, [400,50, 600,550], Doc, false),
 write('Press <ok.> when the changes are completed: '),
 read('ok'), nl,
 stripParen(Document1,Doc1),
 save_window(FEW2, Doc1),
 destroy(FEW1),
 destroy(FEW2),
 write('~~~~~~~~~~~~~~~~~~~~~~~~~~~~~~~~~~~~~~~~~~~~~~~~~~~~'), nl.

modDocAgain(Editor, Document, Comments, NewCR, Document1):-
 write(Editor), write(', please modify the document per the new comments'), nl,
 create(file_edit_window, FEW1, [200,50, 400,550], NewCR, true),
 stripParen(Document,Doc),
 create(file_edit_window, FEW2, [400,50, 600,550], Doc, false),
 stripParen(Comments,Com),
 create(file_edit_window, FEW3, [600,50, 800,550], Com, false),
 write('Press <ok.> when the changes are completed: '),
 read('ok'), nl,
 stripParen(Document1,Doc1),
 save_window(FEW2, Doc1),
 destroy(FEW1),
 destroy(FEW2),
 destroy(FEW3),
 write('~~~~~~~~~~~~~~~~~~~~~~~~~~~~~~~~~~~~~~~~~~~~~~~~~~~~'), nl.

reviewDoc(Reviewer, Document, NewCR, Comments, PassCom):-
 write(Reviewer), write(', please review the document as per the change request'), nl,
 write('Add any comments to the comments window'), nl,
 create(file_edit_window, FEW1, [200,50, 400,550], NewCR, true),
 stripParen(Comments, Com),
 stripParen(Document,Doc),
 fopen('comment', "w+", _),
 create(file_edit_window, FEW2, [400,50, 600,550], 'comment', false),
```

```
create(file_edit_window, FEW3, [600,50, 800,550], Doc, true),
write('Press y if review passes, press n otherwise: ' ), read(Pass),nl,
(Pass='y', PassCom='passReview';
PassCom=Comments, save_window(FEW2, Com)),
close('comment'),
destroy(FEW1),
destroy(FEW2),
destroy(FEW3),
write('~~~~~~~~~~~~~~~~~~~~~~~~~~~~~~~~~~~~~~~~~~~~~~~~~~~~~'), nl.

sendMsgToMgr(Manager, Document):-
    write(Manager), write(', the update of '), write(Document), write(' is now complete'), nl,nl,
    write('~~~~~~~~~~~~~~~~~~~~~~~~~~~~~~~~~~~~~~~~~~~~~~~~~~~~~'), nl.
```

A.3.2   Typical Program Output

The following listing illustrates an interactive session with ProSim, using the process controller program of Section A.1 with the process model of Section A.3.1. The
process model is defined in Figures 2-20, 2-21, and 2-22 as translated into the above
Prolog statements. As in the listing of the previous example, all user input text is in
bold. *alan* is the name of the manager while *paul* and *ed* are the names of the technical writers.

In running this program, text windows containing the documents (e.g. *cr_no_1*)
also appear on the screen. These are not shown below.

```
?- init.
Enter file name of process model: docUpdate.
~~~~~~~~~~~~~~~~~~~~~~~~~~~~~~~~~~~~~~~~~~~~~~~~~
~~~~~~~~~~~~~~~~~~~~~~~~~~~~~~~~~~~~~~~~~~~~~~~~~
alan, do you wish to accept the change request cr_No_1? (y/n):y.
~~~~~~~~~~~~~~~~~~~~~~~~~~~~~~~~~~~~~~~~~~~~~~~~~
alan, who do you wish to selelct as editor: ed or paul
Enter name: ed.
~~~~~~~~~~~~~~~~~~~~~~~~~~~~~~~~~~~~~~~~~~~~~~~~~
ed will you accept the role of editor for cr_No_1? (y/n):n.
~~~~~~~~~~~~~~~~~~~~~~~~~~~~~~~~~~~~~~~~~~~~~~~~~
paul will you accept the role of editor for cr_No_1? (y/n):n.
~~~~~~~~~~~~~~~~~~~~~~~~~~~~~~~~~~~~~~~~~~~~~~~~~
alan, who do you wish to select as editor: ed or paul
Enter name: ed.
~~~~~~~~~~~~~~~~~~~~~~~~~~~~~~~~~~~~~~~~~~~~~~~~~
paul, you have been selected to be reviewer
~~~~~~~~~~~~~~~~~~~~~~~~~~~~~~~~~~~~~~~~~~~~~~~~~
ed, you have been selected to be editor
~~~~~~~~~~~~~~~~~~~~~~~~~~~~~~~~~~~~~~~~~~~~~~~~~
ed, please modify the document per the change request
Press <ok.> when the changes are completed: ok.
~~~~~~~~~~~~~~~~~~~~~~~~~~~~~~~~~~~~~~~~~~~~~~~~~
paul, please review the document as per the change request
Add any comments to the comments window
```

Press y if review passes, press n otherwise: **n.**

~~~~~~

ed, please modify the document per the new comments
Press <ok.> when the changes are completed: **ok.**

~~~~~~

paul, please review the document as per the change request
Add any comments to the comments window
Press y if review passes, press n otherwise: **y.**

~~~~~~

alan, the update of testReport is now complete

~~~~~~

All activities have been completed

Appendix B
The Process Verification Program

The following listing is for the process verification program described in Chapter 2. It is written in Prolog for the Macintosh [AAIS 91]. The program essentially consists of a set of driver functions that are common to any process which is being verified, a set of process-specific clauses, in this case for the *codeDevel* process, and a set of *log* statements that are generated during the execution of the process. As verification proceeds, the program checks the validity of the activities, as reflected though the log statements, against the clauses that define the process. Unlike the process enaction program of appendix A, the listing in this appendix includes both the verification program and the clauses that represent the specific process (*codeDevel*). While these process-specific clauses were written by hand, it is foreseen that they could be generated directly from ProNet diagrams, thus allowing for automated verification.

When the verification program finds an inconsistency, this inconsistency is identified and the program terminates. As an example of a process "error" one of the *log* statements below was commented out of the set of *log* statements that define the process history (see Section 4.1 for description of *log* statements).

This program can be downloaded through Internet's anonymous ftp facility. The ftp address is: *ftp.sei.cmu.edu*. The files are located in the directory: *pub/procauto/execProcs/ProSim.SEI*

The files can also be downloaded through the World Wide Web [Dougherty 94]. Using this approach, the Universal Resource Locator is: *http://www.sei.cmu.edu/SEI/topics/process_auto/ProcAuto.html*

```
/********************** driver functions **********************/

startVerify(FinalEnt):-
                initUserVars,
                assert(FinalEnt),
                verify.


set(X,I):-
/* initialize version number X to value K */
                retractall(ver(X,_)),
                assert(ver(X,I)).
```

```
dec(I,J):-
/* increment version number K by 1 */
                    retract(ver(I,J)),
                    J1 is J-1,
                    assert(ver(I,J1)).

del_ent(Store, Val, Desc):-
/* inverse of put - deletes an element that the put entered into the store*/
                    retract(store(Store, Val_list)),
                    (member(Val, Val_list); escape(Store, Val, Desc)),
                    delete(Val, Val_list, [], Val_list1),
                    assert(store(Store, Val_list1)),
                    assert(Val).

delete(Val1, [Val1|Val_list], Val_listA, X):-
                    delete(Val1, Val_list, Val_listA, X).

delete(Val1, [Val|Val_list], Val_listA, X):-
                    delete(Val1, Val_list, [Val|Val_listA],X).

delete(_, [], Val_list, Val_list).

rem_ent(Store, Val, Val2, Desc):-
/* inverse of get - tests if Val in Store then deletes retrieved copy*/
                    Val,
                    store(Store, Val_list),
                    (member(Val, Val_list); escape(Store, Val, Desc)),
                    retract(Val),
                    assert(Val2).

escape(Store, Val, Desc):-
/* default if del-ent or rem-ent fail */
                    write(Val),
                    write(' is not contained in '),
                    write(Store),nl,
                    write('Cannot perform operation: '),
                    write(Desc), nl,
                    !,
                    abort.

instantiate(VarIn, VarOut):-
                    instantiate1(VarIn,VarOut),
                    !.

instantiate1(VarIn,VarOut):-
/* instantiates a subscripted variable e.g., doc(1) => report(1) */
                    VarIn =.. [Var1, I],
                    Var2 =.. [Var1, X],
                    Var2,
                    string(X),
                    VarOut =.. [X,I].
```

```prolog
instantiate1(VarIn,_):-
                        write('Could not instantiate variable '), write(VarIn),
                        abort.

/********************* verify  predicates **************************/

verify:-
                        ver(i,I),
                        ?(sourcesUpdated),
                        instantiate(codeModule1(I), CodeModule1),
                        instantiate(codeModule2(I), CodeModule2),
                        del_ent(sourceRepos, CodeModule1, 'putSourceCode'),
                        del_ent(sourceRepos, CodeModule2, 'putSourceCode'),
                        retract(log(putSourceCode, [testPasses(I,true)], [sourcesUpdated])),
                        assert(testPasses(I,true)),
                        retractall(sourcesUpdated),
                        write('********* putSourceCode is OK **********'), nl,
                        verify.

verify:-
                        ver(i,I),
                        ?(sourcesUpdated),
                        not(log(putSourceCode, [testPasses(I,true)], [sourcesUpdated])),
                        write('********* putSourceCode not completed **********'), nl,
                        abort.

verify:-
                        ver(i,I),
                        I1 is I+1,
                        instantiate(codeModule1(I1), CodeModuleA),
                        CodeModuleA,
/*                      retract(log(modifyCode1, [X], [CodeModuleA])),
                        asserta(X), */
                        retract(log(modifyCode1, _, [CodeModuleA])),
                        instantiate(codeModule1(I), CodeModuleB),
                        asserta(CodeModuleB),
                        retractall(CodeModuleA),
                        write('********* modifyCode1 is OK **********'), nl,
                        verify.
verify:-
                        ver(i,I),
                        I1 is I+1,
                        instantiate(codeModule1(I1), CodeModuleA),
                        CodeModuleA,
                        not(log(modifyCode1, _, [CodeModuleA])),
                        write('********* modifyCode1 not completed **********'), nl,
                        abort.

verify:-
                        ver(i,I),
                        I1 is I+1,
                        instantiate(codeModule2(I1), CodeModuleA),
                        CodeModuleA,
```

```
                retract(log(modifyCode2, [X], [CodeModuleA])),
                asserta(X),
                instantiate(codeModule2(I), CodeModuleB),
                asserta(CodeModuleB),
                retractall(CodeModuleA),
                write('********* modifyCode2 is OK **********'), nl,
                verify.

verify:-
                ver(i,l),
                l1 is l+1,
                instantiate(codeModule2(l1), CodeModuleA),
                CodeModuleA,
                not(log(modifyCode2, _, [CodeModuleA])),
                write('********** modifyCode2 not completed **********'), nl,
                abort.

verify:-
                ?(sourcesRetrieved(1)),
                retract(log(getSourceCode, [startCodeMod], [sourcesRetrieved(1)])),
                instantiate(codeModule1(1), CodeModule1),
                instantiate(codeModule2(1), CodeModule2),
                rem_ent(sourceRepos, CodeModule1, startCodeMod, 'getSourceCode'),
                rem_ent(sourceRepos, CodeModule2, '', 'getSourceCode'),
                assert(startCodeMod),
                retractall(sourcesRetrieved(1)),
                write('********* getSourceCode  is OK *********'), nl.

verify:-
                ?(sourcesRetrieved(1)),
                not(log(getSourceCode, [startCodeMod], [sourcesRetrieved(1)])),
                write('********* getSourceCode  not completed *********'), nl,
                abort.
verify:-
                ver(i,l),
                (?(testPasses(l,true)), Var=testPasses(l,true);
                           ?(testPasses(l,false)), Var=testPasses(l,false)),
                retract(log(buildAndTestCode, [CodeModule1, CodeModule2], [Var])),
                assert(CodeModule1),
                assert(CodeModule2),
                retractall(Var),
                dec(i,l),
                write('********* buildAndTestCode is OK **********'), nl,
                verify.

verify:-
                ver(i,l),
                (?(testPasses(l,true)), Var=testPasses(l,true);
                               ?(testPasses(l,false)), Var=testPasses(l,false)),
                not(log(buildAndTestCode, _, [Var])),
                write('********* buildAndTestCode not completed *******'), nl,
                abort.
```

```
/*********************** variable initialization ********************/

initUserVars:-
                    retractall(startCodeMod),
                    retractall(sourcesRetrieved(_)),
                    retractall(module1(_)),
                    retractall(module2(_)),
                    retractall(testPasses(_,_)),
                    retractall(sourcesUpdated),
                    set(i,3).

sourcesRetrieved(0).
module1(0).
module2(0).
testPasses(0,false).
codeModule1(module1).
codeModule2(module2).
log(nul, nul, nul).

/*********************** process history ********************/

log(getSourceCode, [startCodeMod], [sourcesRetrieved(1)]).
/*log(modifyCode1, [sourcesRetrieved(1)], [module1(2)]). */
log(modifyCode2, [sourcesRetrieved(1)], [module2(2)]).
log(buildAndTestCode, [module1(2), module2(2)], [testPasses(2, false)]).
log(modifyCode1, [testPasses(2, false)], [module1(3)]).
log(modifyCode2, [testPasses(2, false)], [module2(3)]).
log(buildAndTestCode, [module1(3), module2(3)], [testPasses(3, true)]).
log(putSourceCode, [testPasses(3, true)], [sourcesUpdated]).

store(sourceRepos, [module2(3), module2(1), module1(3), module1(1)]).

/************************* end ************************/
```

The above clauses under *process history* heading were generated from an execution of the *codeDevel* process defined in Appendix A. The only alteration that was made was to comment out the second *log* statement, indicating that this activity was not correctly completed. On running the verification program with this modification, the following output is generated:

```
********* putSourceCode is OK *********
********* buildAndTestCode is OK *********
********* modifyCode1 is OK *********
********* modifyCode2 is OK *********
********* buildAndTestCode is OK *********
********* modifyCode1 not completed *********
```

Appendix C
Vendor Information on PCEs

The following is a list of commercial products that support process automation for software development or business workflow. This list is for tools that provide the explicit capability to define general processes. Thus it does not include the large number of tools that help manage work products but in which there is weak or no explicit capability to define process. For a review of other products (with a focus on document management) [Ayre 94] should be consulted.

Life*Flow
Company: Computer Resources International A/S
245 146th Place SE
Suite 270
Bellevue, WA 98007
Contact: Lynn Campbell
Phone: 206-643-4773
Platforms supported: Sun SPARC, IBM RS/6000, HP9000, PC Windows (client mode).

InConcert
Company: Xerox Corporation
Advanced Information Technology
4 Cambridge Center, 4th floor
Cambridge, MA 02142
Contact: Debra Leigh Henry
Phone: 617-499-4488
Platforms supported: Sun SPARCstations and compatibles, IBM RS/6000 series, HP 9000, and PCs and compatibles (386 and 486) (client mode).

ProcessWeaver
Company: Cap Gemini America
1114 Ave. of the Americas
29th floor
New York, NY 10036
Contact: Larry Proctor
Phone (US): 1-800-759-8255 (pin: 513-3640)
Platforms supported: Unix platforms including HP, Dec, Sun SPARC, IBM RS/6000. The Agenda (client mode) also runs under MicroSoft Windows.

ProcessWise
Company: ICL
ProcessWise Portfolio Center
ICL Waterside Park
Cain Road
Bracknell, Berkshire, RG12 1FA
United Kingdom
Contact: Jane Burns
Phone (UK): 44-0344-711795
Platforms supported: ICL DRS6000, ICL Series 39, Sun, Bull DPX20, IBM RS/6000.

ProSLCSE Vision
Company: International Software Systems Inc.,
9430 Research Blvd., Echelon IV, Suite 250,
Austin TX 78759
Contact: Cecil Martin
Phone: 512-338-5729
Platforms supported: Sun SPARC.

SynerVision
Company: Hewlett-Packard Company
Software Engineering Systems Division
3404 East Harmony St., MS 7
Fort Collins, Colorado 80525
Contact: Dave Pugmire, Process Program Manager
Phone: 303-229-3265
Platforms supported: HP9000, Sun SPARC.

Appendix D
Listing of SynerVision Experiment Script

The following script is for the SynerVision implementation of the experimental model. It is provided a) to illustrate the programming that was required to implement the model and b) as a basis for others who may wish to explore SynerVision's capabilities. Each *AUTOMATIC_ACTION* in the script corresponds to one of the activities in the task hierarchy shown at the beginning of the script. Also provided at the end of the script is a listing of the function *getTerm* that is used in the process model. Clearly the script needs to be modified to be used on other machines, as path names will be different. In addition, the variables *manager*, *person1*, etc., instantiated in the first *AUTOMATIC_ACTION*, need to be defined in SynerVision's *schema* file. This program can be downloaded through Internet's anonymous ftp facility. The ftp address is: *ftp.sei.cmu.edu*. The files are located in the directory: *pub/procauto/execProcs/SynerVision.SEI*

ProcessWeaver defines its graphical model as a series of ASCII files. While these are readable, they are machine-generated, quite lengthy, and thus not provided below. However, they can also be downloaded, in this case from the directory: *pub/procauto/execProcs/ProcessWeaver.SEI*

```
# This is the task hierarchy for the Update Document project
##########################################################

TASK "Initiate Project"
InitProj=$last_TASKID

CHILDREN_BEGIN

        TASK "Review New CR"
        RevNewCR=$last_TASKID

        TASK "Identify Agents For Roles"
        IdenAgForRl=$last_TASKID

        CHILDREN_BEGIN

                TASK "Make Revised Assignments"
                ReviseAssign=$last_TASKID
```

```
                    TASK "Impose Assignments"
                    ImposeAssign=$last_TASKID

                    TASK "Get Editors Reply"
                    GetEdReply=$last_TASKID

                    TASK "Notify Editor"
                    NotifyEd=$last_TASKID

                    TASK "Notify Reviewer"
                    NotifyRev=$last_TASKID

                    TASK "Check If Person A is Editor"
                    CheckA=$last_TASKID

                    TASK "Make Initial Assignments"
                    InitAssign=$last_TASKID

            CHILDREN_END

            TASK "Update Document"
            UpdateDoc=$last_TASKID

              CHILDREN_BEGIN

                    TASK "Get Report"
                    GetReport=$last_TASKID

                    TASK "Initial Mods"
                    InitMod=$last_TASKID

                    TASK "Modify Report"
                    ModReport=$last_TASKID

                    TASK "Review Report"
                    RevReport=$last_TASKID

                    TASK "Put Report"
                    PutReport=$last_TASKID

              CHILDREN_END

CHILDREN_END

# Each AUTOMATIC_ACTION below is associated with one of the tasks above
####################################################################

AUTOMATIC_ACTION -t $InitProj Status New Inprogress perform <<EOF
# Initialize the variables for the project
      ATTRIB -i -v manager "Paul"
      ATTRIB -i -v person1 "Leonard"
      ATTRIB -i -v person2 "Alan"
      ATTRIB -i -v report "TestReport"
```

```
        ATTRIB -i -v CR "CR_No_1"
        ATTRIB -i -v notes "ReviewNotes"
        ATTRIB -i -v inc 0
        ATTRIB -i -v -t $RevNewCR "Executing=Running_Foreground"
EOF


AUTOMATIC_ACTION -t $RevNewCR Status New Inprogress perform <<EOF
# Send a message to the manager requesting him to decide on the acceptability of the
# modification. If the modification is unacceptable, the project terminates here.
        CR=\'GET_ATTRIB CR\'
        report=\'GET_ATTRIB report\'
        manager=\'GET_ATTRIB manager\'
        display=\'getTerm \$manager\'
        DISPLAY=\$display
        export DISPLAY
        cd /users/amc/SVdata
        get -e s.\$report>temp
        chmod a-w \$report
        emacs \$CR &
        emacs \$report &
        result=\'svprompt -p "\$manager, please review the acceptability of change request \$CR
per the document \$report then press either the Accept or Reject button" -L -d "Accept
Reject"\'
# mark this task completed
        ATTRIB -i -v -t $RevNewCR "Status=Completed"
        if [ \$result = "Accept" ]; then
# start the next task
            ATTRIB -i -v -t $IdenAgForRI "Executing=Running_Foreground"
        else
# mark parent task as abandonded
            ATTRIB -i -v -t $InitProj "Status=Abandoned"
        fi
        delta s.\$report>temp
EOF


AUTOMATIC_ACTION -t $IdenAgForRI Status New Inprogress perform <<EOF
# This task is for continuity -- it has no action except to call to a lower-level task
        ATTRIB -i -v -t $InitAssign "Executing=Running_Foreground"
EOF


AUTOMATIC_ACTION -t $UpdateDoc Status New Inprogress perform <<EOF
# This task is for continuity -- it has no action except to call to a lower-level task
        ATTRIB -i -v -t $GetReport "Executing=Running_Foreground"
EOF


AUTOMATIC_ACTION -t $InitAssign Status New Inprogress perform <<EOF
# The manager makes an initial assignment of the proposed editor,and by default, also the
# reviewer.
        report=\'GET_ATTRIB report\'
        manager=\'GET_ATTRIB manager\'
        personA=\'GET_ATTRIB person1\'
        personB=\'GET_ATTRIB person2\'
        display=\'getTerm \$manager\'
```

```
        DISPLAY=\$display
        assign=\'svprompt -p "\$manager, please make an initial assignment of who
will edit the report" \$report" -L -d "\$personA
\$personB"\'
        if [ \$assign = \$personA ]; then
            ATTRIB -i -v -t $InitProj editor \$personA
            ATTRIB -i -v -t $InitProj reviewer \$personB
        else
            ATTRIB -i -v -t $InitProj editor \$personB
            ATTRIB -i -v -t $InitProj reviewer \$personA
        fi
        ATTRIB -i -v -t $InitAssign "Status=Completed"
        ATTRIB -i -v -t $GetEdReply "Executing=Running_Foreground"
EOF

AUTOMATIC_ACTION -t $ReviseAssign Status New Inprogress perform <<EOF
# As a result of the first person refusing the editor role, the second person is chosen to be
# the editor.
        personA=\'GET_ATTRIB reviewer\'
        personB=\'GET_ATTRIB editor\'
        ATTRIB -i -v -t $InitProj editor \$personA
        ATTRIB -i -v -t $InitProj reviewer \$personB
        ATTRIB -i -v -t $ReviseAssign "Status=Completed"
        ATTRIB -i -v -t $CheckA "Status=New"
        ATTRIB -i -v -t $GetEdReply "Status=New"
        ATTRIB -i -v -t $GetEdReply "Executing=Running_Foreground"
EOF

        AUTOMATIC_ACTION -t $ImposeAssign Status New Inprogress perform <<EOF
# As a result of the secon person refusing the editor role, the manager must decide who will be
# the editor (and then by default, who will be reviewer).
        manager=\'GET_ATTRIB manager\'
        personA=\'GET_ATTRIB person1\'
        personB=\'GET_ATTRIB person2\'
        display=\'getTerm \$manager\'
        DISPLAY=\$display
        assign=\'svprompt -p "\$manager, both staff members have refused the editing assign.
Please assign either \$personA or \$personB to be editor" -L -d "\$personA
\$personB"\'
        if [ \$assign = \$personA ]; then
            ATTRIB -i -v -t $InitProj editor \$personA
            ATTRIB -i -v -t $InitProj reviewer \$personB
        else
            ATTRIB -i -v -t $InitProj editor \$personB
            ATTRIB -i -v -t $InitProj reviewer \$personA
        fi
        ATTRIB -i -v -t $NotifyEd "Executing=Running_Foreground"
        ATTRIB -i -v -t $NotifyRev "Executing=Running_Foreground"
        ATTRIB -i -v -t $ImposeAssign "Status=Completed"
EOF

AUTOMATIC_ACTION -t $NotifyEd Status New Inprogress perform <<EOF
# The person selected to be editor is notified of the manager's choice.
```

```
      report=\'GET_ATTRIB report\'
      personA=\'GET_ATTRIB editor\'
      display=\'getTerm \$personA\'
      DISPLAY=\$display
      svprompt -p "\$personA, you have been selected to be editor for report \$report"
      ATTRIB -i -v -t $NotifyEd "Status=Completed"
EOF


AUTOMATIC_ACTION -t $NotifyRev Status New Inprogress perform <<EOF
# The person selected to be reviewer is notified of the manager's choice.
      report=\'GET_ATTRIB report\'
      personB=\'GET_ATTRIB reviewer\'
      display=\'getTerm \$personB\'
      DISPLAY=\$display
      svprompt -p "\$personB, you have been selected to be reviewer for report \$report"
      ATTRIB -i -v -t $UpdateDoc "Executing=Running_Foreground"
      ATTRIB -i -v -t $NotifyRev "Status=Completed"
      ATTRIB -i -v -t $IdenAgForRl "Status=Completed"
EOF


AUTOMATIC_ACTION -t $CheckA Status New Inprogress perform <<EOF
# Select path to next task depending on whether this is the first of second request for a
# volunteer to be editor.
      report=\'GET_ATTRIB report\'
      reviewer=\'GET_ATTRIB reviewer\'
      inc=\'GET_ATTRIB inc\'
      personA=\'GET_ATTRIB editor\'
      display=\'getTerm \$personA\'
      DISPLAY=\$display
      if [ \$inc = 0 ]; then
            ATTRIB -i -v -t $InitProj inc 1
            reviewer=\'GET_ATTRIB reviewer\'
            svprompt -p "I will check to see if \$reviewer will be editor"
            ATTRIB -i -v -t $ReviseAssign "Executing=Running_Foreground"
      else
            manager=\'GET_ATTRIB manager\'
            reportA=\'GET_ATTRIB report\'
            svprompt -p "\$manager will have to decide who will update \$report"
            ATTRIB -i -v -t $ImposeAssign "Executing=Running_Foreground"
      fi
      ATTRIB -i -v -t $CheckA "Status=Completed"
EOF


AUTOMATIC_ACTION -t $GetEdReply Status New Inprogress perform <<EOF
# Send message asking if person will volunteer to be editor. Depending on the result, select
# appropriate next task.
      CR=\'GET_ATTRIB CR\'
      report=\'GET_ATTRIB report\'
      personA=\'GET_ATTRIB editor\'
      reportA=\'GET_ATTRIB report\'
      display=\'getTerm \$personA\'
      DISPLAY=\$display
      reply=\'svprompt -p "\$personA are you willing to act as editor for \$report
```

```
per the change request \$CR" -L -d "accept
reject"\'
     if [ \$reply = "accept" ]; then
          ATTRIB -i -v -t $NotifyRev "Executing=Running_Foreground"
     else
          ATTRIB -i -v -t $CheckA "Executing=Running_Foreground"
     fi
     ATTRIB -i -v -t $GetEdReply "Status=Completed"
EOF


AUTOMATIC_ACTION -t $GetReport Status New Inprogress perform <<EOF
# Retrieve report form repository.
     report=\'GET_ATTRIB report\'
     CR=\'GET_ATTRIB CR\'
     cd /users/amc/SVdata
     get -e s.\$report>temp
     chmod a-w \$CR
     ATTRIB -i -v -t $InitMod "Executing=Running_Foreground"
     ATTRIB -i -v -t $GetReport "Status=Completed"
EOF


AUTOMATIC_ACTION -t $InitMod Status New Inprogress perform <<EOF
# Request the the editor updates the document as requested in the change request.
     editor=\'GET_ATTRIB editor\'
     report=\'GET_ATTRIB report\'
     CR=\'GET_ATTRIB CR\'
     display=\'getTerm \$editor\'
     DISPLAY=\$display
     export DISPLAY
     cd /users/amc/SVdata
     chmod a+w \$report
     emacs \$report &
     emacs \$CR &
     svprompt -p "\$editor, please update \$report, as
requested in the chnage request \$CR. When you are fininshed,
press the OK button"
     ATTRIB -i -v -t $RevReport "Executing=Running_Foreground"
     ATTRIB -i -v -t $InitMod "Status=Completed"
EOF


AUTOMATIC_ACTION -t $ModReport Status New Inprogress perform <<EOF
# A a result of the document review, the document still needs revision. The editor is requested
# to make these revisions.
     editor=\'GET_ATTRIB editor\'
     report=\'GET_ATTRIB report\'
     CR=\'GET_ATTRIB CR\'
     ReviewNotes=\'GET_ATTRIB notes\'
     display=\'getTerm \$editor\'
     DISPLAY=\$display
     export DISPLAY
     cd /users/amc/SVdata
     chmod a+w \$report
     emacs \$report &
```

```
    emacs \$CR &
    chmod a-w \$ReviewNotes
    emacs \$ReviewNotes &
    svprompt -p "\$editor, unfortunately your revisions to \$report did not pass review.
Please modify the document as indicated by the comments in \$ReviewNotes.
When you are finished, press the OK button."
    ATTRIB -i -v -t $RevReport "Status=New"
    ATTRIB -i -v -t $RevReport "Executing=Running_Foreground"
    ATTRIB -i -v -t $ModReport "Status=Completed"
EOF


AUTOMATIC_ACTION -t $RevReport Status New Inprogress perform <<EOF
# The reviewer checks the revised document against the change request. This can result in
# the document passing or the review or requiring further work.
    reviewer=\'GET_ATTRIB reviewer\'
    report=\'GET_ATTRIB report\'
    CR=\'GET_ATTRIB CR\'
    ReviewNotes=\'GET_ATTRIB notes\'
    display=\'getTerm \$reviewer\'
    DISPLAY=\$display
    export DISPLAY
    cd /users/amc/SVdata
    chmod a-w \$report
    emacs \$report &
    emacs \$CR &
    chmod a+w \$ReviewNotes
    emacs \$ReviewNotes &
    reply=\'svprompt -p "\$reviewer, please review this updated version of \$report,
using the change request \$CR, and comments in \$ReviewNotes. Any additional comments
should also go into \$ReviewNotes." -L -d "DocOK
NeedsFurtherWork"\'
    if [ \$reply = "DocOK" ]; then
        chmod a-w \$ReviewNotes
        ATTRIB -i -v -t $PutReport "Executing=Running_Foreground"
    else
        ATTRIB -i -v -t $ModReport "Status=New"
        ATTRIB -i -v -t $ModReport "Executing=Running_Foreground"
    fi
    ATTRIB -i -v -t $RevReport "Status=Completed"
EOF


AUTOMATIC_ACTION -t $PutReport Status New Inprogress perform <<EOF
# The updated document is saved in the repository and the manager is informed of completion
# of the project
    manager=\'GET_ATTRIB manager\'
    report=\'GET_ATTRIB report\'
    display=\'getTerm \$manager\'
    cd /users/amc/SVdata
    delta s.\$report>temp
    DISPLAY=\$display
    svprompt -p "\$manager, the report \$report has been successfully updated"
    ATTRIB -i -v -t $UpdateDoc "Status=Completed"
    ATTRIB -i -v -t $InitProj "Status=Completed"
```

```
EOF
```

The following is a listing of the function getTerm used in the above script.

```
#Given a user's name, return the display they use

user_name=$1
( grep $user_name | awk -F/t '{print $3}' ) <<EOF
Proper Name Login Display
--------------------------------
Alan Christie amc bs
Paul Zarella pfz ncday:0.0
Leonard Green lsg ncday:0.0
EOF
```

Appendix E
Terminology and Concepts

This appendix provides an overview of some of the process-related terminology and concepts used in the body of the report. Definitions of basic terms have been extracted from [Feiler 92] and are used with the same meaning as in that document. However, there are other terms used in the report that need to be explained more fully, since these terms have not gained general acceptance. This appendix also relates some of the process concepts discussed to the process categories defined in [NIST 93]. [Osterweil 87] also provides a good explanation of concepts in this area.

E.1 Basic Terminology

Some basic process-related definitions, extracted from [Feiler 92] are given below.

Process: *A set of partially ordered steps intended to reach a goal.*
 While the term process is used in many different contexts, the context for this definition is software. For software development, the goal is production or enhancement of software products or the provision of services. Other examples are the software maintenance process, the acceptance testing process, or the process development process.

Process automation: *The use of machine process agents in process enactment.*
Here the use of the machine agent is facilitated by a fully-developed process definition embodied in a suitable process program.
 In the body of the book, the term *process automation* is also used in a more general sense. It is used when dealing with the broader organizational context in which the process-centered framework implemented (as in the title of the book).

Process definition: *The implementation of a process design in the form of a partially ordered set of process steps that is enactable.*

At the lower end of abstraction, each process step may be further refined into more detailed process steps. A process definition may consist of (sub)process definitions that can be enacted concurrently. Process definitions whose level of abstraction are refined fully are referred to as complete or fit for enactment. Completeness, however, depends on context since a definition that is complete for one process agent may not be for another. A process definition may be for a class of projects, a specific project team, or an individual professional.

Enactable process: *An instance of a process definition that includes all the elements required for enactment.*
An enactable process consists of a process definition, required process inputs, assigned enactment agents and resources, an initial enactment state, an initial enactment agent and continuation and termination capabilities. A process that lacks any of these capabilities is not enactable.

Process model: *An abstract representation of a process architecture, design, or definition.*
Process models are process elements at the architectural, design, or definitions level, whose abstraction captures those elements of a process relevant to the modeling. Any representation of the process is a process model. Process models are used where use of the complete process is undesirable or impractical. A process model can be analyzed, validated and, if enacted, can simulate the modelled process. Process models may be used to assist in process analysis, to aid in process understanding, or to predict process behavior.

The process examples discussed in Chapter 2 are instances of process models built for a specific applications, and are described using the graphical process notation ProNet.

Process program: *A process definition which is suitably designed and instantiated for enactment by machine.*
Process programs must be designed to fit the particular computing environmental needs for format and generally be tested, debugged, and modified much like computer programs

E.2 Process-Related Concepts

Two related concepts are used throughout this book: process-centered framework (PCF) and process-centered environment (PCE). These terms are defined below and their relationships to other process terms are illustrated through the Entity-Relation model of Figure E.1. These definitions attempt to capture the spirit of the concepts *framework* and *environment* as defined in [Brown 93b]. We also introduce below the term *process template*.

Process centered framework (PCF): *A PCF is a software product that provides the functionality necessary for the definition and enactment of process.*
It includes a process enactment language, mechanisms for process enactment, means to invoke tools, support for communications (between persons and tools), and capabilities to support the debugging the process models described within the process enactment language.

Process-centered environment (PCE): *A PCE is a software product that includes the facilities of a PCF, and also includes application tools.*
Examples of applications that these tools may support are: metrics collection, project management, and software development.

Process template: *A process template is a process program in which the variables have not been instantiated.*

Both a PCF and a PCE must have certain basic functionalities, such as a supporting a process programming language, while only a PCE will have an end-user application as part of the product. ProcessWeaver (Version 1.2) is a PCF since it does not have any application tools embedded in it. On the other hand SynerVision may be considered to be a PCE since it has some end-user applications embedded in it. Either a PCF or a PCE can invoke end-user application tools to support a particular process and this can be seen in Figure E.1.

E.3 Relationship to the NIST/ECMA Reference Model

The report *Reference Model for Frameworks of Software Engineering Environments* [NIST 93] defines a conceptual model that is relevant to the discussions in this appendix. It partitions services needed by a Software Engineering Environment into seven categories. The sixth category, *process management,* is then structured into six process-related services: *development, enactment, visibility, monitoring, transaction,* and *resource.* The [NIST 93] process management categories are similar to those described in Table 3.1 (i.e., *development, enactment, debugging, resource,* and *communication*), that were found to be a useful set of categories in the investigations of SynerVision and ProcessWeaver. A new category, not found in the [NIST 93] model, is *debugging,* while the NIST model defined the category *transaction* which was not needed since neither SynerVision nor ProcessWeaver had mechanisms to support the concept.The NIST category of

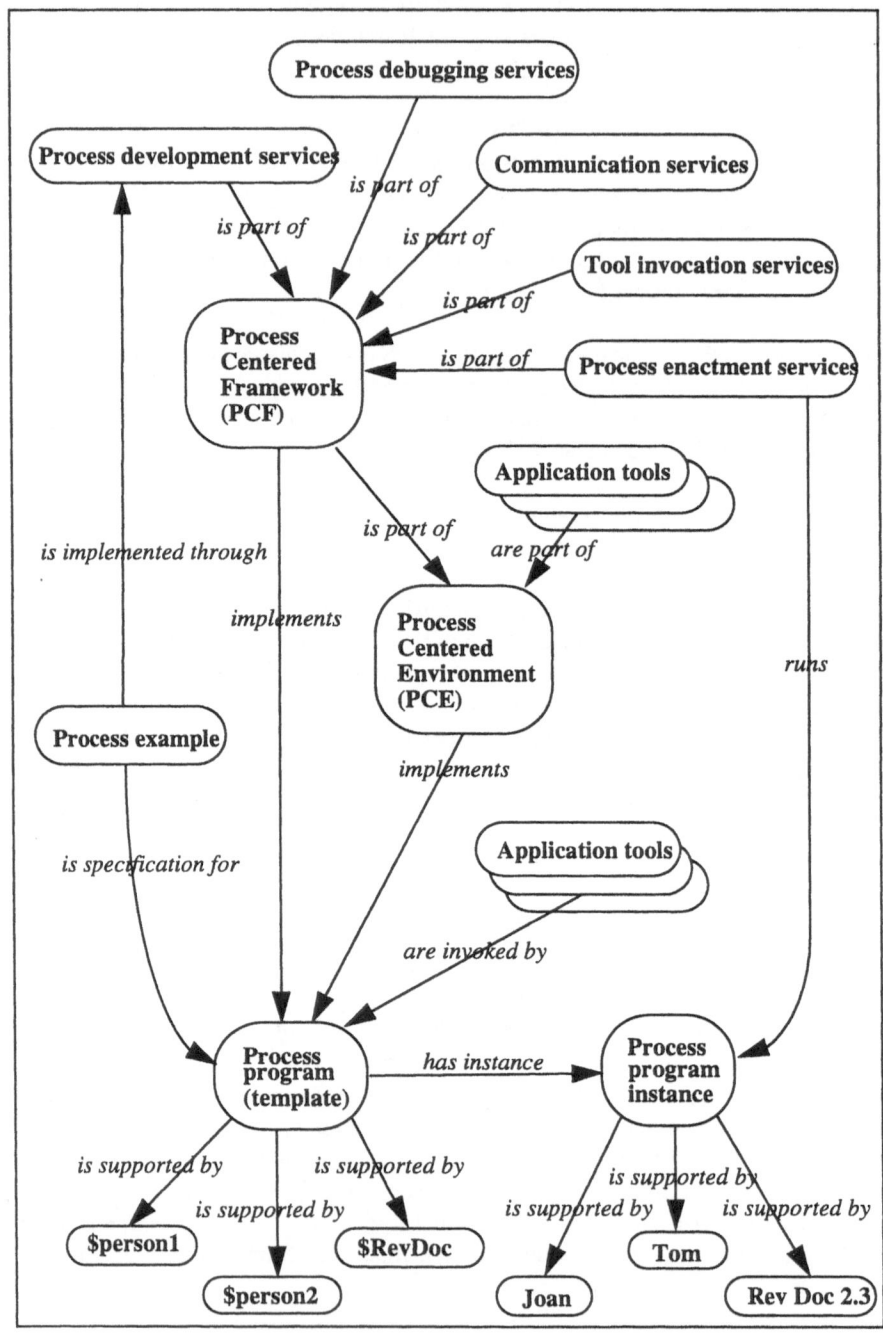

Fig. E.1. Relationship between process enactment concepts

monitoring is similar to the categories of *communication*. A correlation between the NIST process service categories and the elements of Table 3.7 is shown in Table E.1.

Table E.1. Relationship to NIST Service Categories

NIST Service[a]	Item Numbers from Table 3-1
development	1b, 1c, 1d, 1e, 1f, 1g
enactment	2a, 2b, 2c
visibility	1a
monitoring	4a, 4b
transaction	3b[b]
resource	3a

a. Debugging services are not covered in [NIST 93]
b. Neither SynerVision nor ProcessWeaver supports transaction services

Appendix F
End-User Evaluation Materials

Objective: To evaluate the effectiveness of the end-user interface capability provided by SynerVision and Processweaver. Note that the objective is *not* to evaluate the process model itself or its implementations in the products. To this end, the two implementations have been kept as similar as possible.

In order to consider this evaluation of ProcessWeaver and Synervision from an end-user perspective, you are asked to participate in an exercise in which you will act out one of three roles in a simple document update scenario. This scenario, as defined in Figures 2.20 through 2.22, will be enacted twice, once using the process model as implemented in ProcessWeaver, and once using the process model as implemented in SynerVision. You will then be asked to answer some questions about the two versions of the scenario and also about process automation in general.

The scenario deals with updating a document. There are three roles; a manager and two technical writers. Also, there are three documents: the *document* to be modified, the *change request* that contains the modifications to be made, and *review notes* that contain any information that the document reviewer may wish to send to the editor. There are four tasks in the exercise that are:

- to determine if the change request should be implemented (manager's task).
- to select one of the two technical writers as editor and the other as reviewer (manager's task). The sequence of events is as follows. The manager suggests that the first writer be the editor. If the first writer rejects the role, the second writer is automatically asked to be the editor. If the second writer also refuses the role, the manager then dictates which writer will be editor. By default, the other writer becomes reviewer.
- to update the document (editor's task).
- to review and either accept or reject the revisions (reviewer's task). If a review fails, then the document, the change request and a review notes document (in which the reviewer adds review notes) goes back to the editor. The edit/review cycle continues until the reviewer is satisfied.

- In the scenario, many of the administrative tasks (e.g., making sure that the right persons have the right documents at the right times) are automated. The information in Table F.1 provides you with the guidance necessary to follow the scenario. The actions in this table are all sequential. If you are given the role of *Technical Writer A*, then follow the instructions for that role. When an action needs to be performed, guidance is displayed at the terminal of the appropriate person, along with the documents necessary to perform the action.

After performing the scenario, please answer the questions in Table E-2 as fully as possible. Answers to some of these questions may require technical and human insights that stretch the limited scope of the simple scenario. Therefore, please use your own background experience in conjunction with knowledge gained in the role play to answer the questions.

Table F.1. Process Enactment Scenario

#	Role	Action
1	Manager	a. Review the change request *CR_No_1* with respect to document *TestReport*. b. Close both documents (control-x control-c). c. Accept the change request by clicking on *accept* button.
2	Manager	Select Technical Writer A as editor by clicking on button beside *Technical Writer A*.
3	Technical Writer A	Reject role as editor, by clicking on *reject* button.
4	Technical Writer A	Remove the information window by clicking on the OK button.
5	Technical Writer B	Reject role as editor by clicking on *reject* button.
6	Technical Writer B	Remove the information window by clicking on the OK button.
7	Manager	Force selection of *Technical Writer A* as editor by clicking on button beside *Technical Writer A*.
8	Technical Writer A	Remove the information window by clicking on the OK button.
9	Technical Writer B	Remove the information window by clicking on the OK button.
10	Technical Writer A	a. Modify the document *TestReport* as described in *CR_No_1*. b. Save the updated *TestReport* file (control-x control-s). c. Close both documents (control-x control-c). d. Click on the OK button.
11	Technical Writer B	a. Review the document *TestReport* against the modifications in *CR_No_1*. b. In the *ReviewNotes* document add "Replace last period ('.') in report with an exclamation point ('!')". c. Save the updated *ReviewNotes* file (control-x control-s). d. Close all documents (control-x control-c). e. Click on the *NeedsFurtherWork* button.
12	Technical Writer A	a. Modify the document *TestReport* as described in *ReviewNotes*. b. Save the updated *TestReport* file (control-x control-s). c. Close all documents (control-x control-s). d. Click on the *OK* button.
13	Technical Writer B	a. Review the document *TestReport* against the modifications in *ReviewNotes* and in the change request. a. Close all documents (control-x control-c). a. Accept review by clicking on the *DocOK* button.
14	Manager	Click on the OK button.

Table F.2. Questionnaire for End-User Role Plays[a]

A.	Experience with the scenario (ProcessWeaver)						
1	The screen layouts were easy to understand.	1	2	3	4	5
2	The instructional text was well formatted.	1	2	3	4	5
3	The instructional text was easy to read.	1	2	3	4	5
4	The Agenda window was useful in displaying current tasks.	1	2	3	4	5
5	The use of icons was helpful in organizing the task elements.	1	2	3	4	5
6	The use of buttons was effective.	1	2	3	4	5
7	The amount of information in the windows was good.	1	2	3	4	5
8	Computer response times were good.	1	2	3	4	5
9	I found it easy to understand the operating mechanics of the system.	1	2	3	4	5
10	The guided task sequence was helpful in managing the process.	1	2	3	4	5
11	The task sequencing was logical.	1	2	3	4	5
12	I would enjoy working in an environment supported by ProcessWeaver.	1	2	3	4	5

B.	Experience with the scenario (SynerVision)						
1	The screen layouts were easy to understand.	1	2	3	4	5
2	The instructional text was well formatted.	1	2	3	4	5
3	The instructional text was easy to read.	1	2	3	4	5
4	The use of buttons was effective.	1	2	3	4	5
5	The amount of information in the windows was good.	1	2	3	4	5
6	Computer response times were good.	1	2	3	4	5
7	I found it easy to understand the operating mechanics of the system.	1	2	3	4	5
8	The guided task sequence was helpful in managing the process.	1	2	3	4	5
9	The task sequencing was logical.	1	2	3	4	5
10	I would enjoy working in an environment supported by SynerVision.	1	2	3	4	5

Please add any comments here.

a. In ranking your answers, 1 implies total disagreement, 5 represents full agreement

Table F.2. Questionnaire for End-user Role Plays (Continued)

C. Adoption issues

Given your brief experience with the process automation scenario, would you feel comfortable working in a process-centered environment if:

1) it were designed by you and only supported your personal tasks,

| 1 | 2 | 3 | 4 | 5 |

2) you had input to its design, and it were used within your project,

| 1 | 2 | 3 | 4 | 5 |

3) it were predefined, but modified (with your input) for use within
 your project,

| 1 | 2 | 3 | 4 | 5 |

4) you did not have input to its design?

| 1 | 2 | 3 | 4 | 5 |

Do you think that working within a process-centered environment is *necessarily*:

1) too invasive,

| 1 | 2 | 3 | 4 | 5 |

2) too impersonal

| 1 | 2 | 3 | 4 | 5 |

3) too controlling?

| 1 | 2 | 3 | 4 | 5 |

Please explain your reasons.

Table F.2. Questionnaire for End-user Role Plays (Continued)

D.	Applications

Do you think that process automation, as exemplified in the experiment, could be effectively applied to improve productivity and software quality? What would be the drawbacks? Consider such areas as:

1) office paper-routing (e.g., document updating, document sign-offs),

1	2	3	4	5

2) software quality (e.g. inspections, walk-throughs),

1	2	3	4	5

3) software development (e.g., edit/compile/test cycle, system integration),

1	2	3	4	5

4) communications (e.g., subcontractor management., inter-group coordination),

1	2	3	4	5

5) metrics collection and analysis,

1	2	3	4	5

6) process improvement (process definition, reuse, or adaption).

1	2	3	4	5

Please explain your reasons.

E.   Miscellaneous

Please provide any other comments or insights you may have in the area of applying process automation.

References

AAIS, *AAIS reference manual, version 3.0*, Advanced A. I. System's Prolog, Inc., P.O. Box 39-0360, Mountain View CA 94039-0360, 1991.

Ambriola, V., et al., Software process enactment in Oikos, *Proceedings of the Fourth ACM SIGSOFT Symposium on Software Development Environments*, pp. 183-192, Irvine CA, 1990.

Ayre R., Gottesman, B. Z., Workgroup computing: group enabled, *PC Magazine*, 13(11), pp. 171-180, June 1994

Barghouti, N.S., et al., Modeling concurrency in rule-based development environments, *IEEE Expert*, December, 1990.

Basili, V. R., Rombach, H. D., Support for comprehensive reuse, *Software Engineering Journal* 6(5) September 1991.

Bernard, Y., Lavency, P., A process-oriented approach to configuration management, *Trans ACM*, pp. 320-327, 1989.

Block, P., *Flawless Consulting*, San Diego: Pfeiffer and Co., 1981.

Boone, G., CASE and its challenge for change, *International Journal of Software Engineering and Knowledge Engineering* 1(2) 1991: 151-163.

Bouldin B. M., *Agents of Change: Managing the Introduction of Automated Tools*, Yourdon Process Computing Series, Prentice-Hall, 1989.

Brandl D. L., *A Classification for Software Development Methodologies*, Texas Instruments report (un-numbered), November 1990.

Bratko, I., *Prolog Programming for Artificial Intelligence*, Addison-Wesley, 1986.

Brown, A. W., Earl, A. N., McDermid, J. A., *Software Engineering Environments: Automated Support for Software Engineers*, New York: McGraw-Hill, 1992.

Brown, A. W., et al., Experiences with a federated environment testbed, *Proceedings of the European Software Engineering Conference*, Garmisch, Germany: Springer, September 1993(a).

Brown, A., Carney, D., Oberndorf, P., Zelkowitz, M., eds., *Reference Model for Project Support Environments:* (CMU/SEI-93-TR-23). Pittsburgh, PA: Software Engineering Institute, Carnegie Mellon University, November 1993(b).

Brown, A. W., et al., *Principles of CASE Tool Integration*, Oxford University Press, 1994.

Brownston, L., et al., *Programming Expert Systems in OPS5*, Addison-Wesley, 1985.

Brownsword, L., Software Engineering Transition Issues, *4th IEEE Computer Society Conference on Software Engineering Technology Transfer*, Dallas, Texas, April 1994.

Bullen, C. V., Bennett, J. J., Learning from user experience with groupware, *Proceedings of the Conference on Computer-Supported Cooperative Work*, Los Angeles, California, October 1990.

Cagan, M. R., The SOFTBENCH environment: an architecture for a new generation of software tools, *Hewlett-Packard Journal*, 41(3), pp. 36-47, June 1990.

CaseWare User's Guide, CaseWare Inc., Irvine, CA, 1992.

CaseWare/CM Integration. Technical note from CaseWare Inc., 1993.

Chen, P. P., ed. *Entity-Relationship Approach to Information Modeling and Analysis*, Amsterdam: North-Holland, 1983.

Christie, A.M., *Process-Centered Development Environments: An Exploration of Issues*: (CMU/SEI-93-TR-04). Pittsburgh, PA: Software Engineering Institute, Carnegie Mellon University, June 1993(a).

Christie, A.M., A graphical process definition language and its application to a maintenance project. *Information and Software Technology*, 35(6/7) pp. 364-374, (June/July) 1993(b).

Ciancarini, P., Coordinating rule-based software processes with ESP, *ACM Transactions on Software Engineering and Methodology*, 2(3), pp. 203-227, July 1993.

Clough A. J., Choosing an appropriate process modeling technology, *CASE Outlook*, 7(1), pp. 9-27, 1993.

Conradi, R., et al. Towards a reference framework for process concepts, in *Software Process Technology*, pp. 3-17, Springer 1992.

Cook, J. E., Wolf, A. L., "Towards metrics for process validation", *Proceedings of the Third International Conference on Software Process*, IEEE Press, Reston, VA, October, 1994.

Cusumano, M. A., *Japan's Software Factories*, New York: Oxford University Press, 1991.

Dart, S., Concepts in configuration management systems, *Proceedings of the Third International Conference on Software Configuration Management*, ACM Press, Trondheim, Norway, June, 1991.

Dart, S., Adopting an automated configuration management solution, *Sixth Annual Software Technology Conference*, Salt Lake City: Paper presented at STC Conference, April 1994.

Davidow, W. H., Malone M. S., *The Virtual Corporation*, Published by Harper Business, 1993.

DeMarco T., *Structured Analysis and Systems Specifications*, Englewood Cliffs, New Jersey: Prentice-Hall 1979.

Demming W. E., *Out of the Crisis*, MIT Center for Advanced Engineering Study, Cambridge, MA, Press, 1982.

Dewan, P., Toward computer supported software engineering, *IEEE Computer*, January 1993.

Dougherty, D., Koman, R., *The Mosaic Handbook for MicroSoft Windows*. O'Reilly and Associates Inc., 1994. (Companion books are also available for the X Window System and for the Macintosh.)

Dowson, M., ISTAR — an integrated project support environment, *Proceedings of the Second ACM Software Engineering Symposium on Practical Software Development Environments*. ACM SIGPLAN 22(1), pp. 27-34 1987.

Ellis, C. A., et al., GroupWare, Some Issues and Experiences, *Communications of the ACM* 43(1), January 1991.

Emmerich, W., MERLIN: Knowledge-based process modeling, *First European Workshop on Software Process Modeling*, published by Associazione Italiana per I'Informatica ed il Calcolo Automatico, Milan, Italy 1991.

Ett, W.H., Enacting the software process, Washington DC: *STARS '91 Proceedings*, December 1991.

Feiler, P.H., Smeaton, R., *The Project Management Experiment*: (CMU/SEI-88-TR-7, ADA197490), Pittsburgh, PA: Software Engineering Institute, Carnegie Mellon University, July 1988.

Feiler, P., Downey, G., *Transaction-Oriented Configuration Management: A Case Study*: (CMU/SEI-90-TR-23), Pittsburgh, PA: Software Engineering Institute, Carnegie Mellon University, 1990.

Feiler, P.H., Humphrey, W. S., *Software Process Development and Enactment: Concepts and Definitions* (CMU/SEI-92-TR-04, ADA258465). Pittsburgh, PA: Software Engineering Institute, Carnegie Mellon University, September, 1992.

Fernstrom, C., L. Ohlsson, Integration needs in process centered environments, *First International Conference on the Software Process*, Redondo Beach, CA, Published by IEEE Press, October 1991.

Fletcher, T., Hunt, J., *Software Engineering and CASE: Bridging the Cultural Gap*, New York: McGraw-Hill Cap Gemini America Series, 1993.

Finkelstein, A., et. al., *Software Process Modelling and Technology*, John Wiley and Sons Inc., 1994.

Fowler, P., Rifkin, S., *Software Engineering Process Group Guide*, Software Engineering Institute Technical Report CMU/SEI-90-TR-24, 1990.

Gintell, J., et al., Scrutiny: a collaborative inspection and review system, *Fourth European Software Engineering Conference*, Garmisch-Partenkirchen, Germany, September, 1993.

Gray, L., Management and initiative as forms of resistance in software process improvement, *4th IEEE Computer Society Conference on Software Engineering Technology Transfer*, Dallas, Texas, April 1994.

Greis, D., *The Science of Programming*, Springer, 1981.

Grudin, J., Why CSCW applications fail: problems in the design and evaluation of organizational interfaces, *Proceedings of the Conference on Computer-Supported Cooperative Work*, Portland, Oregon. Sponsored by ACM, September, 1988.

Gruhn, V., Jegelka, R., An evaluation of funsoft nets, in *Software Process Technology*, pp. 3-17, Springer 1992.

Harel, D., Statecharts: a visual formalism for complex systems, *Science of Computer Programming*, 8(3), pp. 231-274, 1987.

Harel, D., STATEMATE: a working environment for the development of complex reactive systems, *IEEE Transactions on Software Engineering*, 16(4), pp. 403-414, April 1990.

Heimbigner, D., P4: a logic language for process programming, *Proceedings of the 5th International Software Process Workshop*, pp. 67-70, IEEE Computer Society Press, Kennebunkport, Maine, 1989.

Hoffnagle G. F., Beregi, W. E., Automating the Software Development Process, *IBM Systems Journal*, 24(2), pp. 102-119, 1985.

Hounshell, D. A., *From the American System to Mass Production 1800-1932*, John Hopkins University Press, 1984.

Huff, K. E., Software process initiation and the planning paradigm, *Proceedings of the 5th International Software Process Workshop: Experience with Software Process Models*, pp. 97-106, IEEE Computer Society Press, Kennebunkport, Maine, 1989.

HuckVille, T., Ould M., Process modelling - why, what and how, Chapter 6 of *Software assistance for Business Re-engineering*, Edited by Cathy Spurr, et al., John Wiley and Sons, 1993.

Humphrey, W. S., *Managing the Software Process*, Reading, MA: Addison-Wesley, 1989(a).

Humphrey, W. S., *CASE Planning and the Software Process* (CMU/SEI-89-TR-26), Pittsburgh, PA: Software Engineering Institute, Carnegie Mellon University, May 1989(b).

Humphrey, W. S., Software and the factory paradigm, *Software Engineering Journal*, September 1991(a).

Humphrey, W. S., Kitson, D. H., Gale, J. A., *Comparison of U.S. and Japanese Software Process Maturity* (CMU/SEI-91-TR-27), Pittsburgh, PA: Software Engineering Institute, Carnegie Mellon University, 1991(b).

Humphrey, W., Toward a discipline for software engineering, *Sixth SEI Conference on Software Engineering Education*, San Diego CA, 1992.

ISO, *Guidelines for the application of ISO-9001 to the development, supply and maintenance of software*, ISO-9000-3, International Organization for Standardization, June, 1991.

Juran, J., *Juran on Leadership for Quality*, The Free Press, New York, NY 1989.

Kaiser G. E., Feiler P.H., An architecture for intelligent assistance in software development, *Proceedings of the 9th International Conference on Software Engineering*, IEEE Computer Society Process, 1987.

Kaiser, G.E., Barghouti, N. S., Sokolski, M. H., Preliminary experience with process modeling in the marvel software development environment kernel, *Proceedings of the Twenty-Third Annual Hawaii International Conference on Systems Science*, Vol. 2. IEEE Computer Society Press 1990.

Kaplan. S. M., Supporting collaborative software development with ConversationBuilder, *Proceedings of the Fifth ACM SIGSOFT Symposium on Software Development Environments*, 17(5), Edited by Herbert Weber, ACM Press, December 1992.

Kellner, M. I.,Software process modeling: value and experience, *1989 SEI Technical Review*, Pittsburgh, PA: Software Engineering Institute, Carnegie Mellon University, 1989.

Kellner, M. I., Rombach, H. D., Comparison of software process descriptions, *Proceedings of the 6th International Software Process Workshop: Support for the Software Process*, Hakodate, Japan: IEEE Computer Society Press, October, 1990.

Kellner, M. I., Software process modeling support for management planning and control, *First International Conference on the Software Process*, Redondo Beach CA, IEEE Computer Society Press, October 1991.

Kellner, M. I., Gates, L. P., Evolution of software process, *Proceedings of the International Workshop on the Evolution of Software Process*, Quebec, Canada, January, 1993(a).

Kellner, M. I., Phillips, R. W., Practical technology for process assets, *Proceedings of the 8th International Software Process Workshop*, Wadern, Germany: IEEE Computer Society Press, March, 1993(b).

Lee, S., Sluizer, S., An executable language for modeling simple behavior, *IEEE Transactions on Software Engineering*, 17(6), June 1991.

Liu L., Horowitz, E. A formal model for software project management, *IEEE Trans. Software Eng.* 15(10), pp. 1280-1293, 1989.

Leymann, M., The role of process models in software and systems development nad evolution, *Proceedings of the 5th International Software Process Workshop Experience with Software Process Models*, pp. 91-94, published by IEEE Computer Society Press, Kennebunkport, Maine, 1989.

Mahler, A., Lampen, A., Integrating configuration management into a generic environment, SIGSOFT, 15(6), *Proceedings of the Fourth ACM SIGSOFT Symposium on Software Development Environments*, 1990.

Mi, P., Scacchi, W. Process integration in case environments, *IEEE Software* 9(2) pp. 45-53, March 1992.

Nejmeh B. A, Riddle W. E., *Process Description and Analysis Tool Sets*, Report by INSTEP Inc., and SDA Inc., Ref. No 23-65-4, 1994.

NIST 93 *Reference Model for Frameworks of Software Engineering Environments*, NIST Special Publication 500-211, August, 1993.

Oaks, K. S., Smith, D., Morris, E., *Guide to CASE Adoption*, (CMU/SEI-92-TR-15), Pittsburgh, PA: Software Engineering Institute, Carnegie Mellon University, November, 1992.

Osterweil, L., Software processes are software too, *9th International Conference on Software Engineering*, Monterey, California, IEEE Computer Society Press, 1987.

Page-Jones, M., The CASE manifesto, *CASE Outlook*, pp. 33-42, January-February, 1992.

Paulk, M. C., et. al. *Capability Maturity Model for Software, Version 1.1*, (CMU/SEI-93-TR-24, ADA263403), Pittsburgh, PA: Software Engineering Institute, Carnegie Mellon University, February, 1993(a).

Paulk, M. C., et al., *Key Practices of the Capability Maturity Model, Version 1.1*, (CMU/SEI-93-TR-25, ADA 263432), Pittsburgh, PA: Software Engineering Institute, Carnegie Mellon University, February, 1993(b).

ProcessWeaver *ProcessWeaver User's Manual and Reference Manual, Version PW1.2*. Grenoble, France: Cap Gemini Sogeti, 1992.

Przybylinski, S, Maher, J., Fowler, P., *Software Technology Transition*. Tutorial presented at the 13th International Conference of Software Engineering, Austin Texas, May, 1991.

Rader, J., Morris, E.J., Brown, A.W., An investigation into the state of the practice of case integration, pp. 209-221. *Proceedings of Software Engineering Environments,* '93, IEEE Computer Society, July, 1993.

Radice, R., et al, A programming process architecture, *IBM Systems Journal*, 24(2), pp. 79-90, 1985

Rasmussen, J., *On the structure of knowledge: A morphology of mental models in a man-machine system context*, Technical Report, Riso National Laboratory, Riso, Denmark, November, 1979.

Reisig, W., *Petri Nets*, Springer, 1982.

Ross T. R., Applications and extensions of SADT, IEEE Computer, pp. 25-34, April, 1985.

Rumbaugh, J., et al, *Object Oriented Modeling and Design*, Prentice-Hall Inc., 1991.

Shaw, M., *Prospects for an Engineering Discipline of Software*, Software Engineering Institute report CMU/SEI-90-TR-20, September, 1990.

Singh, B., Rein, G., *Role interaction Nets (RINs): A Process Formalism Description*, Technical Report CT-083092, Microelectronics and Computer Technology Corp., July, 1992.

Slomer, H. M., Christie, A.M., *Analysis of a Software Maintenance System*, (CMU/SEI-92-TR-31), Pittsburgh, PA: Software Engineering Institute, Carnegie Mellon University, 1992.

Sobell, M. G., *A Practical Guide to the Unix System, 2nd Edition*, Redwood City, CA: Benjamin Cummings, 1989.

Soley, R. M., ed., *Object Management Architecture Guide, V2.0*, Object Management Group, September, 1992.

Stanley, M. E., Verifying the design process, *AI Expert*, pp. 42-49, September 1992.

Sutton, S., et al., Language constructs for managing change in process-centered environments, *Proceedings of the 4th SIGSOFT Symposium on Software Development Environments*, Software Engineering Notes 15, pp. 206-217, 1990.

SynerVision, *Introduction to SynerVision: Models of Use*, Hewlett-Packard document B3261-90002, Draft May 5, 1993(a).

Synervision, *Developing SynerVision Processes*, Hewlett-Packard document B3261-90003 Draft May 5, 1993(b).

Taylor, F. W., *Principles of Scientific Management*, New York: Harper and Brothers, 1911.

Tichy W. F., RCS - a system for version control, *Software Practice and Experience* 15(7). pp. 637-654, July, 1985.

Thomas, I., *An Overview of PCTE*, Software Design and Analysis Inc., Ref 21-12-1, April, 1993.

Weiderman, N. H., et al., A methodology for evaluating environments, pp. 199-207, *Proceedings of the ACM SIGSOFT/SIGPLAN Software Engineering Symposium on Practical Software Development Environments*, Palo Alto, CA: ACM Press, December, 1986.

Womack, J. P., Jones D. T., Roos, D., *The Machine that Changed the World*, New York,: Rawson Associates, 1990.

Yourdon, E., *The Decline and Fall of the American Programmer*, Englewood Cliffs, NJ: Prentice Hall, 1992.

Index

Commercial versions of ProNet are available for PC-compatible and SUN platforms. Additional information can be obtained from:

Mark V Systems Limited
16400 Ventura Boulevard
Encino California 91436

Voice: (818) 995-7671 or (800) 995-7671
Fax: (818) 995-4276
e-mail: info@markv.com